TEN MODERN
AMERICAN PLAYWRIGHTS

GARLAND REFERENCE LIBRARY
OF THE HUMANITIES
(VOL. 234)

TEN MODERN
AMERICAN PLAYWRIGHTS
An Annotated Bibliography

Kimball King

GARLAND PUBLISHING, INC. • NEW YORK & LONDON
1982

Library of Congress Cataloging in Publication Data

King, Kimball.
  Ten modern American playwrights.

  (Garland reference library of the humanities ; v. 234)
  Includes index.
  1. Dramatists, American—20th century—Bibliography.
2. American drama—20th century—Bibliography. I. Title.
II. Series.
Z1231.D7K56 [PS351]   016.812'54   80-8498
ISBN 0-8240-9489-1   AACR2

Printed on acid-free, 250-year-life paper
Manufactured in the United States of America

CONTENTS

ACKNOWLEDGMENTS

I am indebted to Lanford Wilson and Ed Bullins who personally checked over the lists of their primary sources included in this volume and to Edward Albee who provided helpful sources of bibliographic materials. The research council of The University of North Carolina gave me additional funds to do research while I was lecturing in Germany in May of 1981, providing me with the opportunity to observe the interest of German critics in American playwrights and to read materials only recently available in America. Many research assistants in the English department deserve credit for their contributions to various parts of this volume. John Kamauff, as noted elsewhere, initiated research on the Albee section. David March worked most of one summer on the Baraka and Bullins bibliographies. Lisa McDonnell, Brent Betit, and Dan Butterworth contributed to the Mamet, Rabe, and Shepard sections and investigated other playwrights who for various reasons were not ultimately included. James East, Ralph Earle and Elizabeth Chambers were especially helpful during the last stages of preparing the manuscript. Mrs. Lana Reichert typed many sections of the original draft, and Mrs. Muriel Dyer, who typed my previous Garland bibliographies, also prepared the final copy on this one.

INTRODUCTION

Historians of American drama, such as Arthur Hobson Quinn, Moses Montrose, Barrett Clark, and, more recently, Walter J. Meserve, have explored the roots of American theatre in colonial days or, even earlier, among native Americans, and have revealed a continuous but erratic attempt to build a theatre tradition. Critics agree that there was little drama of merit prior to this century. The Puritan distrust of theatre, as well as the disapproval of other religious groups, and the dependency of our writers on European models, together with the lack of the sophisticated urban audience generally associated with distinguished theatre movements, caused American playwrights to lag behind poets and novelists in gaining worldwide recognition. Eugene O'Neill, who began writing a little more than sixty years ago, was the first American dramatist to gain respect internationally. After O'Neill a series of eminent playwrights established a forceful American dramatic tradition. Thornton Wilder, Arthur Miller, and Tennessee Williams, as well as O'Neill, are taught in universities from London to Delhi to Tokyo. These dramatists captured the uniqueness of the American nuclear family and revealed the special freedoms and frustrations of life in a pluralistic, capitalistic society. Despite the psychological determinism of O'Neill's character studies or the emphasis on greed and personal disappointment in the corrupt environments described by Miller and Williams, American playwrights have generally expressed a faith in democratic society and have suggested that their countrymen were largely capable of solving their problems, as long as they remained objective and flexible.

From Ibsen's Norway in the 1880s until the second World War, stage action in Western drama tended to be sequential and logical; conflicts moved toward resolution, even when tragic. Following the holocaust, the second World War, and Hiroshima, a fun-

damental distrust in man's ability to control his life or to learn
from his experiences led many sensitive people to a state of
spiritual and emotional despair. Samuel Beckett and Eugene
Ionesco most forcefully expressed the dilemma of alienated man
in a hostile, irrational universe. It was not until nearly a decade
after these two playwrights began what Martin Esslin has called
"the theatre of the absurd" that absurdist techniques and attitudes
were reflected in American drama. Edward Albee, an admirer of
Beckett, began writing plays which differed from the popular
tradition of American family drama. His *Zoo Story* (1959), *The
Sandbox* (1960), and *The American Dream* (1961) were all plays which
seemed to follow recent continental trends. Beginning with Albee, American theatre entered a new phase, one still hard to
define but possessing certain characteristics that suggest the birth
of a movement.

In the United States as in other Western countries naturalism
had been the prevailing dramatic mode during the twentieth
century. Pure naturalism, as presented by the European dramatists—Gerhart Hauptmann; Anton Chekhov, and Maxim Gorky,
among others at the turn of the century—was never popular in
America, but naturalism combined with other concepts and
fetishes has resulted in significant theatre. As early as 1920 O'Neill
blended what he considered to be naturalistic speech with a range
of expressionistic stage devices and visual effects in his play *The
Hairy Ape*. Later, in *Desire Under the Elms,* he grafted the plain New
England speech of Eben Cabot and his family onto the classic
Hippolytus legend, creating a convincing American drama based
on Greek myth. A similar technique, drawing a parallel between
an American family after the Civil War and the story of Agamem-
non's return, resulted in *Mourning Becomes Electra* (1928). In the
1930s political and social realism was well suited to naturalistic
techniques, but dramatists such as Lillian Hellman tempered
their social criticism with Ibsenesque plots, and Clifford Odets
borrowed the *agit prop* techniques of revolutionary playwrights.
Even though America's verse dramatists, Maxwell Anderson, T.S.
Eliot, and Archibald MacLeish, seemed to defy the naturalistic
trend, they attempted to make the words of their verse-speaking
protagonists sound like ordinary speech. And Thornton Wilder,
under the influence of Bertolt Brecht, combined highly theatrical

devices with homey speech and recognizable everyday events in both *Our Town* and *The Skin of Our Teeth.*

Following the second World War, Tennessee Williams, Arthur Miller, and William Inge, all of whom wrote enormously popular plays, resurrected a number of 1920s stage devices to give symbolic resonance to their tales of ordinary, believable people enmeshed in circumstances beyond their control. Albee, however, was the first major dramatist to combine the existential despair and irrational violence of the French absurdists' world with "slice of life" situations and plain talk. In England Harold Pinter, especially in his early plays, blended a comparable absurdist-naturalistic mixture. The majority of dramatists treated in this volume have followed Albee's lead and attempted to offer recognizable American experiences against the backdrop of a world that makes no sense. The titles of their plays reflect this whimsical and distrustful view of life, as well as their receptivity to the argot of the streets and the slogans of popular culture. Claims have been made, for example, that the title of Albee's best-known play, *Who's Afraid of Virginia Woolf?,* was originally graffiti in a public lavatory. Such a source would not be surprising, for as Simon and Garfunkel observe in "Sounds of Silence," the theme song of *The Graduate,* a movie which defined a generation of students, "The words of the prophets are written on subway walls."

Playwrights of the past two decades have been openly critical of their country from the caricatured Americanism of Albee's Mommy and Daddy in *The American Dream,* whose apartment is papered with the American flag, to Sam Shepard's alleged portrait of Howard Hughes in *Seduced,* where a tycoon is pictured as a monster created by American greed and hero-worship. The materialism, racism, anger, and violence of American society since the 1960s have confronted audiences alternately amused or terrified by the artist's satire. The complexity of modern American experience is reflected in the varied ethnic backgrounds of our leading dramatists, and their astute explorations of the cultures or regions they know best. Albee and Arthur Kopit are chroniclers of WASP America and expose the fears and prejudices of educated upper-middle-class Americans. Ed Bullins and Amiri Baraka reveal Black America and the struggle of minorities in a "white" country. To date, David Rabe has concerned himself with the Vietnam War and its aftermath. Jack Gelber and David Mamet are generally apologists for urban lowlife characters; Sam Shepard captures the atmosphere of the drug culture or the rock music scene in several plays, but he and Lanford Wilson return consistently to heartland America—the rural middle west. Neil Simon draws on the milieu of affluent, rootless Americans, urbanites or suburbanites, who worship the trinity of values depicted in television's situation comedies—sentimentality, prurience, and self-satisfaction.

The most substantial body of secondary criticism in this volume is naturally concentrated on the writers who have had the longest careers in the theatre. Thus, there is sufficient bibliography on Edward Albee to warrant perhaps a single volume on his work. By implication his contribution seems to have convinced a majority of scholars in this country and abroad that he is presently America's foremost "young" playwright, although he is now past fifty. But Baraka, Bullins, and Kopit have also been the subjects of extensive research. More recent playwrights, such as Mamet, Shepard, and Wilson, have not yet received wide attention from the scholarly community; they are included here because they are on the verge of worldwide recognition, and a list of their primary works testifies to their energy and accomplishment. I would emphasize also that the playwrights included in this volume are not the only ten significant writers of the American theatre. For example, Jack Richardson, Ronald Tavel, John Guare, Ronald Ribman, and the late Preston Jones have made substantial contributions to the modern theatre. I have not included the late Lorraine Hansberry, for although her birth date of 1930 makes her younger than Albee, her style and subject matter, the conventional narrative portrayal of ethical and moral values, place her in the era of Williams and Miller. Jules Feiffer, though the author of successful plays, is regarded primarily as a cartoonist. Other prominent young playwrights, such as Albert Innaurato, Thomas Babe, Ntozake Shange, or the Chicano dramatist Luis Valdez, have not yet gained sufficient critical recognition to warrant inclusion in a book-length bibliographical study but may well prove major writers in the future.

Interviews, articles, chapters in books, or long segments in books have been annotated. One-page articles have not generally been annotated. I have extensively but selectively listed reviews of individual plays. In general, however, I have chosen to annotate only one review for each play, basing my selection on the typicality of the review and its success in summarizing information useful to students and teachers.

Below is the list of sources used in the preparation of this volume.

Abstracts of English Studies, 1958–. Boulder, Colorado: National Council of Teachers of English.

Afro-American Literature and Culture Since World War II. Charles D. Peavy. Detroit, Michigan: Gale Research Company, 1979.

American Drama Criticism: Interpretations, 1890–1977. Floyd E. Eddleman. Hamden, Connecticut: Shoestring Press, 1979.

American Literary Scholarship. Eds. James Woodress and J. Albert Robbins. Durham, North Carolina: Duke University Press, 1962–.

Articles on American Literature. Lewis Leary. Durham, North Carolina: Duke University Press, 1970 and 1979.

Chicorel Theatre Index to Plays in Anthologies, vols. 1–8. Ed. Marietta Chicorel. New York: Chicorel Library, 1970–.

Comprehensive Index to English Language Little Magazines 1890–1970. Millwood, New York: Kraus-Thomson.

Contemporary Dramatists. Ed. James Vinson. London: St. James Press, 1973.

Dictionary of Literary Biography, vol. 7. Twentieth Century Dramatists. Part 1 and Part 2. Ed. John MacNicholas. Detroit: Gale Research, 1981.

Dissertation Abstracts, 1938–. Ann Arbor, Michigan: University Microfilms.

Dissertations in English and American Literature; Theses Accepted by American, British, and German Universities, 1865–1964. Lawrence F. McNamee. New York and London: R.R. Bowker, 1968.

Drama Criticism Index. Paul Breed and Florence Sniderman. Detroit: Gale Research Company, 1972.

The Drama Scholars' Index to Plays and Filmscripts, vols. 1 and 2. Gordon Sample. Metuchen, New Jersey: Scarecrow Press, 1974 and 1980.

Dramatic Index, 1909–1949. Boston: R.W. Faxon, 1910–1952.

Essay and General Literature Index, 1900–. New York: H.W. Wilson.

A Guide to Critical Reviews. James M. Salem. Metuchen, New Jersey: Scarecrow Press, 1966–1971.

A Guide to the Performing Arts, 1958–1968. S. Yancey Belknap. Metuchen, New Jersey: Scarecrow Press, 1959–1969.

Index to Little Magazines, 1943–. Denver: Alan Swallow.

Index to Plays in Periodicals. Dean H. Keller. Metuchen, New Jersey: Scarecrow Press, 1979.

Index Translationum, 1955–1973. Paris: Unesco Press.

International Index to Periodicals, 1970–. New York: H.W. Wilson. From vol. 19 (April 1965–March 1966) called *Social Sciences and Humanities Index.*

LeRoi Jones (Imamu Amiri Baraka): A Checklist of Works By and About Him. Letitia Dace. London: The Nether Press, 1971.

Masters Abstracts, 1962–. Ann Arbor, Michigan: University Microfilms.

MLA Bibliography. New York: Modern Language Association.

Modern Drama (the periodical's annual checklists).

More Black American Playwrights: A Bibliography. Esther Arata. Metuchen, New Jersey: Scarecrow Press, 1978.

New York Theatre Critics' Reviews.

New York Times Index.

The New York Times Theatre Reviews.

Ottemiller's Index to Plays in Collections, 6th edition. John M. and Billie M. Connor. Metuchen, New Jersey: Scarecrow Press, 1976.

Play Index, 1961–1977. Estelle A. Fidell. New York: H.W. Wilson Co., 1968–1978.

Pownall's Articles on Twentieth Century Literature. David E. Pownall. New York: Kraus-Thomson, 1973–.

Readers' Guide to Periodical Literature, 1900–. New York: H.W. Wilson.

Revue d'Histoire du Théâtre (annual bibliographies).

Subject Index to Periodicals, 1915–1961. London: The Library Association. Continued as *British Humanities Index,* 1962–.

Theatre Dissertations. Ed. Frederic M. Litto. Kent, Ohio: Kent State University Press, 1969.

The Times (London) *Index.*

1 EDWARD ALBEE

Born March 12, 1928, Washington, D.C.

Of all recent American playwrights Edward Albee has been the most persistent interpreter of trends in contemporary theatre. He was the first American to employ the stage techniques of the European absurdists, thereby changing the shape of American drama in works like Zoo Story, The Sandbox, and The American Dream. Although he experimented with the elliptical language, non-sequiturs, and plot forms of Beckett and Ionesco, he fused their continental style with a particularly American social consciousness and optimism. In Who's Afraid of Virginia Woolf? absurdist devices were blended with an arresting naturalism to create the major American play of the past two decades. Albee revived the Gothic spirit in his adaptation of Carson McCullers' Ballad of the Sad Cafe, revitalized dialectical drama in Box Mao Box, and updated surrealism in Seascape. While critics have deplored his experimentation in recent years, preferring, it would seem, the known appeal of his more popular domestic melodramas, Albee, caught in the grasp of a noetic impulse, continues to express his unique vision of American society, its deficiencies and possibilities, and to search for forms which will undergird his perceptions. His canon to date has made him one of the best-known dramatists in the world, especially in Europe where his reputation has eclipsed O'Neill's. Still a relatively young man, Albee retains the ability to surprise audiences; it is possible that his best plays are yet to be written.

PRIMARY SOURCES

I.   STAGE

All Over. Staged New York, 1971. New York: Samuel French, 1970.

2

_____. New York: Atheneum, 1971.

_____. In Best American Plays, Seventh Series, 1967-1973. Ed. Clive Barnes. New York: Crown, 1974.

The American Dream. Staged New York, 1961. Mademoiselle, November 1960, pp. 86-89, 127-35.

_____. New York: Coward-McCann, 1961.

_____. London: Samuel French, 1961.

_____. New York: Pocket Books, 1974.

_____. In The American Dream, The Death of Bessie Smith, Fam and Yam. New York: Dramatists Play Service, 1962. Acting edition.

_____. In The American Dream and The Zoo Story. New York: New American Library, 1963.

_____. In Drama, An Introductory Anthology (alternate edition). Ed. Otto Reinert. Boston: Little, Brown, 1964.

_____. In Great Plays: Sophocles to Albee. Eds. M. W. Bloomfield and R. C. Elliot. New York: Holt, 1975.

_____. In Literary Types and Themes (second edition). Ed. Maurice Basil McNamee. New York: Holt, Rinehart, and Winston, 1971.

_____. In New American Drama. Ed. Charles Marowitz. Harmondsworth, England: Penguin Books, 1966.

The Ballad of the Sad Cafe. Staged New York, 1963. New York: Atheneum and Boston: Houghton Mifflin, co-publishers, 1963.

_____: the Play; Carson McCullers' Novella Adapted to the Stage. London: Jonathan Cape, 1965.

Bartleby. Staged New York, 1961.

Box and Quotations from Chairman Mao Tse-tung: Two Inter-related Plays. Staged Buffalo, N.Y., and New York, 1968.

_____. London: Jonathan Cape, 1970.

_____. New York: Pocket Books, 1970.

Counting the Ways (A vaudeville). Staged Hartford, Conn., 1977. New York: Atheneum, 1977.

_____. In Counting the Ways and Listening. New York:
Atheneum, 1977.

The Death of Bessie Smith. Staged Berlin, 1960; New York,
1961. London: Samuel French, 1962.

_____. In The American Dream, The Death of Bessie
Smith, Fam and Yam. New York: Dramatists Play
Service, 1962. Acting edition.

_____. In The Sandbox, The Death of Bessie Smith, with
Fam and Yam. New York: New American Library, 1963.

_____. In The Sandbox and The Death of Bessie Smith.
New York: New American Library, 1964.

_____. In The Zoo Story, The Death of Bessie Smith,
The Sandbox. New York: Coward-McCann, 1960.

A Delicate Balance. Staged New York, 1966. Pulitzer Prize.
New York: Atheneum, 1966.

_____. New York: Samuel French, 1967. Acting edition.

_____. London: Jonathan Cape, 1968.

_____. New York: Pocket Books, 1968.

_____. In The Best Plays of 1966-1967: The Burns Mantle
Yearbook. Ed. Otis L. Guernsey, Jr. New York and
Toronto: Dodd, Mead, 1967.

Everything in the Garden. Staged New York, 1967. New
York: Atheneum, 1968.

_____. New York: Pocket Books, 1969.

_____. New York: Dramatists Play Service, 1968. Act-
ing edition.

Fam and Yam. Staged Westport, Conn., 1960. Harper's
Bazaar, September 1960.

_____. In The American Dream, The Death of Bessie
Smith, Fam and Yam. New York: Dramatists Play
Service, 1962. Acting edition.

_____. In The Sandbox, The Death of Bessie Smith, with
Fam and Yam. New York: New American Library, 1963.

The Lady from Dubuque. Staged New York, 1980. New York:
Atheneum, 1980.

Listening (A Chamber Play). Staged Hartford, Conn.,
1977. Originally produced in 1976 as a radio play.

_____. In Counting the Ways and Listening. New York: Atheneum, 1977.

Lolita (adapted from the novel by Vladimir Nabokov). Staged New York, 1981.

Malcolm. Staged New York, 1966. New York: Atheneum, 1966.

_____ (adapted by Edward Albee from the novel by James Purdy). London: Jonathan Cape with Secker and Warburg, 1967.

The Sandbox. Staged New York, 1960.

_____. In The Sandbox and The Death of Bessie Smith. New York: New American Library, 1964.

_____. In The Sandbox, The Death of Bessie Smith, with Fam and Yam. New York: New American Library, 1963.

_____. In The American Experience: Drama. Ed. Marjorie Wescott Barrows et al. New York: Macmillan, 1968.

_____. In The Best Short Plays, 1959-1960. Ed. Margaret Mayorga. Boston: Beacon Press, 1957.

_____. In Literature; Structure, Sound and Sense. Ed. Laurence Perrine. New York: Harcourt Brace Jovanovich, 1970; second edition, 1974.

_____. In Modern Drama for Analysis (third edition). Ed. Paul M. Cubeta. New York: Holt, Rinehart and Winston, 1962.

_____. In Reading Literature; Stories, Plays, and Poems. Ed. Joseph Henry Satin. Boston: Houghton Mifflin, 1964; second edition, 1968.

_____. In Theatre Today. Ed. David Thompson. London: Longmans, 1965.

_____. In Twelve American Plays, 1920-1960. Eds. Richard Corbin and Miriam Balk. New York: Scribners, 1969.

Schism. Choate Literary Magazine 20 (May 1946):87-110.

Seascape. Staged New York, 1975. Pulitzer Prize. New York: Atheneum, 1975.

_____. London: Jonathan Cape, 1976.

_____. New York: Dramatists Play Service, 1975. Acting edition.

_____. In The Best Plays of 1974-1975: The Burns Mantle Yearbook. Ed. Otis L. Guernsey, Jr. New York and Toronto: Dodd, Mead, 1975.

Tiny Alice. Staged New York, 1964. New York: Atheneum, 1965.

_____. New York: Dramatists Play Service, 1965. Acting edition.

_____. London: Jonathan Cape, 1966.

_____. New York: Pocket Books, 1966.

_____. In Best American Plays, Sixth Series, 1963-1967. Ed. John Gassner and Clive Barnes. New York: Crown, 1971.

_____. In The Best Plays of 1964-1965: The Burns Mantle Yearbook. Ed. Otis L. Guernsey, Jr. New York and Toronto: Dodd, Mead, 1965.

Who's Afraid of Virginia Woolf? Staged New York, 1962. New York: Atheneum, 1962 and 1964.

_____. New York: Pocket Books, 1963.

_____. London: Jonathan Cape, 1964.

_____. Harmondsworth, England: Penguin, 1965.

_____. In America's Lost Plays. New York: Dodd, Mead, 1963.

_____. In Best American Plays, Fifth Series, 1957-1963. Ed. John Gassner. New York: Crown, 1963.

_____. In The Best Plays of 1962-1963: The Burns Mantle Yearbook. Ed. Henry Hewes. New York and Toronto: Dodd, Mead, 1963.

_____. In Classic Through Modern Drama; an Introductory Anthology. Ed. Otto Reinert. Boston: Little, Brown, 1970.

_____. In Fifty Best Plays of the American Theatre. Ed. John Gassner and Clive Barnes. New York: Crown, 1969.

_____. In A Treasury of the Theatre. Ed. John Gassner and Bernard F. Dukore. Fourth edition. New York: Simon and Schuster, 1970.

The Zoo Story. Staged Berlin, 1959; New York, 1960. Evergreen Review 4 (March-April 1960): 28-52.

_____. In The Zoo Story, The Death of Bessie Smith, The Sandbox. New York: Coward-McCann, 1960.

_____. In The Zoo Story and The Sandbox. New York: Dramatists Play Service, 1961. Acting edition.

_____. In The Zoo Story and Other Plays. London: Jonathan Cape, 1962.

_____. The Zoo Story. London: Samuel French, 1963.

_____. In Absurd Drama. Ed. Martin Esslin. Harmondsworth, England: Penguin Books, 1965.

_____. In Classics of the Modern Theater, Realism and After. Ed. Alvin Bernard Kernan. New York: Harcourt, Brace, World, 1965.

_____. In Contexts of the Drama. Ed. Richard Henry Goldstone. New York: McGraw-Hill, 1968.

_____. In The Dramatic Moment. Ed. Eugene M. Waith. Englewood Cliffs, N.J.: Prentice-Hall, 1967.

_____. In Famous American Plays of the 1950s. New York: Dell, 1962.

_____. In The Literature of America: Twentieth Century. Ed. Mark Schorer. New York: McGraw-Hill, 1970; revised edition, 1971.

_____. In Modern Drama (alternate edition). Ed. Otto Reinert. Boston: Little, Brown, 1966.

_____. In Reading for Understanding: Fiction, Drama, Poetry. Ed. Caroline Shrodes, Justine Van Gundy, and Joel Dorius. New York: Macmillan, 1968.

_____. In Twentieth Century Drama: England, Ireland [and] The United States. Ed. Ruby Cohn, Bernard F. Dukore, and Haskell M. Block. New York: Random House, 1966.

II. FILM

A Delicate Balance, 1973.

Who's Afraid of Virginia Woolf?, 1966 (screenplay by Ernest Lehman).

III. MISCELLANEOUS AND UNPUBLISHED WRITINGS

"Bartleby." An unpublished libretto, 1961. Adapted from
    Melville's story, "Bartleby The Scrivener."

"Breakfast at Tiffany's" (also called "Holly Golightly").
    See the New York Times, 14 November 1966, p. 52;
    24 November 1966, p. 63; and 15 December 1966, p. 60.

"The Dancer." An unpublished screenplay, 1971.

"The Fate of the Idle Merrymakers." An unpublished novel,
    1944.

"The Flesh of Unbelievers." An unpublished novel, 1942.

"A Novel Beginning; Excerpt from First Novel." Esquire,
    July 1963, pp. 59-60.

Short stories and poems published in Choate Literary
    Magazine 1945-1946.

"The Tenant." An unpublished screenplay, 1971.

IV. NONFICTION

"Albee Says 'No Thanks' to John Simon." New York Times,
    10 September 1967, II:1.

Antoni Tapies: Paintings, Collages, and Works on Paper
    1966-1968. Introduction by Edward Albee. New York:
    Martha Jackson Gallery, 1968.

"Apartheid in the Theater." New York Times, 30 July
    1967, II:1.

"Carson McCullers--the Case of the Curious Magician."
    Harper's Bazaar, January 1963, p. 98.

"Creativity and Commitment." Saturday Review, 4 June
    1966, p. 26. Written for the series on the general
    theme of "The Writer as Independent Spirit" which
    was also the theme of the Thirty-fourth International
    P.E.N. Congress that met in New York City June 12-18,
    1966.

"The Decade of Engagement." Saturday Review, 24 January
    1970, pp. 19-20.

"The Future Belongs to Youth." New York Times, 26 Novem-
    ber 1967, II:1.

"Judy Garland." In Double Exposure. Ed. Roddy McDowell. New York: Delacorte Press, 1966. Pp. 198-99.

"Just What Is the Theater of the Absurd?" Dramatists' Bulletin 2 (April 1962):104.

"Program Notes on Box-Mao-Box." Playbill (Studio Arena Theater, Buffalo, New York) (March 1968). Written for the world première of the play.

Review of Sam Shepard's play Icarus's Mother. Village Voice, 25 November 1965, p. 19.

Review of Lilian Ross's novel The Vertical and the Horizontal. Village Voice, 11 July 1963, p. 7.

"Some Notes on Non-Conformity." Harper's Bazaar, August 1962, p. 104.

"Stars of the Future. Talented Males the Pros Think Will Make It on Broadway." Playbill, 1 (February 1964).

Three Plays by Noel Coward. Introduction by Edward Albee. New York: Dell Publishing Co. and Boulder: Delta Publishing Co., 1965.

"What's It About?--A Playwright Tries to Tell." New York Herald Tribune Magazine, "The Lively Arts," 22 January 1961, p. 5.

"Which Theatre Is the Absurd One?" New York Times Magazine, 25 February 1962, pp. 30-31, 64, 66. Reprinted in Horst Frenz' American Playwrights on Drama, pp. 168-74, and John Gassner's Directions in Modern Theater and Drama, pp. 329-36.

"Who Is James Purdy?" New York Times, 9 January 1966, II:1 and 3.

"Who's Afraid of the Truth?" New York Times, 18 August 1963, II:1.

V. TRANSLATIONS

ALL OVER

    Alles voor de tuin. Tr. Ernst van Altena. 'S-Grav: Daamen, 1967. Dutch.

THE AMERICAN DREAM

    "Der amerikanische Traum." In Theater im S. Fischer Verlag I. Frankfurt am Main: S. Fischer Verlag, 1962. Pp. 393-433. German.

Der amerikanische Traum. Der Tod von Bessie Smith.
Die Zoogeschichte. Der Sanderkasten. Tr.
Pinkas Braum. Frankfurt am Main: S. Fischer
Verlag, 1962. German.

Het verhaal van de dierentuin. Tr. Gerard Kornelis
van het Reve. Amsterdam: Corvey, 1965. Dutch.

Het verhaal van de dierentuin. De dood van Bessie
Smith. De Droom Amerika. Tr. Gerard Kornelis
van het Reve. Amsterdam: Van Ditmar, 1964.
Dutch.

Il Sogna Americano e altre commedie. Tr. Ettore
Capriolo. Milan: Bompiani, 1963. Italian.

La Rêve de l'Amérique. Zoo Story. La Morte de
Bessie Smith. Le Tas de sable. Tr. George
Belmont and Elisabeth Janvier. Paris: Laffont,
1965. French.

THE BALLAD OF THE SAD CAFE

Balada o smutne Kavarne. Tr. Luba and Rudolf Pellar.
Prague: Dilia, 1964. Czech.

Die Ballade vom Traurigen Cafe. Tr. Pinkas Braum.
Frankfurt am Main: S. Fischer Verlag, 1964.
German.

BOX-MAO-BOX

Kiste, Worte des Vorsitz enden Mao Tse-tung, Kiste.
Tr. Pinkas Braum. Frankfurt am Main: S.
Fischer Verlag, 1969. German.

Kiste und Worte des Vorsitzenden Mao Tse-tung. Tr.
Pinkas Braum. Theater heute 10 (March 1969):
47-55. German.

THE DEATH OF BESSIE SMITH

Nuovo teatro americano: La morte de Bessie Smith, et
al. Tr. Furio Columbo. Milan: Bompiani,
1963. Italian.

Smrt Bessie Smithove. Tr. Bedrich Becher. Prague:
Dilia, 1965. Czech.

See The American Dream above.

A DELICATE BALANCE

Délicate Balance. Tr. Matthieu Galey. Paris:
Lafont, 1967. French.

Empfindliches Gleichgewicht. Winzige Alice. Tr.
    Pinkas Braum. Frankfurt am Main: S. Fischer
    Verlag, 1967. German.

En Harfin Balance. Tr. Frederik Dessau. Copenhagen:
    Gyldendal, 1967. Danish.

Um Equilibro Delicado. Tr. Sergio Viotti. Rio de
    Janeiro, 1968. Spanish.

In wankel evenwicht. Tr. Ernst van Altena. Amster-
    dam: Van Ditmar, 1967. Dutch.

Issorropia Tromou. Tr. Frontas Kondyles. Athens,
    1968. Greek.

Kenyes Egyensuly. Tr. Adam Rez. Budapest, 1968.
    Hungarian.

Kil Payi. Tr. Sevgi Sanli. Ankara, 1968. Turkish.

Krehka Rovnovaha. Tr. Luba and Rudolf Pellar.
    Prague: Dilia, 1968. Czech.

THE SANDBOX

See The American Dream above.

TINY ALICE

Kleine Alice. Tr. Ernest van Altena. Amsterdam:
    Van Ditmar, 1965. Dutch.

Winzige Alice. Frankfurt am Main: S. Fischer
    Verlag, 1965. Acting edition. German.

"Winzige Alice." In Theater 1966 Chronik und Bilanz
    eines Buehnenjahres, special yearly issue of
    Theater heute, 20 August 1966, pp. 85-103.
    German.

See A Delicate Balance above.

WHO'S AFRAID OF VIRGINIA WOOLF?

Chi ha paura di Virginia Woolf? Tr. Ettore Capriolo.
    Milan: Bompiani, 1963. Italian.

Hvem er bange for Virginia Woolf? Tr. Astra Hoff-
    Jørgenson. Copenhagen: Gyldendal, 1964.
    Danish.

Hvem er redd for Virginia Woolf? Tr. Peter Magus.
    Oslo: Gyldendal, 1964. Norwegian.

Kdo se boji Virginie Woolfove? (Kdo by se Kafky
bal). Tr. Luba and Rudolf Pellar. Prague:
Dilia, 1964. Czech.

Qui a peur de Virginia Woolf? Tr. Jean Cau. Paris:
Laffont, 1964. French.

"Qui a peur de Virginia Woolf?" Tr. Jean Cau.
L'Avant-Scène 339 (August 1965):10-51. French.

Sui P'a Wu Erh Fu. Tr. Yuan Chen. Taipei: Student's Book Company, 1968. Chinese.

Vem aer raedd foer Virginia Woolf? Tr. Oesten
Sjoestrand. Stockholm: Bonniers, 1964.
Swedish.

Virginia Woolf. Nanka Kowakunai. Tr. Narumi Shiro.
Tokyo, 1968. Japanese.

Wer hat Angst vor Virginia Woolf? Frankfurt am Main:
S. Fischer Verlag, 1964. German.

"Wer hat Angst vor Virginia Woolf?" In Spectaculum
7. Stuttgart: Suhrkamp Verlag, 1964. Pp. 7-
101. German.

Wie is er bang voor Virginia Woolf? Tr. Gerard
Kornelis van het Reve. Amsterdam: Van Ditmar,
1964 (1st through 4th printing) and 1965 (5th
printing). German.

THE ZOO STORY

Stalo se v zoo. Trans. Wanda Zamecka. Prague:
Dilia, 1964. Czech.

Zoo Story. Tr. Matthieu Galey. L'Avant-Scène 334
(May 1965):9-16. French.

Zoo Story. Tr. John Hahn-Petersen and Preben Harris.
Copenhagen: Gyldendal, 1966. Danish.

"Die Zoogeschichte." In Theatrum Mundi: amerikanische Dramen der Gegenwart. Frankfurt am Main:
S. Fischer Verlag, 1961. Pp. 427-50. German.

See The American Dream above.

VI. INTERVIEWS

"Albee." New Yorker, 25 March 1961, pp. 30-32.
This interview, containing pertinent information
regarding the playwright's life, including his educa-

tional failures, indicates Albee's liking for adopted
cats, modern painting, music, and art. He also discusses his work in progress at the time.

"Albee: Anger Between the Acts." Chicago Literary Times,
October 1963, pp. 1, 11, and 14.

"Albee Revisited." New Yorker, 19 December 1964, pp. 31-
33.
Albee discusses his forthcoming production of
Tiny Alice in an interview conducted during a rehearsal.

Arthur, Thomas H. "Edward Albee: auto, if not biographical." Dramatics 51 (November/December 1979):3-4.
With regard to the commercialism of his works
Albee claims that had he been smart, he "would have
written 'Son of Who's Afraid of Virginia Woolf?,'
then 'Virginia Woolf, Part 2.'" He asserts that the
ideas in his plays are filtered through himself so
they are certainly "auto; whether it's biographical
or not is another matter." Although he has little
formal education, Choate did teach him something
about self-education and he now spends a great
deal of time reading, listening to music, and getting involved in public affairs. He adds that he
has stayed away from television because there is
simply not much room there for serious playwriting.

Berkvist, Robert. "Nabokov's Lolita Becomes a Play by
Albee." New York Times, 1 March 1981, II:1:5 and
p. 4:1.
Albee says Lolita is "not the story of a dirty
old man," but he claims it is "about an obsession
with the past" and "essentially Proustian." Albee
tries to match Nabokov's style so that the dialogue
will seem "as though it was taken directly from the
book."

Booth, John E. "Albee and Schneider Observe: 'Something's
Stirring.'" Theatre Arts 45 (March 1961):22-24 and
78-79.
This interview with the playwright and the
director of most of his staged productions is concerned with determining the advances made by the new
theater and the direction in which it is going.

Clarkson, Adrienne. "Private World of Edward Albee."
Montrealer 41 (October 1967):42-45 and 47-49.
This article provides a transcript of a tele-
vision interview conducted by Clarkson.

Diehl, Digby. "Edward Albee Interviewed." Transatlantic
Review, No. 12 (Spring 1963), 57-72. Also included
in Behind the Scenes. Ed. Joseph McCrindle. New

York: Holt, Rinehart & Winston, 1971. Pp. 223-42.
In this interview Albee asserts that audiences
prefer vicarious experience to genuine involvement.
He indicates that although he writes for himself
and not for the audience, he still "does not wish
to leave them indifferent." He compares himself to
a musical composer in the manner with which he
treats his part and maintains that the playwright
should "notate" his lines in such a way "that it's
impossible for an actor to say the line incorrectly."
Albee reveals his opinion that Americans are too
much interested in writers and too little interested
in their works. At this point he emphasizes that
his dissatisfaction with American society is the
motive for his writings and he predicts that there
is still a great deal about which he can write.

Downer, Alan. "An Interview with Edward Albee." The
American Theatre Today. New York: Basic Books, 1967.
Pp. 111-23.

"Edward Albee." New Yorker, 3 June 1974, pp. 29-30.

"Edward Albee: An Interview." Times of India, 28 September 1969, pp. 5-8.

Flanagan, William. "The Art of the Theater: IV." Paris
Review 9 (Winter 1966):93-121. Reprinted as "William
Flanagan interroge Edward Albee." Tr. Claude Clergé.
In Cahiers de La Compagnie Madeleine Renaud-Jean
Louis Barrault 63 (1967):3-10. In French.
In this interview with a friend and former roommate, Albee discusses his plays, his varied theatrical experiences, and his work in progress at the
time. He also develops his principles of critical
theory with regard to the bad reviews of Malcolm and
the film version of Who's Afraid of Virginia Woolf?
In assessing the responsibilities of critics, Albee
stated that they have sold their profession short
with caustic and derogatory remarks. The article
also includes a revised manuscript of A Delicate Balance.

Gardner, Paul. "'Tiny Alice' Mystifies Albee, Too." New
York Times, 21 January 1965, p. 22.

Gelb, Arthur. "Dramatists Deny Nihilistic Trend." New
York Times, 15 February 1960, p. 23.
In this interview, Gelb discusses the trend in
American theater with two of its proponents, Edward
Albee and Jack Gelber.

Gussow, Mel. "Albee: Odd Man In on Broadway." Newsweek,
4 February 1963, pp. 49-52.
This interview includes pictures of Albee and
his mother, Frances Albee. Gussow relates him to

other young American dramatists like Gelber, Kopit, and Richardson who have also helped to establish new trends in theater.

"Is the American Youth in a Vacuum?" Albee's comments on the Dorothy Gordon Youth Forum Television Program, WNBC T.V. (25 November 1965). A transcript is available from the Zimmer Reporting Service, New York City.

Kosner, Edward. "Social Critics, Like Prophets, Are Often Honored from Afar." New York Post, 31 March 1961, p. 38.
This early interview with the playwright includes some pictures.

Lester, Elenore. New York Times, 16 August 1966, p. 35.
This interview with Albee was conducted at his new home.

"Lisby, R. Barr, M. Gottfried, and Others on Interview with Edward Albee." New York Times, 9 May 1971, II: 6.

Lukas, Mary. "Who Isn't Afraid of Edward Albee?" Show (February 1963), 83, 112-14.
This interview was occasioned by the success of Who's Afraid of Virginia Woolf? and it contains a great deal of biographical information. This material is applied in conjunction with modern psychological theories in an effort to relate Albee's early life to its effect on his artistic temperament.

Meehan, Thomas. "Edward Albee and a Mystery." New York Times, 27 December 1964, II:1 and 16.
This interview with the playwright occurs on the eve of the premiere of Tiny Alice and indicates the play is a real mystery.

Le Monde, 28 October 1967, p. 15a.

Morgan, T. B. "Angry Playwright in a Soft Spell." Life, 26 May 1967, pp. 90-90B, 93-94, 96, 97.
This interview contains pictures and relates relevant biographical material.

Newquist, Roy. "Interview with Edward Albee." In Showcase. New York: William Morrow, 1966. Pp. 17-29.

New York Times, 22 January 1961, II:1.

New York Times, 9 February 1971, p. 32.
This interview was conducted during a rehearsal of All Over and includes comments by Albee regarding the production.

New York Times, 18 April 1971, II:6.

New York Times, 18 July 1971, II:4.
    Albee is interviewed at the Flanagan Center for
    Creative Persons.

New York Times Magazine, 20 October 1963, p. 27.
    This interview is with director Alan Schneider.

Saponta, Marc. "Edward Albee." Informations et Docu-
    ments 187 (1963):20-22.

Skow, J. "Broadway's Hottest Playwright, Edward Albee."
    Saturday Evening Post 237 (1964):32-33.
        In this interview, complete with pictures, Skow
    reveals the growth of Albee's reputation.

Smith, Michael. "Edward Albee in Conversation with
    Michael Smith." Plays and Players (March 1964):12-
    14.
        This interview was conducted in England.

Stewart, R. S., ed. "John Gielgud and Edward Albee Talk
    about the Theater." Atlantic, April 1965, pp. 61-68.
        These interviews are in connection with the pro-
    duction of Tiny Alice. Albee reveals his theories of
    writing and indicates the responsibilities of modern
    playwrights.

Tallmer, Jerry. "Edward Albee, Playwright." New York
    Post, 4 November 1962, p. 10.

Terzieff, L. Le Monde, 11-12 February 1965.

Wager, Walter. "Playwright at Work: Edward Albee."
    Playbill, 1 (May 1964).

_____, ed. Playwrights Speak. New York: Delacorte
    Press, 1967. Pp. 25-67. An interview with Albee
    reprinted from Beverwyck (Siena College), (Winter
    1965).

Weatherby, W. J. "Do You Like Cats?" Manchester Guardian,
    19 June 1962.
        This interview contains pictures of Albee and
    discusses his personal qualities, such as his fond-
    ness for cats.

"Who's Afraid of Success?" Newsweek, 4 January 1965, p. 51.
        This interview was conducted on the eve of the
    premiere of Tiny Alice.

Zindel, Paul, and Loree Yerby. "Interview with Edward
    Albee." Wagner Literary Magazine, No. 3, 1962-63.

SECONDARY SOURCES

I. CRITICISM

Acharya, Shanta. "The Drama of Confrontation: A Study of
    Edward Albee." Indian Journal of English Studies 18
    (1978-1979):83-96.
        Albee himself confronts the major social issues
    of American life. His characters, such as George in
    Who's Afraid of Virginia Woolf?, Grandma in The
    American Dream, and Jerry in The Zoo Story, all
    force confrontations with callous, uncaring people,
    making them aware of their own humanness and of
    life's complexities.

_____. "The Zoo Story: Alienation and Love." Literary
    Criticism 12 (1978):27-36.
        Albee experiments with various dramatic tech-
    niques of the Absurd Theater, but he refuses to in-
    dulge in its metaphysics. Since his concern is pri-
    marily social, his plays serve to re-establish the
    overriding significance of individual human relation-
    ships.

_____. "The Zoo Story and the Myth of the Garden Set-
    ting." Rajasthan Journal of English Studies 7-8
    (1978):29-35.
        Acharya discusses the garden archetype and its
    symbolic function in The Zoo Story.

Adams, H. R. "Albee, the Absurdists and High School Eng-
    lish?" English Journal 55 (November 1966):1045-48.
        The suitability of Albee and other absurdists
    for study by high school students and other adoles-
    cents is questioned.

Adler, Thomas P. "Albee's Seascape: Humanity at a Second
    Threshold." Renascence 31 (1979):107-14.
        Though Adler sees the tone of the maturing Albee
    as increasingly somber, he views Seascape as a funda-
    mentally optimistic work; he feels the play can best
    be approached "as a reverse mirror image of the ear-
    lier play," All Over. After drawing parallels be-
    tween the two, he likens the struggling optimism of
    Seascape to certain attitudes of Thornton Wilder.

_____. "Albee's Who's Afraid of Virginia Woolf?: A
    Long Night's Journey into Day." Educational Theatre
    Journal 25 (March 1973):66-70.
        Most critics have agreed that the illusion/
    reality dichotomy in Who's Afraid of Virginia Woolf?
    is the central thematic motif, yet there has been
    considerable discussion as to which one Albee pre-

ferred. A re-examination of the play with greater emphasis on the character development of Nick and Honey renders the conclusion less ambiguous by revealing its basically optimistic position. George observes a radical change in the young couple as Honey moves from a fear of pregnancy to a desire for a child and Nick undergoes a rebirth of creativity. And George exorcises the imaginary child in the destruction of an illusion in order to create a new reality, his renewed marriage.

Agnihotri, S. M. "Child-Symbol and Imagery in Edward Albee's Who's Afraid of Virginia Woolf?" Punjab University Research Bulletin (Arts) 3 (October 1972):108-11.
    Agnihotri disagrees with Richard Schechner who has branded this play as escapist in his essay "Who's Afraid of Edward Albee?" The symbolic overtones of character and image, particularly the dominating image of parenthood, establish this play as a tragic myth of a barren civilization.

"Albee vs. Chester." Letters from readers, Commentary 36 (October 1963):272-75.
    Readers react to Alfred Chester's attack on Who's Afraid of Virginia Woolf? in his review (April 1963, pp. 296-301).

Amacher, Richard E. Edward Albee. New York: Twayne Publishers, 1969.
    The first two chapters concentrate on biographical information and present Albee's literary theory. In the remainder of the book, Amacher analyzes each of the plays. He also endeavors to relate Albee's life to his works and draws a respectable picture of the man as an important figure in literary circles.

"American Playwrights." Times Literary Supplement (London), 8 June 1962, p. 428.
    This article offers brief criticism of Albee's first four plays published in book form in England.

Anderson, Mary C. "Staging the Unconscious: Edward Albee's Tiny Alice." Renascence 32 (1980):178-92.
    Anderson cleverly shows that Tiny Alice is a dramatized model of the worship of the unconscious with ego, id, and superego in conflict.

Armstrong, Madeleine. "Edward Albee and the American Dream." Quadrant 9 (March 1965):62-67.
    In questioning the rationale behind Who's Afraid of Virginia Woolf?'s appeal to both middle-class and avant-garde audiences, Armstrong endeavors to relate the play to Albee's earlier works. She claims that its success results from the playwright's ability to break down the barriers of the living

room and to familiarize his characters with the audience. He also continues to provide relevant social criticism and suggestions for improvement.

Ballew, Leighton M. "Who's Afraid of Tiny Alice?" Georgia Review 20 (Fall 1966):292-99.
Reviewers and critics--even Albee himself--have been unable to decide upon the central thematic motif of this play. Ballew suggests that the entire play takes place in Julian's mind. Blending techniques of reality and fantasy, Albee deals with problems of illusion and reality, existential agony, and the nature of God. Albee provides no solutions to these problems but rather he indicates the essential absurdity of the human condition.

_____, and Gerald Kahan. "The AETA Production Lists Project Survey: 1969." Educational Theatre Journal 23 (October 1971):298-306.
This article lists the results of tabulations compiled over the season of 1969-70 regarding theater performances throughout the country. It reveals that seven full-length plays by Albee had a total of 53 different productions during the time frame. It also indicates that Albee had the greatest number of one-act plays produced with five plays being produced 90 times. In all categories, works by Albee ranked behind only those of Shakespeare and Tennessee Williams.

Bauzyte, Galina. "Illiuzijos ir tikroves konflictas Edvardo Olbio dramaturgijoje." Literature: Lietuvos TSR Aukstuju Mokyklu Mokslo Darbai (Vilnius) 15 (1973):79-94. In Russian.
This article indicates the response in Russia to the plays of Edward Albee. Summaries in both Russian and English are appended to the text. Emphasis is placed on Albee's criticisms of American society.

Baxandall, Lee. "The Theatre of Edward Albee." Tulane Drama Review 9 (Summer 1965):19-40.
Freudian criticism provides the focal point for analysis of Albee's early plays. His characters show the moral degeneration of America. The action of his plays symbolically represents repugnant aspects of society while at the same time it remains theatrical. Nonetheless, his power to affirm values or to offer suggestions is limited.

_____. "Theatre and Affliction." Encore 10 (May-June 1963):8-13.
The American theater is an ailing institution because of a disease in the society that produces it. Only because drama is such an integral facet of society does it survive. There is no tradition, nor

can there be, until subsidized repertory companies appear. Inge and Williams present realistic dramatic structures that condemn, but are restricted to "limited allusion to basic social forces." On the other hand, Albee's Who's Afraid of Virginia Woolf? is an allegorical anti-myth that captures the "ghoulish spectacle of our decline and collapse." Still, no one offers an adequate diagnosis of the causes of social affliction.

Bennett, Robert B. "Tragic Vision in The Zoo Story." Modern Drama 20 (1977):55-66.
Bennett calls for a re-examination of Jerry's death in The Zoo Story based on Albee's own stage directions which are included "in order to prevent us and the actor who plays Jerry from either sentimentalizing his death scene or regarding it purely as a Christ-like sacrifice." He claims that Jerry, and Albee, are quite conscious of the frailty of the symbolic solution. Most critics see Jerry as the victim of a ruthless society, but Bennett maintains that he brings his burdens to bear upon himself because of his overwhelming apathy and aloofness; only through his aggressive encounter with Peter does he find solace and a possible transference of attitudes.

Bernstein, Samuel. The Strands Entwined: A New Direction in American Drama. Boston: Northeastern University Press, 1980.
In all of his essays on the drama Bernstein shows that naturalism and absurdism are blended to produce powerful new plays. In his detailed discussion of Seascape, which includes a plot summary and a lengthy pastiche of critical assessment, he notes that while Seascape has realistic dialogue, it also has surrealistic characters in lizard suits and is therefore typical of the 1970s.

Besdine, Matthew. "The Jocasta Complex, Mothering and Genius (Part II)." Psychoanalytic Review 55 (Winter 1968-69):547-600.
The salient features of a typical personality resulting from Jocasta mothering are quite evident in certain characters of Albee's plays. These characteristics develop in the child when the family is dominated by an affection-hungry mother and an absent, inept, distant, or aloof father. Also cited as confirming evidence of this facet of modern fiction are Shaw, Conrad, Tennessee Williams, Whitman, Maugham, Poe, and Wilde.

Bierhaus, E. G., Jr. "Strangers in a Room: A Delicate Balance Revisited." Modern Drama 17 (1974):199-206.
In his re-examination, Bierhaus focuses on the significance of the characters' names, the surprising permutations of the characters, and, finally,

the parable of Tobias and the cat. "The Players" in
A Delicate Balance evoke biblical, historical, and
sexual references through their naming and add to the
ironic incongruities of character development. Ultimately, Bierhaus maintains that Tobias' parable of
the cat is an analogue of the whole play, and he further illustrates this point through an in-depth study
of its "eleven salient points."

Bigsby, C. W. E. Albee. Edinburgh: Oliver and Boyd,
    1969.
        Bigsby discusses Albee's role as the leading
    young American dramatist. He focuses on the play-
    wright's early life as a factor in his later develop-
    ment and argues that Albee is not an absurdist; he
    only exhibits some similarities to this European
    form in some of his work. Bigsby provides a short
    biography, bibliography, and briefly analyzes each
    of Albee's plays and adaptations through A Delicate
    Balance.

_____. Confrontation and Commitment: A Study of Ameri-
    can Drama: 1959-66. New York: MacGibbon and Kee,
    1967. Pp. 71-92.
        This collection of essays includes revisions of
    earlier printed criticism of Albee.

_____. "Curiouser and Curiouser: Edward Albee and the
    Great God Reality." Modern Drama 10 (December 1967):
    258-66.
        However serious the faults of Tiny Alice, the
    play nonetheless represents a logical extension of
    the theme of reality and illusion developed in Al-
    bee's earlier works. In Who's Afraid of Virginia
    Woolf?, for instance, he expresses the need to face
    reality but does not establish precisely what that
    reality is. In Tiny Alice he sets out to find it and
    discovers that the "symbolic pattern is essentially
    Platonic"--a revelation of the "dilemma of modern
    society in retreat from reality" or truth.

_____. "Edward Albee's Georgia Ballad." Twentieth
    Century Literature 13 (January 1968):229-36.
        Bigsby provides part defense and part censure of
    Albee and McCullers as writers in the absurdist tra-
    dition. The Albee adaptation of McCullers' The Bal-
    lad of the Sad Cafe does represent a further exten-
    sion on the theme of isolation accompanied by a
    slight hope for amelioration and human exchange. The
    play suffers in several of the changes instigated by
    Albee: the history of Marvin's relationship to Ame-
    lia is given too great a role; turning narration in-
    to rural idiom is a weakness; and the introduction
    of a Negro narrator into the drama brings in extra-
    neous considerations.

_____. "The Strategy of Madness: An Analysis of Edward Albee's A Delicate Balance." Contemporary Literature 9 (Spring 1968):223-35.
Where Who's Afraid of Virginia Woolf? had examined "the impotence of contemporary society, A Delicate Balance attempts to penetrate to the fear of which this impotence is merely one expression." Albee affirms the freedom of man to grapple with such fear and its attendant guilt. Individuals can only deal with reality by renewing "love even in the face of inevitable failure." An analysis of the play shows that it justifies the Pulitzer Prize Committee's belated selection.

_____. "Who's Afraid of Virginia Woolf?: Edward Albee's Morality Play." Journal of American Studies 1 (October 1967):257-68.
Bigsby penetrates into the play as "a modern secular morality play." He sees Albee accepting and transcending the absurdist vision by teaching the secular gospel regarding the primacy of human interchange based on a complete acceptance of reality. The games help to bring about a gradual disintegration of illusion that leads from humiliation to humility.

_____, ed. Edward Albee: A Collection of Critical Essays. Englewood Cliffs, N.J.: Prentice-Hall, 1975.
Bigsby includes essays from some of the most renowned theater critics. Nonetheless he attacks modern academic and theatrical criticism in his introductory remarks. He adds that "few playwrights can have been so frequently and mischievously misunderstood, misrepresented, overpraised, denigrated, and precipitately dismissed." He includes a chronology of important dates in Albee's life and a selected bibliography.

Blau, Herbert. The Impossible Theater. New York: Macmillan, 1964. Pp. 39-42.
Blau discusses Albee's critical theory and early development. He also adds a brief analysis of Who's Afraid of Virginia Woolf?

Bowers, Faubion, and Glen M. Loney. "Theatre of the Absurd: It is Only a Fad (Loney). It Is Here to Stay (Bowers)." Theatre Arts 46 (November 1962):20-24.
Loney writes approvingly of Albee's work with regard to a Theater of the Absurd which has no real context. Bowers focuses on The Zoo Story as an important piece of absurdist drama.

Brede, Regine. "Edward Albee." Literatur in Wissenschaft und Unterricht (Kiel) 8 (1975):30-46.
Brede surveys Albee's achievements from The Zoo Story to Everything in the Garden. A brief biography

of the playwright is provided as well as a concise
history of American critical opinion regarding his
works. The question of whether Albee is a nihilist
or an engaged humanist is debated. Through descriptions of Albee's themes and techniques Brede attempts
to show Albee's commitment to intellectual honesty
and social reform. There is a four-page bibliography
at the conclusion of the article.

Brody, Jane E. "The Case Is Familiar, but the Theater Is
Absurd." New York Times, 15 July 1967, p. 15.
    Brody takes a psychiatric approach to The Zoo
Story in order to understand its significance as ab-
surdist drama.

Brown, Daniel R. "Albee's Targets." Satire Newsletter 6
(Spring 1969):46-52.
    Albee sympathizes with his characters to achieve
his satiric ends. They are witty, almost never crude,
opaquely obscene--for Albee is not disgusted with
everything human, only those humans whose behavior
warrants his animosity. His objects of attack are,
more uncomfortably, specific rather than "mankind";
he criticizes the basic values most readers unconsciously accept: class virtues, marriage, and moth-
erhood. Nonetheless, his belief in the correctabil-
ity of man is evident, and although he rarely offers
suggestions for improvements, his empathy for the
human situation emerges through the satire.

Brown, Terence. "Harmonic Discord and Stochastic Process:
Edward Albee's A Delicate Balance." Re: Arts and
Letters 3 (1970):54-60.
    Recognizing the nature of the human condition is
the theme of A Delicate Balance where the characters
have an inherent commitment to mutual aggression.
The play is a realistic, yet allegorical, modern
tragedy revealing man's loss of humanity until con-
tention and confrontation are the only acts which
lend meaning to his existence.

Brunkhorst, Martin. "Albees Frühwerk in Kontext des
absurden Theaters: Etappen der Deutungsgeschichte."
Literatur in Wissenschaft und Unterricht 12 (1979):
304-18.
    Brunkhorst concerns himself with Albee's five
early one-act plays, two of which were first performed in Berlin. He is particularly interested in
The Zoo Story, reviewing both audience and critical
responses to it in Germany and the United States. He
compares The Zoo Story to Krapp's Last Tape and evaluates Albee's early works as leading examples of
American Theatre of the Absurd.

Brustein, Robert. "The New American Playwrights." In
    Modern Occasions. Ed. Philip Rahv. New York:
    Farrar, Straus and Giroux, 1966. Pp. 124-27.
        Brustein focuses on Albee as "the logical start-
    ing point for any discussion of the new dramatic
    writing," suggesting that his major qualities are an
    "instinct for the theater" and a control of the lan-
    guage. Albee's verbal and visual images impact upon
    audiences, yet few of his works "can be readily iden-
    tified as the expression of a single playwright; and
    no two works seem to be written in the same style."
    Brustein also implies that Albee relies on others be-
    cause he has nothing significant to communicate.
    Nonetheless, he admits that Albee is still one of the
    rare American playwrights with whom one can interact
    and show "more than apathy and indifference."

_____. Seasons of Discontent. New York: Simon and
    Schuster, 1965. Pp. 28-29, 46-49, 145-48, 155-58,
    and 304-11.
        All sections on Albee have been published sepa-
    rately and are listed in this bibliography individu-
    ally as reviews. These include: (1) "Albee and the
    Medusa-Head," (2) "Fragments from a Cultural Explosion,"
    (3) "Krapp and a Little Claptrap," (4) "The Playwright
    as Impersonator," and (5) "Three Plays and a Protest."

Busch, Frieder. "Albees A Delicate Balance: Balanceakt
    mit oder ohne Netz?" In Geschichte und Gesellschaft
    in der amerikanischen Literatur. Ed. Karl Schubert
    and Ursula Müller-Richter. Heidelberg: Quelle and
    Meyer, 1975.

Byars, John A. "Taming of the Shrew and Who's Afraid of
    Virginia Woolf?" Cimarron Review 21 (October 1972):
    41-48.
        Byars examines a series of allusions in Who's
    Afraid of Virginia Woolf? to illustrate the universal
    theme of male domination he finds in the play. He
    believes the legend of St. George and the dragon,
    the novels of Virginia Woolf, and the Oedipus myth
    are carefully planned allusions in the play. But
    the most significant allusion is to The Taming of
    the Shrew. George's games are compared to Petruchio's
    and we are meant to believe that Martha has become
    obedient at the play's conclusion.

Calta, Louis. "Albee Lectures Critics on Taste." New
    York Times, 23 March 1965, p. 33.
        Calta reports on Albee's press conference fol-
    lowing the opening of Tiny Alice at the Billy Rose
    Theater.

Campbell, Mary E. "The Statement of Edward Albee's Tiny
Alice." Papers on Language and Literature 10 (Winter
1968):85-100.
Campbell endeavors to clarify the meaning and
value of Tiny Alice by focusing on the structural
lines of the play, "allowing the sense of Albee's
intent for the play to rise from this kind of focus."
In this light, she suggests the theme to be one of
meeting the ever-increasing dilemmas confronting
modern Western man. She sketches out the main struc-
turing in the play and analyzes its thematic content
from this vantage point, concluding that the play
has some real virtues in spite of a glaring inconsis-
tency in the roles of the minor characters.

_____. "Tempters in Albee's Tiny Alice." Modern Drama
13 (1970):22-33.
The character Julian, an Everyman with a touch
of superiority, seems to be created to challenge the
power of evil to seduce him. Certainly Albee presents a workable framework in which the surrounding
characters personify an assortment of modern tempta-
tions. The allegory presents them functioning alone
and at different levels. In any case, the analogy
is appropriate if Julian is regarded in this manner.

Capellán, Gonzalo Angel. "Albee: Una década." Primer
Acto (Madrid) 116 (1969):67-74.
One decade after The Zoo Story Albee has been
recognized as America's major new dramatic talent.
The spectacular success of Virginia Woolf is noted
and the more mixed reception of Tiny Alice. The
question is, will Albee move on to theatre immortal-
ity, or is his best work behind him?

Cappelletti, John. "Are You Afraid of Edward Albee?"
Drama Critique 6 (Spring 1963):84-88.
Cappelletti defends Albee's attack on artificial
values in American society, "its complacency, cruelty, emasculation, vacuity." And in spite of the
scathing critical remarks that he is nihilistic, de-
featist, and immoral, the audience will "stay and
listen."

Carr, Duane R. "St. George and the Snapdragons: The Influence of Unamuno on Who's Afraid of Virginia
Woolf?" Arizona Quarterly 29 (1973):5-13.
A comparison between this play and Miguel de
Unamuno's "Saint Emmanuel the Good, Martyr" reveals
a strong influence of the Spanish existentialist on
Albee. Don Emmanuel protects those around him from
experiencing the nothingness of existence by allowing
them to maintain the illusion that God exists, although he knows this to be untrue. In the same way,
George helps sustain Martha's illusions and protects
her from the existential despair he constantly en-

counters until she retreats too far into her fantasy
world. Only then does he act, and, like Saint Emmanuel who attained salvation, George achieves a
"hint of communion" with Martha.

Chabrowe, L. E. "The Pains of Being Demystified." Kenyon
Review 25 (1963):142-49.
Chabrowe indicates that he finds the Theater of
the Absurd unsatisfying although he does show some
appreciation of Albee's work in his criticism of The
American Dream and Who's Afraid of Virginia Woolf?

Chamberlain, Lowell. "Pismo ot Nyu York: Novi piesi na
stsente v Broduey (Letter from New York: New Plays
on Broadway Stages)." Plamuk, No. 10 (1968):87.
Two plays presented on Broadway this season
were Miller's The Price and Albee's Everything in
the Garden. The public expects Albee to satirize
American society with greater weapons than sheer wit,
but he, like Miller, stops short of radical analysis
or suggestion. Nonetheless, the drama enables the
audience to ascertain the situation and to provide
the resolutions themselves.

Chester, Alfred. "Edward Albee: Red Herrings and White
Whales." Commentary 35 (April 1963):296-301.
Chester sees Albee assuming the role of "the
artist as judge." Albee despises rather than com-
prehends, and by limiting himself to this judgment,
he confines himself to the study of the irrelevant.
A passion for symbolism has overshadowed the real
meaning of art and rendered Albee's works impotent.

Choudhuri, A. D. The Face of Illusion in American Drama.
Atlantic Highlands, N.J.: Humanities Press, 1979.
Pp. 129-43.
Choudhuri surveys the important role which illusion plays in modern American drama from The Adding
Machine, where machines create illusion, through the
work of O'Neill, Miller, and Williams. In his last
chapter he discusses the death of illusion in Who's
Afraid of Virginia Woolf?, but he asks whether in-
deed life will be tolerable for George and Martha
without their illusion.

Clurman, Harold. The Naked Image: Observations on the
Modern Theatre. New York: Macmillan, 1966.
Pp. 13-24.
In this book, Clurman reprints his reviews of
The Zoo Story, The American Dream, The Death of
Bessie Smith, and Tiny Alice.

Cohen, Marshall. "Theater '67." Partisan Review 34
(1969):436-44.
In this view of the theater scene, Cohen contrasts Albee with Pinter, indicating that the

American playwright "has never quite succeeded in domesticating his European sources and, if he frees himself from one influence, it is only to subject himself to another." He goes on to illustrate his point but still concedes to Albee a singularly American significance. In any case, he devotes a large portion of the analysis to the study of A Delicate Balance.

Cohn, Ruby. "Albee's Box and Ours." Modern Drama 14 (1971):137-43.
    By applying musical form to dramatic structure, Albee has at last escaped the criticism that he is imitative. In Box and in the play that it encloses, Quotations from Chairman Mao Tse-tung, the audience is presented with two realistic characters who frequently quote supposedly definitive sources as though they were unaware of the other one. This action is played against a complex pattern of symbolic objects. Albee portrays man as being "boxed in" much in the same manner as a composer might do within a musical piece.

_____. Edward Albee. Minneapolis: University of Minnesota Press, 1969.
    In this pamphlet on Albee, Cohn includes a brief biography of the playwright prior to her analyses of the ten plays, opera libretto, and three adaptations created by Albee during his first decade as a professional playwright. "Although Albee has provoked extravagant praise and venomous dispraise," Cohn suggests his "drama merits dispassionate analysis."

_____. Dialogue in American Drama. Bloomington: Indiana University Press, 1971. Pp. 130-69.
    Cohn calls Albee "the most skillful composer of dialogue that America has produced," but his very facility with language has allowed him "to deny subsurface search." She analyzes the major plays through Box-Mao-Box, emphasizing the playwright's mastery of the colloquial idiom.

Cole, Douglas. "Albee's Virginia Woolf and Steele's Tatler." American Literature 40 (March 1968):81-82.
    Cole suggests that Steele's Tatler, Number 85, where Steele likens certain marital relationships to a game he calls "Snapdragon," is a possible source for one of the games in Who's Afraid of Virginia Woolf?

Coleman, D. C. "Fun and Games: Two Pictures of Heartbreak House." Drama Survey 5 (Winter 1966-67):223-36.
    Although many similarities have been drawn between Albee's early plays and those of George Bernard Shaw, it is Who's Afraid of Virginia Woolf? which is

so much like Shaw's <u>Heartbreak House</u>. The form,
structures, characters, and, in particular, the sad
games which end on a serious note are essentially
the same.

Corona, Mario. "Edward Albee." <u>Studi Americani</u> 10
    (1963):369-94.
        Corona provides an introduction to Albee with a
    survey of his works from <u>Zoo Story</u> to <u>Who's Afraid
    of Virginia Woolf?</u>

Corrigan, Robert W. "The Soulscape of Contemporary
    American Drama." <u>World Theatre</u> 11 (Winter 1962-63):
    316-28.
        Corrigan criticizes existential theater and
    contemporary dramatists who nearly all "express ...
    tremendous concern to find a metaphor for universal
    modern man as he lives on the brink of disaster."
    The "condition" replaces all traditional form and
    action and the secret of dramatic effect lies in
    prolonging the effect of a single situation. Some
    writers like Edward Albee and Jack Gelber have made
    advances in the realm of the theater but even they
    are too self-conscious and imitative. Though the
    stage increasingly attracts poets, it is not creative
    enough, but rather it remains a "theatre without com-
    mitment ... existential without being engaged."

Coy, Javier, and Juan José Coy. "Edward Albee, el primero
    Pulitzer 1967." <u>Sic</u>: <u>Revista Venezolana de Orienta-
    ción</u> 30 (1967):408-9. Teatro Norteamericano Actual:
    Miller-Inge-Albee. Madrid: Editorial Prensa Es-
    pañol, 1967. Pp. 241-78.
        Coy provides a biographical sketch of Albee,
    recalls the theatrical debut of <u>The Zoo Story</u>, and
    recounts the plots of <u>The Death of Bessie Smith</u> and
    <u>The Sandbox</u>. He notes the enormous power and popu-
    larity of <u>Who's Afraid of Virginia Woolf?</u>

Cruz, Jorge. "Teatro: Singularidad de Albee." <u>Sur</u>
    (Buenos Aires) 284 (September-October 1963):108-10.
    In Spanish.
        Albee is shown to be a highly original writer
    on the New York scene. Although he is critical of
    American society, his technique departs from the
    usual social realism and has more in common with
    avant-garde continental dramatists. His latest play,
    <u>Who's Afraid of Virginia Woolf?</u>, stands as his most
    impressive achievement to date.

Cubeta, Paul M. <u>Modern Drama for Analysis</u>. 3rd ed. New
    York: Holt, Rinehart and Winston, 1967. Pp. 591-
    602.
        Cubeta includes <u>The Sandbox</u> in this anthology
    and provides an in-depth analysis of the plays, fo-
    cusing on Albee's efforts "to find a new dramatic

mode to contain his view of the world." He compares
the young playwright to Arthur Miller and suggests
that this play is only a natural transition from a
play like A View from the Bridge. Albee's chief
means of erecting a world devoid of spirit and humanity
are his structural and verbal vacuums.

Curry, Ryder Hector, and Michael Porte. "The Surprising
Unconscious of Edward Albee." Drama Survey 7
(Winter 1968-69):59-68.
Tiny Alice is a dramatic representation of
Jung's theory of the collective unconscious as the
basis for artistic form. Albee presents a challenge
to faith "which takes the form of a Gnostic ritual
whereby the soul is released from existence." He
also attacks the fundamental beliefs of Christendom
through the realization in Tiny Alice of "inversion,
that reversal of value which takes place at what
might be described as, quite literally, the point
of reductio ad absurdum."

Daniel, Walter C. "Absurdity in The Death of Bessie
Smith." College Language Association Journal 8
(September 1964):78-80.
Through the development of his central character, the ambitious Negro orderly who believes in the
American dream, Albee creates a concrete image of
the absurd. The orderly's dilemma can be compared
to Camus' doctrine of absurdity expressed in The
Myth of Sisyphus; his efforts to free himself force
him into the degrading stereotype which Southern
society demands.

Davison, Richard Alan. "Edward Albee's Tiny Alice: A
Note of Re-examination." Modern Drama 9 (1968):54-
60.
By most standards of recent drama Tiny Alice is
reasonably successful. Davison views it as an interpretation of symbols in "Albee's aesthetically
unified view of man's tragic struggle in an equivocal
and enigmatic universe." What renders the play at-
tractive is Albee's unfailing sense of the "ingredi-
ents of good drama--that action and language can be
made doubly resilient if plot, character, diction,
thought, spectacle, and song are tuned to vibrate
sympathetically."

Debusscher, Gilbert. Edward Albee: Tradition and Renewal.
Brussels: American Studies Center, 1967.
Debusscher endeavors to determine Albee's
achievements to date along with his indebtedness to
his American predecessors and to some European playwrights. He directs his attention to Albee's "often
highly successful union of expression and thematic
content" in presenting themes, symbols, and structure. Biographical material is limited and Debusscher

stresses analysis of Albee's early one-act plays "since most of his more recent offerings have been dealt with extensively by his critics." He comments on each work, including adaptations, written through 1966.

De Ruyter, V. "Tiny Alice." De Vlaamse Gids 51 (February 1967):86-91.
    Although the play has initiated considerable critical controversy, De Ruyter maintains that Albee intends it to be Brother Julian's dream vision: the lawyer is God, the Butler is the Holy Ghost, Tiny Alice is the Virgin Mary, and the Cardinal is the Catholic Church. Brother Julian has been chosen by the Virgin Mary to be the new Messiah, and he ultimately sacrifices himself.

Deutsch, Robert H. "Writers Maturing in the Theater of the Absurd." Discourse 7 (Spring 1964):181-87.
    He compares Edward Albee with Eugene Ionesco and says that each expresses the same message concerning a world without meaning. Our lives have no significance; we cannot communicate and we are inwardly corrupt. Finally, and most importantly, we are unable to believe.

Dias, Earl J. "Full-Scale Albee." Drama Critique 8 (Fall 1965):107-12.
    In an effort to discover Albee's theatrical ambitions and his achievements to date, Dias examines technique and theme in Who's Afraid of Virginia Woolf?, The Ballad of the Sad Cafe, and Tiny Alice. The Ballad, though bizarre, is skillful; Tiny Alice carries all the significant Albee themes; but the one "undeniable masterpiece" is still Virginia Woolf.

Dollard, John. "The Hidden Meaning of Who's Afraid ...?" Connecticut Review 7 (October 1973):24-48.
    Behind the stormy scenes of Who's Afraid of Virginia Woolf?, Dollard sees a writer expressing loving motives. Albee is viewed as a genius in the use of deep psychological insight and as a playwright of great poetic power.

Dommergues, Pierre. "La Conscience Magique d'Edward Albee." Cahiers de la Compagnie Madeleine Renaud-Jean Louis Barrault 63 (1967):18-22.
    Dommergues believes American drama has a social conscience—as in Arthur Miller's plays—or a sense of theatre magic—as in Tennessee Williams' work. Albee is unique in that he combines both a social conscience and a magical quality.

Downer, Alan S. The American Theater Today. New York:
Basic Books, 1967. Pp. 111-23.
Downer covers Albee's biography and analyzes
his views on theater and movies. He emphasizes Albee's importance as a contemporary American dramatist
and also Albee's influence in shaping the new American
theater.

_____. "The Doctor's Dilemma: Notes on the New York
Theatre, 1966-67." Quarterly Journal of Speech 53
(1967):213-33.
Downer finds Albee's A Delicate Balance weak in
the area of character motivation but notes that "the
focal family was written and played with such skill
as to retain for Albee his appointment as the somewhat desperate hope of the American theatre."

Dozier, Richard J. "Adultery and Disappointment in Who's
Afraid of Virginia Woolf?" Modern Drama 11 (1969):
432-36.
Although Dozier recognizes the admirable quality
of Albee's characterization and dialogue, he sees
Who's Afraid of Virginia Woolf? as ".an unsatisfactory
play, a play of half-heartedly developed ideas, a
play that does not live up to its promise." He is
appalled at the sudden and unconvincing shift of
values in the third act. Instead of permitting the
audience to draw its own conclusions from the conflicts and revelations of the second act, Albee pro-
ceeds to show that, after examining their inner
selves, the characters can come together. In so doing, he threatens "the dramatic integrity of the
first two acts."

Driver, Tom F. Romantic Quest and Modern Query. New
York: Delacorte Press, 1970. Pp. 316-17 et passim.
Driver suggests that Albee became a culture
hero early in his playwrighting career by satisfying
the need to have a popular American dramatist of the
absurd. Although Kopit had temporarily rivaled him
for public accolade, Albee has dominated the American
theater since he came upon the scene with The Zoo
Story. His reputation has not even been diminished
by the patent inadequacies of his later plays. Driver
also implies that Albee's work is open to criticism
because it is derivative and also because "his mixture is a brew that seems calculated, consciously or
unconsciously, to cater to a debased popular taste."

_____. "What's the Matter with Edward Albee?" Reporter
30 (1964):38-39. Reprinted in Alan S. Downer's
American Drama and Its Critics. Chicago: University
of Chicago Press, 1965, pp. 240-44.
Driver quite bitterly criticizes Albee's failure
to maintain realistic conventions in the theater and
he associates him with "the dream" of the bourgeois
theater. "Four of Edward Albee's six plays are too

short to fill an evening. Another is a dead adaptation of a famous story. The sixth is the most pretentious American play since Mourning Becomes Electra." (See pages 10 and 12 of Reporter 30 [January 1964] issue for three letters in response to Driver's article.)

Dukore, Bernard F. "Tiny Albee." Drama Survey 5 (Spring 1966):60-66.
Tiny Alice can only be understood as a symbolic play. Even there the play still fails because its religious meanings are obscure and inconsistent; its character motivation is undiscoverable. When taken on a level of homosexual symbolism, the imagery and thematic structure are clouded by the complicated homosexual argot.

_____. "A Warp in Albee's Woolf." Southern Speech Journal 30 (Winter 1964):261-68.
Dukore discerns strong parallels between the plots of Who's Afraid of Virginia Woolf? and Euripides' Medea, but adds that there are significant differences as well. The Jason-Medea roles are split between George and Martha, and unlike Medea, Albee's play is "essentially a detective story."

Duplessis, Rachel Blau. "In the Bosom of the Family: Evasions in Edward Albee." Recherches Anglaises et Américaines 5 (1972):85-96.
This essay discusses Albee's family plays including Who's Afraid of Virginia Woolf?, A Delicate Balance, and The American Dream. Albee transforms problems "which do not have their origin in the family into family problems," thereby confusing psychological with social issues. In essence, he solves the contradictions in his plays by evasion and at the end they simply go away.

Duprey, Richard A. "The Battle for the American Stage." Catholic World 197 (July 1963):180.
Having tired of realism, today's theater needs intellectual, spiritual, and emotional stimulus. Traditional theater reveals man's shortcomings and offers suggestions for improvement. Avant-garde or absurdist writers such as Ionesco, Beckett, Albee, and Genet show existence to be meaningless--a world without purpose. Although these writers quite effectively use symbols, understatement, and surprise, they frequently do not communicate their intentions. Whatever lies ahead, theater should be designed for and of men.

_____. "Today's Dramatists." In American Theatre.
Stratford-Upon-Avon Studies 10. New York: St. Martin's Press, 1967. Pp. 212-16.
     Duprey recognizes the controversy generated by
Albee's works and adds that it is "most difficult to
assign any fixed position" to his technique. By
analyzing his plays through Tiny Alice, Duprey determines that Albee may or may not be an absurdist.
It matters not what he is, only that he had adequately expressed his dissatisfaction with the world as
it is and, more importantly, that he is shouting out
"in the hope of changing it."

Echeverria, José. "Le tenemos miedo a Albee? (Tentavia
de autocritica frente a nuestra situacion cultural)."
Anales de la Universidad de Chile 122 (July-September
1964):5-22. In Spanish.
     Albee is seen as the new enfant terrible of the
New York dramatists. His scolding criticisms of
American society are discussed from Zoo Story to
Who's Afraid of Virginia Woolf?

"Edward (Franklin) Albee." Current Biography (February
1963):3-5. (Pages 1-3 in bound volume.)
     This article serves as a brief introduction to
Albee's life and his works to date and has been
drawn from six sources.

Elizalde, Ignacio, S.J. "Un teatro de denuncia y de
sexo." Arbor: Revista General de Investigación y
Cultura 304 (1971):67-74. In Spanish.
     This article compares and contrasts the works
of Valle-Inclán, Salacru, Albee, and Mrôżek.

Esslin, Martin. The Theatre of the Absurd. Garden City,
N.Y.: Doubleday, 1969. Pp. 266-70.
     Esslin mentions Albee in the absurdist tradition
because his works attack the very foundations of
American optimism. Included is a brief discussion
of The Zoo Story, The Death of Bessie Smith, and The
American Dream and their relationship to the works
of Pinter and Ionesco. With Who's Afraid of Virginia
Woolf?, Albee achieved his breakthrough "into the
first rank of contemporary playwrights" and yet he
still retained the elements of absurdism evident in
his earlier works. In Tiny Alice, Albee developed a
complex image of man's search for truth and certainty
in a constantly changing world although he returned
to a more realistic setting in A Delicate Balance.
Nonetheless, his latest endeavor, Box-Mao-Box, re-
turns to the familiar absurdist tradition.

Evans, Arthur. "Love, History and Edward Albee." Renascence 19 (Spring 1967):115-18 and 131.
     Central to Albee's Who's Afraid of Virginia
Woolf? is the biblical concept of man as a creature

of History and of man as a "creature in love." The
characters are trapped by their past in the temporal
historical process and tragically suffer for failing
to overcome these forces. With the Dies Irae, they
face their failure, their self-contempt, and their
deluding myths in an endeavor to transcend history
and free themselves through divine love.

Falk, E. H. "No Exit and Who's Afraid of Virginia Woolf?:
    A Thematic Comparison." Studies in Philology 67
    (July 1970):406-17.
        One common feature of the two plays is the
    represented time dimension because each gives the
    impression of infernal eternity. The characters also
    vainly attempt to determine their self-image with re-
    gard to the true reflection of their beings. They
    are unable to transcend their limitations or to exer-
    cise any freedom in choosing acceptable commitments.
    While these two works emphasize that there is no
    exit once man has abdicated his freedom, they also
    imply that his freedom is accessible if he is willing
    to pay the price.

Felandro, Anthony and Dorothy. Letter to editor, Commen-
    tary 36 (1963):272-73.
        The Felandros relate Who's Afraid of Virginia
    Woolf? to the Jason and Medea story in Euripides'
    Medea.

Ferguson, Francis R. "A Conversation with Digby R. Diehl."
    Transatlantic Review (Spring 1965):115-21.
        Diehl criticizes Who's Afraid of Virginia Woolf?
    as narrow, unsophisticated, and unrelated to our time.

Finkelstein, Sidney Walter. Existentialism and Alienation
    in American Literature. New York: International
    Publishers, 1965. Pp. 234-42.
        Finkelstein analyzes Albee's works in an effort
    to illustrate the intellectual "deep freeze" asso-
    ciated with the cold war. Who's Afraid of Virginia
    Woolf? concretely depicts familial alienation, and
    its real value is that its "psychological revelations
    are organically connected to a very real, historical-
    ly emergent social situation." Tiny Alice shows Al-
    bee to be making existential assumptions and giving
    the questions of "existence" and the "absurdity" of
    life precedence over all others. He indicates that
    there is a type of God, a force external to this ab-
    surd universe, but to gain acceptance by this God,
    one "must go through the most terrible suffering and
    anguish, including the loss of every shred of his
    previous faith and of hope itself."

_____. "Norman Mailer and Edward Albee." American Dialog 1 (October-November 1964):23-28.
Finkelstein compares the different brands of existentialism apparent in the two writers. Mailer holds that the individual loses freedom because all conventions are oppressive, but he fails to recognize that society moves freely and collectively away from oppression. On the other hand, Albee maintains that the individual often gives up his freedom to another or to society under pressures of the "cold war" era.

Fischer, Gretl Kraus. "Edward Albee and Virginia Woolf." Dalhousie Review 49 (Summer 1969):196-207.
The inclusion of her name in the title of his play Who's Afraid of Virginia Woolf? is "an open acknowledgement" of Virginia Woolf's influence on Albee. The equal importance attached to realism and symbolism in Albee's work illustrates his association with Woolf and, in particular, "Lappin and Lapinova." They are both concerned with the destiny of the species, with its ultimate goals, and with elemental forces necessary to its progress. Their works "seem to suggest that healthful conditions will exist only where the principles of imagination and fervor combine with those of reason and action."

Fission, Pierre. "Edward Albee veut être le numero un ... ou rien." Figaro Litteraire, 23 October 1967, pp. 40-41. In French.
This Figaro article discusses Albee's aspiration to be America's leading dramatist. Some of his recent plays, such as Tiny Alice, appear controversial, but he continues to be the center of attention.

Flanagan, William. "Albee in the Village." New York Herald Tribune, 27 October 1963, p. 27.
Albee's roommate for nine years gives his own impressions of the playwright and his art now that he has become "successful."

Flasch, Joy. "Games People Play in Who's Afraid of Virginia Woolf?" Modern Drama 10 (December 1967):280-88.
Eric Berne's Games People Play offers some useful insights into the character development and interaction in Albee's Who's Afraid of Virginia Woolf? Flasch maintains that one can recognize a nearly continuous series of games and relationships running throughout the play by using the classifications made famous by Berne.

Force, William. "The 'What' Story? or Who's Who at the Zoo?" Studies in the Humanities 1 (Winter 1969):47-53.
The diverse criticism generated in response to

The Zoo Story suggests that there may be more than
one play. Force questions whether the work is so
symbolically important that it possesses several levels of meaning and perhaps a sub-text or whether some
critics have read too much into the play. Perhaps it
is merely a play which is "less clear" than confusing, and "inclined to be pretentious where it seeks
to be profound."

Franzblau, Abraham N. "A Psychiatrist Looks at 'Tiny
    Alice.'" Saturday Review, 30 January 1965, p. 39.
        Franzblau speculates on certain meanings of the
    play by looking at it psychoanalytically.

Fruchter, Norm. "Albee's Broadway Break-Thru." Encore
    10 (January-February 1963):44-48.
        Albee's first full-length play on Broadway,
    Who's Afraid of Virginia Woolf?, expands upon the
    themes and structures expressed in his earlier, and
    relatively unnoticed, one-act plays, The Zoo Story
    and The American Dream, but not completely to Fruch-
    ter's satisfaction. The games and, in particular,
    the role-playing and the fantasy-son construction
    remain quite weak. Perhaps Albee's success on Broad-
    way is merely an indication of "how rotten, debili-
    tated, and manipulative ... official American culture
    has become."

Gabbard, Lucina P. "Albee's Seascape: An Adult Fairy
    Tale." Modern Drama 21 (September 1978):307-17.
        Using Bruno Bettelheim's definition of a fairy
    tale as a "work of art which teaches about inner
    problems through the language of symbols and, there-
    fore, communicates various depths of meaning to vari-
    ous levels of the personality at various times,"
    Gabbard shows that Albee has cast all semblance of
    reality aside and has created an adult fairy tale.
    She recognizes the central motif to be the realiza-
    tion of the proximity of death that comes with the
    passing of middle age. Symbols are the play's basic
    medium and several levels of meaning are communicated
    simultaneously when the play is interpreted as an
    initiation rite--an initiation which has its final
    stage embedded in the transcendence of evolution.

_____. "At the Zoo: From O'Neill to Albee." Modern
    Drama 19 (1976):365-74.
        O'Neill was unquestionably the first American
    playwright to become a major literary figure and
    Edward Albee is the most recent important dramatist.
    The Hairy Ape and The Zoo Story also have so much in
    common that they and the playwrights become ideal
    partners for comparison. The most striking parallel,
    however, is that "each, in one of his earliest liter-
    ary efforts, wrote a play based on the same metaphor:
    man imprisoned within himself equals an animal caged

at the zoo." This common metaphor leads to similar situations, settings, and plots and shows Albee to be a social dramatist in his concern for the demise of communication within and between social classes.

Gale, Steven H. "Breakers of Illusion: George in Edward Albee's Who's Afraid of Virginia Woolf? and Richard in Harold Pinter's The Lover." Vision 1 (1979):70-77.
     Gale, an authority on Pinter, compares the roles of Pinter's Richard and Albee's George showing how they first play desperate games to preserve their marriages but ultimately are forced to shatter their wives' illusions.

Galey, Matthieu. "Albee sur le chemin de la Gloire." Nouvelles Littéraires 43 (1965):13. In French.

Gardner, R. H. The Splintered Stage: The Decline of the American Theater. New York: Macmillan, 1965. Pp. 146-53.
     Gardner attempts to show what drama should be and what it has become. He suggests that Karl Marx and Sigmund Freud have retarded the development of great drama, and to support this view he surveys modern drama from the birth of naturalism to the "impasse of the absurd" and, in particular, the works of Tennessee Williams, Arthur Miller, and Edward Albee. He includes brief discussions of The Zoo Story, The Death of Bessie Smith, The American Dream, Who's Afraid of Virginia Woolf? and The Ballad of the Sad Café to help illustrate his proposition that American theater is on the decline.

Gassner, John. Directions in Modern Theatre and Drama. New York: Holt, Rinehart and Winston, 1965. Pp. 326-36.
     Gassner includes a brief introduction to the Theater of the Absurd using Albee's works to illustrate his thesis. He also reprints Albee's article entitled "Which Theatre Is the Absurd One?"

_____. "Who's Afraid of Virginia Woolf?" In his Best American Plays, Fifth Series, 1957-1963. New York: Crown Publishers, 1963. Pp. 144-46.
     Gassner's introductory article for Who's Afraid of Virginia Woolf? deals primarily with Albee's life in the theater, although he does provide brief analyses of his earlier works. He also reprints passages from his review of the Columbia recording of the play.

Gilman, Richard. "The Drama Is Coming Now." Tulane Drama Review 7 (Summer 1963):27-42.
     Gilman sees Albee in the continuing tradition of American dramatists rather than in that of the "more

meaningful" European theater. These playwrights lack "significant" intellectuality; they fail to re-interpret and to re-locate man; their characters remain "substitute persons ... identifiable by comparison or reference to figures in the world"; and their traditional plotting has not been "repudiated" sufficiently for allegorical development.

G[ingrich], A[rnold]. "Publisher's Page: A Lively and Responsive Weekend at Princeton." Esquire, July 1963, pp. 111-12.
  Gingrich reports on Albee's participation in the seminars devoted to excellence in the fine arts, which attracted students from fifty colleges besides Princeton.

Goetsch, Paul. "Edward Albees zoogeschichten: Zur ein gelagerten Erzählung im Modernen Drama." In Amerikanisches Drama und Theater im 20. Jahrhundert. Ed. Alfred Weber and Siegfried Neuweiler. Göttingen: Vandenhoeck, 1975. Pp. 289-318.

_____. "Edward Albee: Who's Afraid of Virginia Woolf?" in Das Amerikanische Drama. Ed. Paul Goetsch. Dusseldorf: August Bagel Verlag, 1974. Pp. 295-318.
  Goetsch discusses the popularity of the play and sees in it literary influences as divergent as Strindberg and Noel Coward. He praises the clever blending of conventional realism with psychodrama and social satire.

Goodman, Henry. "The New Dramatists: 4. Edward Albee." Drama Survey 2 (Spring 1962):72-79.
  Albee's plays are "ferocious attacks" on American society and its false values and illusions. His criticism of the lethargy and complacency of Americans evolves from a private hatred. Albee is pre- -occupied with "mutilation, emasculation, and sexual warfare." Albee blends naturalism with "the poetic, the fanciful, and the grotesque, not to say a healthy measure of the satirical."

Goodman, Randolph. "Playwriting with a Third Eye: Fun and Games with Albee, Ibsen, and Strindberg." Columbia University Forum 10 (Spring 1967):18-22.
  The Strindbergian spirit found in Albee's Who's Afraid of Virginia Woolf? was derived through Ibsen's own interpretation. The play contains characters and situations parallel to those expressed in Hedda Gabler, which Ibsen purportedly based on the life and autobiographical writings of Strindberg.

Gottfried, Martin. A Theater Divided: The Postwar American Stage. Boston: Little, Brown, 1967. Pp. 262-73.
  Gottfried provides one of the most negative appraisals of Albee's work. He stresses the shallow-

ness of Albee's ideas and insists his plays are cultist dramas, best understood by homosexuals.

Gould, Jean R. "Edward Albee and the Current Scene." In Modern American Playwrights. New York: Dodd, Mead, 1966. Pp. 273-90.
 Gould points to events in Albee's early life which reveal him to be "The Poor Little Rich Boy." In endeavoring to draw comparisons between Albee's later biography and the characters in his plays, Gould is able to illustrate certain predominant themes and to show that he has shed many of the traits acquired during his "pudding years" in order to become the leading American dramatist of the era.

_____. "Pauvre petit garçon riche." Trans. Simone Benmussa. In Cahiers de la Compagnie Madeleine Renaud-Jean Louis Barrault 63 (1967):11-17.
 Same article as above.

Gray, Wallace. "The Uses of Incongruity." Educational Theatre Journal 15 (December 1963):343-47.
 Albee's use of incongruity is an important technique in modern drama employed by such writers as Beckett, Ionesco, and Pinter. There are three basic types: "Rational and meaningful, irrational and meaningless, and irrational and apparently meaningless." All types are really metaphors in that they imply or actually present the affinity between dissimilar things. For Albee it is the third type which serves both as a source of humor and as a basis for making a meaningful point, although this type of incongruity is most frequently termed "meaningless," "bewildering," or "nonsensical" by critics.

Guthke, Karl S. "Die metaphysische Farce im Theater der Gegenwart." Deutsche Shakespeare-Gesellschaft West. Jahrbuch, 1970. Pp. 49-76. In German.
 Guthke describes many modern plays as metaphysical farces or plays in which man is the victim of an absurd tragedy from which the gods withdraw in cruel delight. The transcendental world, however, is man-made. Shakespeare provides early examples and Guthke discusses the plays of Salacrou, Stoppard, Bridie, Ionesco, Pinter, Albee, and MacLeish at length to illustrate his proposition.

Haas, Rudolf. "Wer hat Angst vor Edward Albee?" In Das Amerikanische Drama. Ed. Hans Itschert. Darmstadt: Wissenschaftliche Buchgesellschaft, 1972. Pp. 420-35.
 In his analysis of Albee's contribution to modern drama, "Who Is Afraid of Edward Albee?," Haas notes that the playwright has received more enthusiastic criticism outside the United States than within his own country. Considering O'Neill and the

Absurdists as influences on Albee, Haas explores
the themes of matriarchy, the "box," death, the
American Dream and a new Eden--as evident in Albee's
major plays.

_____. "Wer hat Angst vor Edward Albee? Gedanken zum
modern amerikanischen Drama." Universitas 25 (1969):
347-62. In German. See article above.

Hafley, James. "The Human Image in Contemporary Art."
Kerygma 3 (Summer 1963):25-34.
Hafley uses Albee's work as an example of the
Theater of the Absurd which reveals itself as abstract expression in art. Man is portrayed as being
in an extra-intellectual, concrete quest for his
identity. He adds that it and the nouvelle vague
have in common themes of quest and question. What
seems obscure in art is very possibly our own ob-
scurity which the artist has successfully expressed.

Halperen, Max. "What Happens in Who's Afraid ...?" In
Modern American Drama: Essays in Criticism. Ed.
William Taylor. Deland, Florida: Everett/Edwards,
1968. Pp. 129-44.
Halperen's close reading of Who's Afraid of
Virginia Woolf? posits that George and Nick are
turning their women into monsters out of a false
sense of chivalry. They shield them from a confrontation with their own sterility and hence thwart
psychological or spiritual growth.

Hamblen, Abigail Ann. "Edward Albee ... And the Fear of
Virginia Woolf." Trace 2 (1968):198-203.
Hamblen sees the themes of loneliness, suffer-
ing, and the anguish of heightened perceptiveness
which provide the foundation of Virginia Woolf's work
to be at the core of Albee's dramas. She draws comparisons between the two writers and compliments Albee on forcing us to face the truth in ourselves.

Hamilton, Kenneth. "Mr. Albee's Dream." Queen's Quarterly 70 (1963):393-99.
Albee fails to clearly separate his characters
in The American Dream into Good and Bad. Daddy,
Mommy, and Mrs. Barker, upon re-examination, appear
more human than the Young Man and Grandma, contrary
to Albee's intentions. He makes his mistake by
superficially diagnosing the American social scene
and by failing to make any relevant social criticism.
Albee himself is the victim of a dream "no less hol-
low than that which he attacks."

Hankiss, Elemér. "Who's Afraid of Edward Albee?" New
Hampshire Quarterly 5 (Autumn 1964):168-74.
A few years ago, Albee would have been pro-
claimed a "nihilist" or "pessimist" and he would

have been shunned publicly; now he is accorded note-
worthy mention. Hankiss discusses his entry into
the international theatre and, in particular, he
analyzes the impact of Who's Afraid of Virginia Woolf?
on audiences and critics alike. Albee's social protest and his search for something different and new
has been realized in this drama, "which though
gloomy is yet full of hidden and radiating lights."

Harris, James Neill. "Edward Albee and Maurice Maeterlinck: All Over as Symbolism." Theatre Research
International 3 (1978):200-208.
    Harris opens by attributing All Over's critical
rejection to its being judged by the tenets of naturalism. He argues that the play is more properly a
symbolist drama, and after acknowledging its debt to
Waiting for Godot, he builds a case for the influence of Maeterlinck on its composition--thematically,
philosophically, and even biographically.

Harris, Wendell V. "Morality, Absurdity, and Albee."
Southwest Review 49 (Summer 1964):249-56.
    In his earlier one-act plays, Albee either de-
nies or ignores the possibility of making a choice
between good and evil. For example, he asserts that
The Zoo Story is merely a brutal attack "on humanity
itself." However, in Who's Afraid of Virginia
Woolf? he confines his "absurdity" to the stage and
directs George toward a meaningful human relationship by allowing him a consciously willed choice in
the matter.

Hatanaka, Takami. "On 'It will be better' in Who's
Afraid of Virginia Woolf?" Essays and Studies in
English Language and Literature 56 (1970):59-74. In
Japanese.
    Hatanaka argues that while George's actions in
killing the imaginary son may seem harsh, he has
finally achieved adulthood and will be able to create a more realistic basis for his and Martha's life
together.

Hays, H. R. "Transcending Naturalism." Modern Drama 5
(1962):27-36.
    Hays notes that Albee combines naturalistic
dialogue with bizarre circumstances, symbolism, and
existential philosophy in a kind of blending of absurdist and naturalistic devices.

Heiberg, Inger. "Theaterbev Fra Los Angeles--Sommeren
1967." Samtiden (Norway) 76 (1967):526-30. In Norwegian.

Heilman, Robert B. "The Dream Metaphor: Some Ramifica-
    tions." In American Dreams, American Nightmares.
    Ed. David Madden. Carbondale: University of Southern
    Illinois Press, 1970. Pp. 1-18.
        Heilman explores literary works which reflect
    the modern writer's disillusionment with American so-
    ciety. Each generation has posited its ideal program
    for a good life but recent authors, like Albee, have
    concentrated on grotesque parodies of American expe-
    rience to reveal their disappointment with current
    values and trends.

Herron, Ima Honaker. The Small Town in American Drama.
    Dallas: Southern Methodist University Press, 1968.
    Pp. 467-74.
        As a satirist without peer among his contempo-
    raries, Albee is quite capable of scathing examina-
    tions of the American scene. Herron focuses on
    Who's Afraid of Virginia Woolf?, both the stage and
    film versions, to illustrate Albee's poetic insight
    and his equally evident sardonic view of life which
    "offers little hope for the solution of our natural
    dilemma, except perhaps through an escape into the
    world cf imagination, the best means of survival
    among people living with false values."

Hilfer, Anthony Channel. "George and Martha: Sad, Sad,
    Sad." In Seven Contemporary Authors: Essays on Coz-
    zens, Miller, West, Golding, Heller, Albee, and
    Powers. Ed. Thomas B. Whitbread. Austin: Univer-
    sity of Texas Press, 1966. Pp. 119-39.
        Hilfer defends Who's Afraid of Virginia Woolf?
    against critics who view it as decadent; decadence
    is merely a theme in the play, a secondary one at
    that. He also points out Strindberg's The Dance of
    Death and O'Neill's Long Day's Journey into Night as
    influences on content and form, respectively, in
    this drama of psychological warfare.

Hill, Carol D. Letter to the Editor, Massachusetts Re-
    view 6 (1965):649-50.
        Hill acknowledges her agreement with Charles T.
    Samuels in "The Theatre of Edward Albee," Massachu-
    setts Review 6 (1964-65):187-201, when he calls Al-
    bee's works "poor social satires."

Hinds, Carolyn Myers. "Albee's The American Dream."
    Explicator 30 (October 1971): Item 17.
        The definition given the word "bumble" by James
    Thomson ("B.V.") in an essay published in 1865 makes
    meaningful Albee's use of the word in The American
    Dream. Thomson describes the "bumble" as a product
    and perpetuation of middle-class values. Opposed to
    new ideas and moral freedom, the "bumble" admires
    material success as well as the industrious manner
    in which it is obtained. Thus, when the couple in

Albee's play request a "bumble of joy" from the adoption service, they are asking for a child prefabricated to conform to their superficial values.

Hirsch, Foster. Who's Afraid of Edward Albee? Berkeley: Creative Arts Book Co., 1978.
Who's Afraid of Virginia Woolf? and A Delicate Balance are great modern plays and are assured of maintaining the reputation of Albee as a significant American playwright. His one-act plays are particularly impressive in performance and provide a view of Albee's "surging rhetorical power." Tiny Alice and Box-Mao-Box have their moments as true dramatic experimentation into the realm of language and of design. But All Over, Seascape, Counting the Ways, Listening, and the three adaptations are disappointments.

Holtan, Orley. "Who's Afraid of Virginia Woolf? and the Pattern of History." Educational Theatre Journal 25 (March 1973):46-52.
In Who's Afraid of Virginia Woolf? Albee has managed to render the events of the family drama with a deeper significance suggestive of larger events and movements. Holtan indicates that "one of the most profitable ways of looking at Who's Afraid of Virginia Woolf? is to see it as an allegory for the American historical experience." He lays the groundwork for this type of study by elaborating upon this theme in the context of Albee's earlier works and fortifies his proposition with illustrations from this play. Holtan concludes that Albee has erected "a rich and troubling allegory for the American historical experience" revealing a nation which "must cast away its comforting dreams and look reality in the face."

Hopkins, Anthony. "Conventional Albee: Box and Chairman Mao." Modern Drama 16 (September 1973):141-48.
Here, Albee further refines the techniques and images he has favored in early creations. The box especially intrigues him as a symbol of the constricting forces of modern life. The monologues in Chairman Mao are reminiscent of earlier plays and, taken together, they illustrate the failure of American ideals as measures against the pronouncements of Chairman Mao.

Hopper, Stanley Romaine. "How People Live Without Gods: Albee's Tiny Alice." American Poetry Review 2 (March/April 1973):35-38.
Albee wrote Tiny Alice as a mystery and morality play revealing the story of Julian's quest for vocation through sacrifice. The manner in which the medieval allegory is adapted to a modern cosmology renders it radically innovative but difficult to

implement. It posits immanence rather than tran-
scendence, but fails because its form detracts from
its dramatic power. The numerous metaphors are confusing because Albee could not reconcile a disjunc-
tion between medieval and modern modes.

Hübner, Paul. "Prekäre Gleichgewichte: Albee, Hofmannsthal,
and Camus." Wirkendes Wort 19 (1969):28-34.
Albee, along with the Austrian playwright Hofmannsthal and the French novelist and philosopher
Camus, expresses contemporary man's profound sense
of alienation.

Hughes, Catharine. American Playwrights 1954-1975. London: Pitman Publishing, 1976.
Hughes observes that Albee's early dramas, such
as Zoo Story and Who's Afraid of Virginia Woolf?, are
"vital and profound," but she laments the fact that
his more recent works, All Over and Seascape, are
"devoid of life and artificial."

_____. "Edward Albee: Who's Afraid of What?" Critic
21 (March 1963):16-19.
Hughes looks at Albee's early plays and endeavors to place them in the context of the themes and
techniques utilized in Who's Afraid of Virginia
Woolf? In particular, the failure of true human
contact, which dominates both The American Dream and
The Zoo Story, is adequately expressed in Who's
Afraid of Virginia Woolf? and it is Albee's total involvement with the audience which will propel him
toward greatness.

Hull, Elizabeth Anne. "A Popular Psychology Illuminates
an 'Elite' Art Medium: A Look at Albee's A Delicate
Balance Through Transactional Analysis." In Pro-
ceedings of the Sixth National Convention of the
Popular Culture Association. Comp. Michael T. Mars-
den. Bowling Green: Bowling Green State University
Press, 1976. Pp 1071-86.

Hurley, Paul J. See under Gelber, below, p. 160.

Inge, M. Thomas. "Edward Albee: La historia de amor en
la era del absurdo." In Sextas jornadas de historia
y literatura norteamericana y rioplatense. Buenos
Aires: Associación Argentina de Estudios Americanos,
1971. See translation below.

_____. "Edward Albee's Love Story of the Age of the
Absurd." Notes on Contemporary Literature 8 (1978):
4-9.
Inge emphasizes the positive aspects of George
and Martha's relationship and marriage in Who's
Afraid of Virginia Woolf? and suggests that some old-
fashioned emotions exist in the barren modern world.

Irwin, Ray. "Who's Afraid of Virginia Woolf, Hunh?" Atlantic 213 (1964):122-24.
        Irwin satirizes close textual criticism as he
is ridiculing Albee's diction. He finds the word
"hunh" used 55 times during the play and comments,
"Mr. Albee clearly has something in mind."

Itschert, Hans, ed. Das Amerikanische Drama von den An-
fangen bis zur Gegenwart. Darmstadt: Wissenshaft-
liche Buchgesellschaft, 1972.
        Itschert discusses Albee's major plays, survey-
ing his development from the writing of The Zoo
Story through Box-Mao-Box. He considers him the most
important American playwright since O'Neill, one who
blends cogent social satire with original aesthetic
perception.

Jain, Jaskir. "Procreation and Infertility in Albee's
Plays." Rajasthan Journal of English Studies 7-8
(1978):24-28.
        Jain discusses the recurrent theme of childless-
ness in several Albee plays, finding it emblematic
of a barren society. Who's Afraid of Virginia Woolf?
and The American Dream are among his major plays
which exploit this theme.

Jamieson, D. J. "On Edward Albee." Teachers College
Record 68 (January 1967):352-53.
        Jamieson considers the problems of truth vs. il-
lusion in The American Dream, Who's Afraid of Virginia Woolf?, Tiny Alice, and A Delicate Balance.
The discussions of the material are quite brief.

Johnson, Carolyn E. "In Defense of Albee." English
Journal 57 (January 1968):21-23 and 29.
        Johnson considers Albee's place in the classroom
and evaluates The Zoo Story and Who's Afraid of Virginia Woolf? with regard to their impact upon impres-
sionable high school students.

Johnson, Martha J. "Note on a Possible Source for Who's
Afraid of Virginia Woolf?" Radford Review 21 (1967):
231-33.
        Johnson suggests that Virginia Woolf's "Lappin
and Lapinova" is quite similar in form and thematic
development to Albee's Who's Afraid of Virginia
Woolf? and could possibly be an important source
which critics have previously overlooked.

Kai-Ho-Mah. "Albee's Who's Afraid of Virginia Woolf?"
Explicator 35 (Summer 1977):10-11.
        Kai-Ho-Mah endeavors to explain Albee's meta-
phorical allusion in Who's Afraid of Virginia Woolf?
to the lamps of China with regard to other motifs in
the play. "Iced drinks help them to maintain their
illusions, and like horses on the inner cylinder of

the lamps of China, the characters have long been
going round in circles and never getting anywhere."

Kamauff, John. "Edward Albee: A Chronology and Bibliography of His Works." M.A. Thesis, North Carolina, 1980.
      Kamauff wrote this thesis while he was a re-
   search assistant on this book. The core of his thesis entries are included in this section.

Kaplan, Donald M. "Homosexuality and American Theatre: A
   Psychoanalytic Comment." Tulane Drama Review 9
   (1965):25-55.
      Kaplan discusses homosexuality in the modern
   theater using very general terms. He regards it as
   an infantile means of creating "rebellion without
   revolution." Kaplan devotes two pages to the discussion of George and Martha and concludes that they
   are merely victims and propagators of this infantile,
   pregenital sexuality.

Kerjan, Lilliane. Edward Albee. Paris: Seghers, 1971.
   In French.
      Kerjan maintains that Albee's classic works
   provide a significant body of American social criticism. In asserting that Albee's theater is one of
   tempest and incandescence, she interprets the playwright's contributions in the context of worldwide
   drama and suggests that Albee is quite important as
   an international dramatist. Kerjan also analyzes
   his works from Zoo Story to Box-Mao-Box in this context and provides illustrations from several sources,
   particularly French productions.

Kerr, Walter. The Theater in Spite of Itself. New York:
   Simon and Schuster, 1963. Pp. 122-26 et passim.
      Kerr addresses Albee as a major proponent of
   absurdity in his "The Ambiguity of the Theater of
   the Absurd" and more specifically discusses Who's
   Afraid of Virginia Woolf? and its impact on the
   theater later in the book.

Kilker, Marie J. "Children and Childishness in the Plays
   of Edward Albee." Players 46 (August-September
   1971):252-56.
      In spite of the fact that children and childish
   behavior figure importantly in Albee's total work,
   most critics have neglected the other plays in defer-
   ence to the imaginary child in Who's Afraid of
   Virginia Woolf? In developing this overall theme,
   Kilker analyzes each of his plays through Box-Mao-
   Box indicating that all of his works are at least
   partially concerned with childhood, children, and
   childishness.

"King of Off-Broadway." Newsweek, 13 March 1961, p. 90.
This article concentrates on Albee's early success with his off-Broadway productions and his work
in progress. It also offers brief criticism of The
Death of Bessie Smith.

Kingsley, Lawrence. "Reality and Illusion: Continuity of
a Theme in Albee." Educational Theatre Journal 25
(March 1975):71-79.
Albee's plays (Kingsley excludes the adaptations
from consideration) are thematically similar in that
they are "preoccupied with the disparity Albee discerns between a fantasy world and the world in which
his characters must live." Kingsley suggests that
Albee's concern was brought out in response to the
Nietzschean distinction between Apollonian and Dionysian tragedy and he analyzes Albee's plays under
these guidelines, concluding that "the Apollonian
paradise ... in The American Dream is demolished in
Who's Afraid of Virginia Woolf? and in Tiny Alice,
with The Zoo Story acting as prologue to the search
for meaningful reality and A Delicate Balance an
epilogue in which that reality is, in some measure,
found."

Kishi, Tetsuo. "Coward to Albee." Eigo Seinen [The Ris-
ing Generation] (Tokyo) 114 (1968):308-09. In
Japanese.
Kishi notes that Who's Afraid of Virginia Woolf?
uses sophisticated characters and a cocktail party
setting as Noel Coward had once done; but Albee's
indictment of society, coarse language, and explicit
sexuality indicate a revolution of manners in the
West.

Klaus, Rudolf U. "Edward Albee: Eine psychologische
Studie." Ciba Symposium (Basel) 3 (1966):105-12.

Knepler, Henry. "Conflict of Tradition in Edward Albee."
Modern Drama 10 (December 1967):274-79.
Albee thus far has been trapped between two ir-
reconcilable traditions. Based on his strictly
American background, he places a premium on making
sense of his environment; on the other hand, he con-
ceives of reality as essentially meaningless, an
absurdist convention. Consequently, Albee's drama
displays a "desire to get behind things," a desire
to understand totally, while at the same time showing
the absurdist preoccupation with isolation, illusion,
and repetition.

Köhler, Klaus. "Das Underground Theatre." In Eberhard
Brüning, Klaus Köhler, and Bernard Scheller. Studien
zum amerikanischen Drama nach dem zweiten Weltkrieg.
Berlin: Rütten and Loening, 1977.

Köhler cites the influence of Beckett on The
Zoo Story and The American Dream and sees The Sandbox as an "underground" play.

Kolin, Philip C. "Two Early Poems by Edward Albee."
Resources for American Literary Study 5 (Spring 1975):
95-97.
Kolin suggests that two of Albee's early poems,
"Eighteen" and "Chopin," merit attention "not only
for the biographical inferences that might be drawn
from them but also for their relationship to the
plays which they distantly prefigure." He reprints
both works exactly as they appeared in 1944 and 1945
respectively in a poetry magazine entitled Kaleido-
graph: A National Magazine.

Kostelanetz, Richard. "American Theater--Performance,
Not Literature." Re: Arts and Letters 5 (Fall 1971):
41-49.
Kostelanetz mentions Albee as an example of the
literary theater, devoted strictly to literature
rather than to an exploration of American experience.
He is also a proponent of the new theater of mixed
means, which "communicates through kinetic movements,
all of which, in realized pieces, evoke some kind of
coherence." Some writers endeavor to make literary
a theater which is not literature. Kostelanetz adds
that lively performances cannot exist in print, and
we should recognize that European standards of literary theater cannot be transferred to performance-
oriented American theater.

_____. "The Art of Total No." Contact 4 (October/
November 1963):62-70.
The playwrights of the New American Theatre are
unified in "shouting a vociferous 'No' to the common
theatrical currency of the post-war years." Kostelanetz delves into the mysteries of this theatrical
movement and determines that Albee is the most promising of the playwrights. In his analysis of Albee's
first play he endeavors "to lift the critical veil
and, once and for all, Spell the Play Out. The Zoo
Story describes an unsuccessful homosexual pass." He
continues to develop the thematic motifs of the play
in this manner and concludes that "once you catch on
to Albee's symbolic way of telling the hidden tale,
everything slightly masked becomes apparent and meaningful." All in all, with Albee at the forefront,
the future of the New American Theatre looks to be
quite successful.

_____, ed. "Edward Albee." In On Contemporary Litera-
ture. New York: Avon, 1964. Pp. 225-31.
Kostelanetz views Albee as the most promising
and substantial young dramatist while the playwright
is at a relatively early juncture in his career.

He suggests that Albee's "themes are as diverse as his subjects" and predicts that continued dramatic excellence can be expected of the young man. In providing brief analyses of the plays, Kostelanetz illustrates several of Albee's thematic and technical achievements, points out some minor flaws, and endeavors to comprehend exactly what in the plays "sustains our interest," a fact which he claims no critic can deny.

_____, ed. "The New American Theatre." In The New American Arts. New York: Horizon Press, 1965. Pp. 52-62.
     Kostelanetz analyzes Who's Afraid of Virginia Woolf? and the shorter plays with regard to thematic content and structure. He criticizes the one-acters for a definite lack of unified action.

La Belle, Jenijoy. "Albee's Who's Afraid of Virginia Woolf?" Explicator 15 (Fall 1976):8-9.
     La Belle suggests that the key to relating Virginia Woolf to the title of the play is in her short story "Lappin and Lapinova."

La Fontane, B. "Triple Threat, On, Off, and Off-Off Broadway." New York Times Magazine, 25 February 1968, pp. 36-37, 39-40, 42, 44, and 46.
     La Fontane focuses on Albee as a person. The article also treats the new Albee-Barr-Wilder producing agency and its encouragement to young dramatists.

Lahr, John. "The Adaptable Mr. Albee." Evergreen Review 12 (May 1968):37-39 and 82-87.
     A careful examination of Albee's three adaptations for Broadway reveals that he cannot in practice meet the standards which he has set for the playwright of vision. Lahr calls him an entertainer rather than an artist and his failure to recognize his limitations is reflected in the product; he tries to impose a depth and vision which are simply not there. "He speaks out for honesty in plays which are dishonest at their core."

_____. "Theater: A Question Long Overdue." Arts Magazine 12 (May 1967):21-23.
     Lahr unfavorably compares Albee's works and his contributions to the new theater with those of Beckett and Pinter in their respective arenas.

Lamport, Harold. "Who's Afraid of Virginia Woolf?" In John Gassner's Best American Plays, Fifth Series, 1957-1963. New York: Crown Publishers, 1965. Pp. 81-98.
     Lamport suggests that Albee intended his plays to be more than a drama of marital conflict or even a battle between the sexes. This intention is re-

vealed in its title. He also points to the various
means of expressing hostility in the play and concludes that the most shattering method is "the statement of an unpleasant, hidden truth either to the
concerned individual alone or before others where
its impact is to castigate that individual without
mercy."

Laufe, Abe. Anatomy of a Hit: Long-Run Plays on Broadway
from 1900 to the Present Day. New York: Hawthorn
Books, 1966. Pp. 302-09.
    In this book devoted to significant dramatic
events of the twentieth century, Laufe singles out
Who's Afraid of Virginia Woolf? as Albee's greatest
contribution to date. He reviews the performance
and includes a list of the numerous dramatic awards
accrued by the playwright, director, cast, and others
associated with the production.

Lawson, John Howard. "Modern U.S. Dramaturgy." Inostrannaya Literatura (Foreign Literature) No. 8 (August
1962):186-96. In Russian.
    The work of the best modern artists in American
theater is permeated by the protests of hopeless
people in a vain assertion of human values. Influenced by Beckett, Ionesco, and Genet, young dramatists such as Edward Albee and Jack Gelber attempt
to combine a resolute rejection of contemporary society with a destruction of "the canonic forms of
the play."

Lee, A. Robert. "Illusion and Betrayal: Edward Albee's
Theatre." Studies: An Irish Quarterly Review 59
(Spring 1970):53-67.
    Albee's particular strength is the dramatization
of betrayal using masks, games, rituals, and charac-
ter-stripping while frequently working in the "tradition of Ionesco and the 'absurd' theater." He has
emphasized that his concern is with self-cheating
and that he rejects the "resolution and catharsis"
of the naturalistic theater.

Leff, Leonard J. "Albee's Who's Afraid of Virginia
Woolf?" Explicator 35 (Winter 1976):8-10.
    Were it not for Martha's allusion to the film
Beyond the Forest in Albee's Who's Afraid of Virginia
Woolf?--"an allusion whose source critics have over-
looked--King Vidor's seamy melodrama would be wholly
forgettable." Leff endeavors to draw out the similarities between the two in an indomitable fashion.

Lenz, Harold. "At Sixes and Sevens--A Modern Theatrical
Structure." Forum (Houston) 11 (Summer-Fall 1973
and Winter 1974):73-79.
    A number of commentary plays currently being
staged, including Albee's All Over, have six or seven

central characters. They all exhibit similarities
which show them to be commentaries representing humanity "at sixes and sevens" with the world.

Lester, Elenore. "The Final Decline and Total Collapse
    of the American Avant-Garde." Esquire, May 1969,
    pp. 142-43 and 148-49.
        Although related to European-oriented phenomena
    such as Futurism, Dadaism, and Surrealism and de-
    spite its "uniquely American characteristics," the
    New Theatre is floundering. Powerful playwrights
    like Antonin Artaud and John Cage, possessing a
    "large shaping intelligence," are needed; Albee,
    once promising, has not fulfilled that promise. His
    gimmicks are not nearly enough to make the New Thea-
    tre meaningful.

Levine, Mordecai H. "Albee's Liebestod." College Lan-
    guage Association Journal 10 (March 1967):252-55.
        Levine recalls that the first production of
    Albee's The Zoo Story was acclaimed in its German
    translation before it received any recognition in
    the United States. He recognizes religious, socio-
    logical, and psychological overtones which are not
    usually perceived and he indicates that its over-
    whelming reception in Berlin may have been in part a
    result of its similarity to Thomas Mann's short
    story "Tobias Mindernickel."

Levy, Maurice. "Albee: un théâtre qui fait peur." Cali-
    ban 8 (1971):151-64. In French.
        Because Albee places the most fundamental of
    problems before his audience in unequivocal terms,
    his plays constitute a "théâtre politique." Allud-
    ing to Marx, Nietzsche, Freud, and Mao, he endeavors
    to destroy the myths and the illusions of security--
    those traditional prefabrications by which man re-
    mains aloof. His characters are rarely allowed a
    choice and if they are, existential anguish usually
    results. Although he does not approach cruelty,
    Albee's plays create a theater of alarm.

Lewis, Allen. American Plays and Playwrights of the Con-
    temporary Theatre. New York: Crown Publishers,
    1965. Pp. 81-98 et passim.
        Lewis reprints his article "The Fun and Games
    of Edward Albee" and also mentions the playwright
    throughout the book with regard to other dramatists
    of the contemporary theater.

_____. "The Fun and Games of Edward Albee." Educa-
    tional Theatre Journal 16 (March 1964):29-39. Re-
    printed in his American Plays and Playwrights of the
    Contemporary Theatre New York: Crown Publishers,
    1965. Pp. 81-98.
        Based on the limited quantity of his work to this

point--four one-acts, one full-length play, and one
adaptation--Lewis feels that Albee's rise to international stardom has been premature. The influence
of Ionesco, Beckett, Strindberg, and particularly
Genet is indelibly stamped upon his plays and Albee
has failed to implement new techniques on the stage.
Lewis sees impotence as his central thematic motif
because Albee confines himself to portraying anti-
heroic characters. Nonetheless, Lewis admits that
the playwright does "subtly and relentlessly search
for the truth of the human condition without fear or
compromise in a manner that grips audiences."

Lipton, Edward. "The Tiny Alice Enigma." Saturday Review, 20 February 1965, p. 21.
     This letter to the editor from an established
physician offers insight into the problems of the
play by using a psychoanalytical approach to the
character of Julian.

Lucey, William Frederick. "Albee's Tiny Alice: Truth and
Appearance." Renascence 21 (Winter 1969):76-80 and
110.
     Lucey suggests that Tiny Alice, "while not an
immediate success as entertainment, is a notable contribution to the American stage." He analyzes the
play and determines that Albee truly probes reality
as he had fully intended in this situation.

Lumley, F. New Trends in Twentieth Century Drama: A Survey Since Ibsen and Shaw. New York: Oxford University Press, 1972. Pp. 319-24 et passim.
     Albee has endeavored to equate legend and real-
ity in order to fabricate the American dream. For
him, misogynism is an obsession. Lumley implies that
the playwright certainly does not fit into any cate-
gory of the American dramatic experience and he suggests that Albee is more closely aligned to "the
theatre of disturbance, or if you prefer, the theatre
of the Absurd." Finally, he analyzes the plays
through Tiny Alice, offers suggestions to Albee, and
labels him "one of the most stimulating, provocative
and controversial playwrights in the post-war theatre."

Luri, S. "Griaz'na podmostkakh (Khellman, Iul'iams,
Elbi)." Izvestia, Moscow Evening Edition, 39 May
1963. In Russian.
     Luri attacks Albee and others for writing and
producing filth.

Lyons, Charles R. Bertolt Brecht's The Despair and the
Polemic. Carbondale and Edwardsville, Illinois:
Southern Illinois University Press, 1968, pp. 5, 25.
     In his book on Brecht, Lyons points out that
Brecht and Albee share a vision "held in a nihilist

imagination." The works of Albee and the continental absurdists, like Brecht's, "derive from a vision of a senseless universe in which man suffers an unredeemable isolation."

_____. "Some Variations of 'Kindermord' as Dramatic Archetype." Comparative Drama 1 (Spring 1967):56-71.
Lyons uses Albee's Who's Afraid of Virginia Woolf? as a modern example of "Kindermord" used as a dramatic archetype. The child in drama, whether actual or imaginative, is often a projection of the will, and "kindermord" frequently indicates "the purging or destruction of that aspect of his psyche," evident in the play when George "kills" the imaginary son. Lyons adds that the act usually reveals the conflict between male and female and, in modern drama in particular, the child is usually associated with regenerative power or impotency.

_____. "Two Projections of the Isolation of the Human Soul: Brecht and Albee." Drama Survey 4 (Summer 1965):121-37.
Both Brecht's and Albee's plays depict a chaotic universe in which an idealistic but alienated individual accepts the terror of isolation.

Macklin, Anthony. "The Flagrant Albatross." College English 28 (October 1966):58-59.
Macklin argues that Peter Spielberg's article in the April 1966 issue of College English is not responsible in comparing Coleridge's Ancient Mariner to Jerry in the Zoo Story. Macklin believes that an attempt to explore the Christian allegory in Albee's play would be more fruitful.

Mandanis, Alice. "Symbol and Substance in Tiny Alice." Modern Drama 12 (May 1969):92-98.
In Tiny Alice, Albee asks "whether or not man is actually prepared to abandon the illusions of established religious symbols for the kind of abstract religious energy which the new age of science proposes to him." Mandanis sees Julian as the representative of this scientific age so that his death constitutes a conflict with "the abstraction of a primordial religious instinct." Nonetheless, Albee does not decide the matter for us; we are forced into a decision because we never know whether the abstraction is real or simply one more illusion.

Markson, John W. "Tiny Alice: Edward Albee's Negative Oedipal Enigma." American Imago 23 (Spring 1966):3-21.
Markson believes Tiny Alice may be interpreted as an intense representation of a chaotic, passively resolved oedipal conflict. The confusion in the play dominates its staging.

Markus, Thomas B. "Tiny Alice and Tragic Catharsis."
Educational Theatre Journal 17 (October 1965):225-33.
        Markus praises Albee's most puzzling play to
date because he has achieved the greatest balance
possible between the world of reality and that of
the play. Its inherent ambiguities are a necessary
reflection of the play's essence and, in addition,
by evoking both fear and pity, Albee has written the
first tragedy to adorn the stage in hundreds of
years.

Marshall, Thomas F. "Edward Albee and the Nowhere Genera-
    tion." Mexico Quarterly Review 3 (1968):39-47.
        Albee portrays three generations--"Then," "Now,"
and "Nowhere"--in their movement toward a state of
debilitated amorality. The past generation cannot
communicate with the younger generations and is
doomed to self-annihilation. Women have been pres-
sured into masculine positions by the present con-
formist generation in a fruitless role reversal; it
will lead ultimately to destruction. Finally, the
"sterile self-complacent future generation is the
very embodiment of passive nihilism."

Martin, Von Richard. "One v. One, or Two Against All? A
    Note on Edward Albee's Who's Afraid of Virginia
    Woolf?" Die Neueren Sprachen N.S. 22 (October 1973):
    535-38.
        Martin believes that game-playing leads George
back to the ultimate game--the destruction of the
imaginary child, which George must accomplish before
he can be a husband rather than a son to Martha.
Martin stresses the close-binding, emotional relationship of the marriage which many critics have
overlooked.

McDonald, Daniel. "Truth and Illusion in Who's Afraid of
    Virginia Woolf?" Renascence 17 (Winter 1964):63-69.
        Who's Afraid of Virginia Woolf? is a quite real-
istic dramatic encounter and its central thematic
motif is the necessity of illusion to sustain life;
its inherent symbolism merely reinforces this theme.
All four characters hold on to and lose their illusions prior to finding it necessary to create new
ones. Finally, they discover that, while necessary,
illusions can have very little positive influence
because the world is simply not a nice place in
which to live.

Macleans, 6 April 1981, p. 62.
        Though essentially a review of Lolita this
article discusses the moral issues raised in the
play.

Meyer, Ruth. "Language: Truth and Illusion in Who's
    Afraid of Virginia Woolf?" Educational Theatre
    Journal 20 (March 1968):60-69.
        Meyer insists that Albee is less interested in
    exploring fact and fantasy in George's and Martha's
    lives than he is in showing how they use their verbal
    abilities to shield themselves from outside scrutiny.
    They defend their egos by creating illusions, such
    as the imaginary child, which then become their sus-
    taining reality.

Michaelis, Rolf. "Albees Spiel in den Tod. Ein Vergleich
    der Auffuhrungen 'Wer hat Angst vor Virginia Woolf.'"
    Theater heute 6 (June 1964):12-20.
        In order to "live" their lives, George and
    Martha must come to terms with their fear of death.

Miller, Jordan Y. "Myth and the American Dream: O'Neill
    to Albee." Modern Drama 7 (September 1964):190-98.
        Miller compares Albee's handling of this subject
    in The American Dream to that of Williams in his
    Camino Real and with that of O'Neill in The Great God
    Brown. In their plays, they warn of the "fatal pos-
    sibility of losing everything in the process of try-
    ing to achieve the goals of the Myth of the American
    Dream." The Myth is that of success based on a clean
    mind and strong body fortified by youthful determina-
    tion. The cost of this success is the loss of the
    soul or the existential anguish accompanying an im-
    portant decision.

Missey, James. "A McCullers Influence on Albee's The Zoo
    Story." American Notes and Queries (New Haven) 13
    (April 1975):121-23.
        Missey suggests that McCullers' short story "A
    Tree. A Rock. A Cloud." specifically influences Al-
    bee's The Zoo Story. The main similarity between
    the two works is the attitude towards love developed
    within the principal characters. The overall effect
    of each work, however, "is to present the idea dif-
    ferently--ironically in the McCullers story and
    straightforwardly in the Albee play."

Moore, Don D. "Albee's The American Dream." Explicator
    30 (1972): Item 44.
        Grandma is the wisest and most endearing figure
    in the play and it seems quite possible that when
    her bedtime is mentioned as being at noon, Albee may
    have had in mind the last utterance of Lear's fool
    that he will go to bed at noon. Even if the verbal
    parallel is accidental, for many critics, the fool,
    not unlike Grandma, speaks his bitter, jesting
    truths against a similar accidental void representa-
    tive of a society in turmoil.

Morsberger, Robert E. "The Movie Game in Who's Afraid of
Virginia Woolf? and The Boys in the Band." Costerus:
Essays in English and American Language and Literature 8 (1973):89-99.
Who's Afraid of Virginia Woolf? consists largely of the sort of neurotic dramas analyzed in Berne's
Games People Play (1964). Morsberger focuses on the
movie game in which, appropriately enough, Martha
indulges at the beginning of the play. This game at
its best is a "source of innocent merriment" and at
its worst it "combines aggression with self-decep-
tion." Morsberger goes on to compare it with Mart
Crowley's play about homosexuality, The Boys in the
Band. He also suggests that the movie mentioned in
the play is Beyond the Forest. By alluding to one
of Davis' more forgettable films, Albee forces the
viewer to fit Martha into a certain role from the
start. The allusion is no mistake. Beyond specific
analogies, Morsberger implies that "the movie game
is an effective introduction to George and Martha,
whose entire relationship is theatrical and made up
of fantasy and illusion."

Moses, Robbie Odom. "Death as a Mirror of Life: Edward
Albee's All Over." Modern Drama 19 (1976):67-77.
The death struggle in All Over is indicative of
"man's final confrontation with life." Albee evaluates the acceptance of death with regard to psychological maturity, the modern tendency to dehumanize
death, and, in particular, the individual notion of
what the death ritual entails. Ironically, there is
more life in the dead man than in all of the survi-
vors combined. For Albee, their actions can be applied to American society and his insidious view of
death "encompasses those who have died, those who
are dying, and those who are dead to life." In this
drama it is then quite apparent that death is merely
a metaphor for "the quality of life."

_____. "Edward Albee: A Voice in the Wasteland." Forum
(Houston) 12 (Winter 1975):35-40.
In the nine plays which Moses analyzes, death
is the metaphor with which Albee assesses the quality of life. The playwright's chief concern, however,
is with the symbolic mode of death in which human
beings are dead to life. In the spiritual wasteland
Albee depicts, love either does not exist at all, or
only the destructive side is evident. For Albee,
life without meaning is death, and life without love
is absolute death. Only a man re-born through divine love can render the life-lie helpless. Through
his fusion of the humanism of existentialism and the
theism of Christianity, Albee reveals that redemption
from death-in-life existence lies in the defiance of
death through love.

Mottram, Eric. "The New American Wave." Encore 11
(January-February 1964):22-41.
Mottram points to the dichotomy between serious
theatrical writing and entertainment following the
Second World War which caused social problems to be
treated merely on a personal level. Now, for the
first time since, playwrights like Lionel Abel,
Edward Albee, Kenneth Brown, Jack Gelber, Arthur
Kopit, and Jack Richardson have entered into a new
era of social drama. These men, unlike their immediate predecessors such as Arthur Miller and William
Inge, refuse to believe "it will all work out with
self-therapy." For example, Albee is concerned with
making "a serious comment on killing without false
tragedy," in The Zoo Story.

Mussorf, Lenore. "Medium Is the Absurd." English Journal
58 (April 1969):566-70 and 576.
Mussorf, a high school English teacher, reflects
that students react more positively to Albee's plays
and to the whole Theater of the Absurd than to any
other type of literature. One reason why it "works
in the classroom is because it's new, it's fresh,
it's different, and, most of all, it communicates an
immediate reality." And of the absurdist literature,
Albee's works are the easiest to follow. Her own
curriculum includes both The Zoo Story and The American Dream and she proposes further study including
The Sandbox and The Death of Bessie Smith. Since
this theater speaks to students "of the present and
in the present" it is the theater to which they
should have access.

Nagel, Ivan. "Requiem für die Seele: Uber Albee's Wer
Hat Angst vor Virginia Woolf?" Neue Rundschau 74
(1963):646-51. In German.
Nagel describes the exorcism scene in Virginia
Woolf, where George and Honey repeat parts of the
burial mass after the imaginary son is "killed."
Nagel believes that George has finally faced his
guilt over his parents' deaths and his own failure;
at last he is ready to begin a new, more realistic
life with Martha.

Narumi, Hiroshi. "Edward Albee no Mondaiten." Eigo
Seinen (Tokyo) 114 (1968):220-21. In Japanese.

Nelson, Benjamin. "Avant-Garde Dramatists from Ibsen to
Ionesco." Psychoanalytic Review 55 (1968):505-12.
Nelson sees Albee as representative of modern
dramatists who are like psychoanalysts or would-be
therapists by depicting the alienated states of
their audiences in mass therapy sessions. He suggests that Albee and others have adopted a variety
of roles and techniques for their therapeutic purposes in much the same manner as a licensed practi-

tioner would treat an individual with similar symptoms.

Newman, David. "Four Make a Wave." Esquire, April 1961, pp. 45-51.
Newman argues that Albee, Gelber, Richardson, and Kopit constitute the new wave in American theater as well as the American component of the Theater of the Absurd. He also includes a review of The Zoo Story to support this claim.

New York Times, 16 January 1968, p. 1.
Albee reveals his plans for a new art center to be developed in conjunction with Barr and Wilder.

_____, 24 July 1969, p. 13.
This article focuses on the recent action taken by the Singapore government to ban the production of Tiny Alice within their jurisdiction.

Nilan, Mary M. "Albee's The Zoo Story: Alienated Man and the Nature of Love." Modern Drama 16 (June 1973): 55-60.
Nilan argues that critics who see the character Jerry as a victim of his compassion fail to recognize that Albee clearly presents him as incapable of love and denies him any hope of success in his search for belonging. The encounter with Peter and Jerry's death serve only as an effort to bridge a communication gap which is a metaphor for the schism between social classes and is not intended to be at all sacrificial.

Normand, J. "L'Homme mystifié: Les heros de The Mystified Man: The Heroes of Bellow, Albee, Styron, and Mailer." Etudes Anglaises 22 (October-December 1969):370-85. In French.
Normand recognizes the need for writers to raise the human consciousness to a verbal level because people wish to understand that anguish which enchants them. Writers endeavor to comprehend, and yet cannot, that phenomenon which mystifies. Thus we have characters on the stage like Albee's Julian, "the apostate from divine love, devoured by Tiny Alice," who leaves audiences groping for the meaning of the unanswerable.

Norton, Rictor. "Folklore and Myth in Who's Afraid of Virginia Woolf?" Renascence 23 (Spring 1971):159-67.
Folklore, myth, and realism are dynamically intertwined in Albee's ritualistic drama. Norton maintains that through close textual reference to the folklore and myth underlying the play's title, its primordial setting, its characters and their actions, Albee establishes a coherent pattern which illustrates its affirmative Dionysian theme of rebirth.

Oberg, Arthur K. "Edward Albee: His Language and Imagination." Prairie Schooner 40 (Summer 1966):139-46.
  Albee's keen dialogue tends to cloud the overall theatrical power of his plays. His characters are "inflicted with the burden of consciousness." Albee's language is often wit, instruction, and satire simultaneously. Oberg holds that conversations in the plays are sheer art and are blunted in their impact only by Albee's poor revelation "of what they might have been like," had anyone else attempted a similar endeavor.

Otten, Terry. "Ibsen and Albee's Spurious Children." Comparative Drama 2 (Summer 1968):83-93.
  Who's Afraid of Virginia Woolf? and Little Eyolf are both realistic-ritualistic plays having birth and regeneration as their central thematic motif. The spurious children in the plays symbolize the characters' many-faceted failures. Honey, Nick, and Martha vainly attempt to save the imaginary child and in so doing they affirm the importance of life and love. The dead "child" is then potentially resurrected in Honey's desire for a child and in the revitalized relationship between George and Martha. This situation is quite similar to that presented in the Ibsen play when Rita reaffirms her love for Asta and the poor boys of the town after Eyolf dies. In both plays, "Kindermord" is the prelude to an "ambiguous birth" and a happy ending.

_____. "'Played to the Finish': Coward and Albee." Studies in the Humanities (Indiana University) 6 (1977):31-36.
  Albee's Who's Afraid of Virginia Woolf? is similar to Noel Coward's Hay Fever in characterization, situation, and theme. However, it is the differences in the plays which are most important: Coward's game-playing defends characters from the truth by their comic nature, while Albee's games are used to reveal the true ineptness of the characters. Coward's characters continue on in their ignorant bliss; Albee's must face reality and all its fears.

Pallavinci, Roberto. "Aspetti della dramaturgia contemporanea." Aut Aut, No. 81 (May 1964):68-73.
  Pallavinci finds fault in Miller and Brecht for failing totally to involve the spectator in their dramatic endeavors. He asks where one can find a theater with a true social function and answers the question himself--almost nowhere. He claims that Albee and Pinter remain too much under the influence of past theater traditions and therefore do not qualify under his guidelines. Only Beckett occasionally enables the audience to participate completely in the drama in what Pallavinci labels the "ultimate realization."

Paolucci, Anne. _From Tension to Tonic: The Plays of Edward Albee._ Carbondale: Southern Illinois University Press, 1972.
Paolucci claims that she pursues no theses or
formal patterns of criticism, not as a reflection on
the content and form of Albee's plays, but rather to
share her own enjoyment of them with others. She
asserts that "Albee has done more than any other recent author to revive the glorious tradition of poly-
semous writing, in a modern vein." In an effort to
illustrate various aspects of his writing, she analyzes his works from _The Zoo Story_ to _All Over._

Pardi, Frencesca. _Nuova Antologia_, No. 1964 (August
1964):554-56.
Unlike the self-made American writers young
in the first half of the century, writers today develop experiences reminiscent of their college days.
Salinger and Kopit have put forth their views of
college life from the outside, while Albee's _Who's
Afraid of Virginia Woolf?_ and Malamud's _A New Life_
depict the internal struggles.

Parone, Edward, ed. Introduction to _New Theater in
America._ New York: Dell, 1965. Pp. 2-13.
Parone uses Albee, Beckett, Genet, and Ionesco
as sources of information to which he can compare
new playwrights included in this anthology. In this
context, Albee "shot straight up out of American
soil, with that peculiar American talent for catch-
ing on to what's happening at the moment it happens."

Parsatharathy, R. "Who's Afraid of Edward Albee? (American Drama in the Sixties)." _Quest_, No. 55 (Autumn
1967):53-55.
Albee's _The Zoo Story_ initiated the new American
theater and was made possible by recent European absurdist theater, off-Broadway productions, and a dissatisfaction with older American playwrights. Albee
is not merely an intellectual writer, rather his
imaginative plays are characteristically marked by
extraordinarily forceful dialogue and "an ability
to draw the emotions of actors into a vortex of violence."

Paul, Louis. "A Game Analysis of _Who's Afraid of Virginia
Woolf?_: The Core of Grief." _Literature and Psychol-
ogy_ 17 (1967):47-51.
Albee's play enacts life games of which the
players are only faintly aware and which may be interpreted using Berne's _Games People Play._ One such
game, "Our son the Pretend Child, is of special interest because it points to a major defect in identity, the lack of procreation and generativity, which
is repaired by imaginary restitution; and ... this

game or life project or script represses a core of grief."

Phillips, Elizabeth C. "Albee and the Theatre of the Absurd." Tennessee Studies in Literature 10 (1965): 73-80.

Phillips uses Albee's plays to illustrate Esslin's list of techniques as implemented by European absurdists: The Zoo Story uses a communication gap; The Death of Bessie Smith is without a plot; The Sandbox conveys the deterioration of language; The American Dream conveys a "horror pervading and permeating the comic"; and Who's Afraid of Virginia Woolf? indicates symbolism projecting "Man's deepest fears and anxieties." She also states that this alignment with European playwrights alienates him from American writers pursuing the same goal.

Plotinsky, Melvin L. "The Transformation of Understanding: Edward Albee in the Theatre of the Irresolute." Drama Survey 4 (Winter 1965):220-32.

The Zoo Story is a work of art and in its focus on the breakdown of communication it foreshadows Albee's later drama. It is quite feasible that his inherent imaginative ideas have detracted from the critical acclaim he deserves--for example, his "comprehensive denial of intellect establishes a theatre incapable of resolution...." Nonetheless, his desire to relate the central character's predicament to the audience may in part make his drama believable, at least to them.

Porter, M. Gilbert. "Toby's Last Stand: The Evanescence of Commitment in A Delicate Balance." Educational Theatre Journal 31 (October 1979):398-408.

Porter reads the "emptiness" in the play to which many critics have objected as an emotional and moral vacuum serving as the center of the dramatic plot. Also, Tobias is the main figure, not Agnes, since his "dawning recognition of his own emptiness provides the dramatic tension in the play." His relationship with each of the other characters also reveals an added dimension of the weakness or failure in both. The circularity of the play is maintained by a series of role reversals, one character becoming another and then returning to his original role. Thus, through "a circular strategy involving plot, space, role-exchanges, and imagery--with Tobias at the center--A Delicate Balance catalogues the price of false values, evasion, and non-commitment." Albee's development from "thematic abstraction into intense presentational immediacy" provides the sheer power of the drama.

Porter, Thomas E. _Myth_ and _Modern_ _American_ _Drama_.
Detroit: Wayne State University Press, 1969.
Pp. 225-47.
Porter entitles his chapter on _Who's_ _Afraid_ _of_
Virginia _Woolf?_ "Fun and Games in Suburbia." He de-
scribes the social and moral climate of the early
1960s as a period of deep alienation, and compares
Albee to the continental absurdists, who share his
love of games, rituals, and word-play.

Post, Robert M. "Cognitive Dissonance in the Plays of
Edward Albee." _Quarterly_ _Journal_ _of_ _Speech_ 55
(February 1969):54-60.
Using the definition that "cognitive dissonance"
refers to inconsistencies between people's beliefs
and their actions, Post shows that several of Albee's
characters exhibit differing degrees of this phenomenon in such things as reversed sex roles and marital
mutability. Thus, in an effort to synthesize differing aspects of their persona, Albee's characters re-
treat into a world of illusion and actually increase
the cognitive dissonance.

_____. "Fear Itself: Edward Albee's _A_ _Delicate_ _Bal_-
ance." _College_ _Language_ _Association_ _Journal_ 13
(December 1969):163-71.
Fear is the most poignant aspect of the play
and it is the fear of loneliness and isolation which
enters into every relationship. This theme and the
realization of total apathy between human beings
forms the dramatic core and provides its overall
impact.

Pradhan, N. S. _Modern_ _American_ Drama: _A_ _Study_ _in_ _Myth_
and _Tradition_. New Delhi: Arnold-Heinemann, 1978.
Pradhan comments on Albee's use of the American
Dream, noting that the Puritan's search for a new
Eden has been so corrupted in modern society that
the Garden in contemporary American drama is more
like purgatory. In Albee's plays an innocent person
has "no place in the New World and has to be destroyed." Jerry, Grandma, and Julian are sacrificed
in this way. _Everything_ _in_ _the_ _Garden_, _Tiny_ _Alice_,
and _Seascape_ are discussed as plays which are set in
a perverted Eden.

Quackenbush, L. Howard. "The Legacy of Albee's _Who's_
Afraid _of_ _Virginia_ _Woolf?_ in the Spanish American
Absurdist Theatre." _Revista/Review_ _Interamericana_ 9
(1979):57-71.
Albee's play has had a long-lasting impact in
South America.

62

Quinn, James P. "Myth and Romance in Albee's Who's
Afraid of Virginia Woolf?" Arizona Quarterly 30
(1974):197-204.
    Albee is one of the few dramatists who is capa-
ble of achieving an aesthetic balance between his
irrational existential assumptions and the rational
art forms he employs. In this play, Albee depicts
existentialism by creating an ironic parody of Western civilization using romantic mythic inversion and
role reversals. Although they cannot be sure that
the night of introspection will absolve them, Albee's
characters must face existential anguish simply because they made the effort.

Rael, Elsa. "Joseph Conrad, Master Absurdist." Conradi-
ana 2 (Spring 1969-70):163-70.
    Conrad's Heart of Darkness and The Secret Sharer
contain excellent examples of absurdist techniques.
Marlow, in the former, who has been described as
Conrad himself, does not know who he is at the beginning of the work and he only achieves a glimpse
of recognition through a brutal encounter, quite like
Jerry's confrontation in The Zoo Story. Also the
knitting fates which he describes are as repugnant
and "terrifying as Edward Albee's janitoress and
dog" in the modern drama.

Ramsey, Roger. "Jerry's Northerly Madness." Notes on
Contemporary Literature 1 (September 1971):7-8.
    Jerry's use of the word "northerly" in The Zoo
Story brings to mind Hamlet's north-northwest madness. Ramsey suggests that other comparisons in the
works substantiate this interpretation.

Rand, Calvin. "Albee's Musical Box-Mao-Box." Humanist
29 (January-February 1969):27.
    Calvin considers that the only standard for
judging this kind of play is with regard to its total
dramatic impact. Box-Mao-Box has a certain force,
but not enough in the long run. The form is different but the content is the same old thing: the chaos
of life and the debility of Western society. It may
take more than one viewing of this work to fully
comprehend its meaning.

Rauter, Herbert. "Edward Albee." In Amerikanische
Literatur der Gegenwart. Ed. Martin Christadler.
Stuttgart: Alfred Kröner, 1973. Pp. 488-505. In
German.
    Rauter provides a fine summary of Albee's
achievement in American drama.

Raymont, Henry. "Campaign by Artists." New York Times,
14 July 1967, p. 9.
    This article includes the text of Albee's let-
ter to Isaac Stern, urging a boycott of the summer

music festival in Athens to protest Melina Mercouri's loss of citizenship. He indicates that he has already refused to allow his work to be performed in Athens as an indication of his support for the proposed boycott.

Razum, Hannes. "Edward Albee und die Metaphisik." In Theater und Drama in Amerika: Aspekte und Interpretation. Ed. Edgar Lohner and Rudolf Haas. Berlin: Schmidt, 1978. Pp. 353-63.
    Razum's study focuses on Tiny Alice as a statement of Albee's metaphysics. Razum places the work in the tradition of Ibsen's Peer Gynt, Beckett's Waiting for Godot, and Eliot's Cocktail Party because it involves an existential search for meaning and purpose in life and explores the implications of Julian's choices in the play.

Reinert, Otto. Drama, An Introductory Anthology. Alternate Edition. Boston: Little, Brown, 1964. Pp. 866-71 et passim.
    Reinert analyzes The American Dream and endeavors to relate Albee's ties to the absurdist movement. Although the article is brief, it does point out some significant aspects of the play and of Albee in the absurdist tradition.

Rewald, Alice. "Albee et l'Avant Garde." Quinzaine Litteraire, 1 January 1968, p. 26.
    Rewald notes Albee's departure from conventional social realism and comments on his affinities with the absurdists.

Rissover, Fredric. "Beat Poetry, The American Dream, and the Alienation Effect." Speech Teacher 20 (January 1971):36-43.
    Rissover comments on his production of The American Dream in combination with a reading of Beat poetry for a college experimental theater performance. He suggests that there is a significant similarity between the play and the poems in their observations of American society and their parallel sense of critical or emotional detachment from the mainstream of society. Rissover also includes portions of the integrated text to illustrate this belief.

Robertson, Roderick. "A Theatre for the Absurd: The Passionate Equation." Drama Survey 2 (June 1962):24-43.
    Robertson makes a very brief reference to The American Dream as a play with a single room setting which, as in many absurdist plays, operates on a primarily metaphorical level.

Robinson, Brian. "De Qui a peur de Virginia Woolf à Delicate Balance: Le talent d'Edward Albee sur le declin." Revue de l'Université d'Ottawa 43 (1973): 270-76.

   Robinson believes Albee has taken to imitating (unsuccessfully) the themes, stage devices, and even jokes of his earlier play.

Rocha Filho, Rubem. "Albee: Processo e Tentativa." Tempo Brasileiro: Revista de Cultura, No 3 (1963):161-72.

Rothenberg, Michael. "Ha-kol Ba-Gan Le-Albee; Lyun Hashva'ati [Comparison of Edward Albee's Adaptation Everything in the Garden and Its Source by Giles Cooper]." Bama 53-54 (1972):64-72.

Roy, Emil. "Who's Afraid of Virginia Woolf? and the Tradition." Bucknell Review 13 (March 1965):27-36.

   Roy maintains that in a tradition of great American plays Who's Afraid of Virginia Woolf? signifies no radical departure in theatrical conventions. He indicates similarities in technique between this play and earlier works of naturalistic, realistic, existentialist, and absurdist traditions. He also analyzes the plot and thematic development in the play.

Rutenberg, Michael. "Edward Albee: Playwright in Protest." Players Magazine 44 (October-November 1968):28-34.

   This article is an excerpt from his book. He is concerned here with elaborating upon the fact that he views A Delicate Balance as Albee's most underrated play. "Misunderstood from the first, and superficially analyzed by critics, Albee's most mature play has not been held up as a dramaturgical prototype for future Pulitzer choices."

_____. Edward Albee: Playwright in Protest. New York: Drama Book Specialists, 1969.

   Rutenberg proposes that Albee writes social protest dramas which succeed because "they touch the pulse of change in our time." He analyzes the plays from The Zoo Story to Box-Mao-Box in an effort to support his claim that it has been Edward Albee who has shown the theater, and America in general, that dramatists must establish the same vital social and political commitment accepted by their predecessors prior to the demise of social drama in the late thirties. He also includes the texts of two interviews he conducted with the playwright on 17 March 1965 and 7 August 1968.

Samuels, Charles Thomas. "The Theatre of Edward Albee." Massachusetts Review 6 (Autumn-Winter 1964-1965): 187-201.

   Samuels argues that Albee's dramas are poor

social satires and worse plays. They are "gothic in their violence, sentimental in their adulation of self-pity and in their melodrama, naturalistic only in their emphasis on invincible social force and their exculpating pity of the poor and maimed, and absurdist only in mannerisms." Albee's most redeeming quality as a playwright is that he excels at being ugly to others. He is unable to initiate new drama, serving only to perpetuate the post-war drama of "sentimentalism and sentimentality."

_____. "The Theatre of Edward Albee." In Das Amerikanische Drama. Ed. Hans Itschert. Darmstadt: Wissenschaftliche Buchgesellschaft, 1972. Pp. 385-400.
Samuels provides a hostile appraisal of Albee's work. Of The Sandbox he writes, "One could not escape the blurred mixture of sociological cartoon and arch lyricism." He adds that Albee's works from The Zoo Story to Virginia Woolf are "grounded in the last of all sentimentalities: the notion that life is thoroughly bad, and that people are thoroughly nasty."

Sarotte, Georges M. "Edward Albee: Homosexual Playwright in Spite of Himself." In his Like a Brother, Like a Lover: Male Homosexuality in the American Novel and Theater from Herman Melville to James Baldwin. Tr. Richard Miller. Garden City, N.Y.: Anchor Press/ Doubleday, 1978. Pp. 134-49.
In the part of the book devoted to homosexuality and the theater, Sarotte analyzes the works of Williams, Inge, and Albee from a psychological viewpoint in an effort to determine their sexual content. He claims that Albee is the "least overtly sexual" and therefore requires a more subtle analysis of the "symbols and dramatic situations." Using the interpretations of numerous critics from The Zoo Story to Malcolm, he endeavors to develop the connection between Albee and the homosexual theater.

Sato, Susumu. "The Fourth Wall in an Age of Alienation: The Zoo Story and The Connection." In American Literature in the 1950's. Annual Report 1976. Tokyo: Tokyo Chapter, American Literature Society of Japan, 1977. Pp. 161-66.
Both Albee's and Gelber's plays are openly theatrical but Gelber's go even further in terms of audience involvement.

Saurel, Renée. "Frisch, Miller and Albee." Les Temps Modernes 226 (March 1965):1696-99.
Saurel suggests that The American Dream and The Zoo Story form a very homogeneous spectacle because one is able to move quite naturally from one play to the other. She recognizes that Albee's talent for social drama is not new; psychological exploration

and social denunciation have been available in the
American novel for some time. It is Albee's significant dramaturgical expertise which distinguishes him
in the realm of the international theater.

Sawyer, Paul. "Some Observations on the Character of
George in Who's Afraid of Virginia Woolf?" CEA
Critic 42 (1980):15-19.

Schechner, Richard. "Who's Afraid of Edward Albee?"
Tulane Drama Review 7 (Spring 1963):7-10.
Albee continues to influence the theater because "we see in his work a reflection of a sentimental view of ourselves, a view which pleases us."
Albee succeeds in gratifying an adolescent culture
which likes to think of itself as decadent. The
only problem is that Albee may have the ability to
foresee the near future; "we are on the verge of becoming the silly role we are playing." Schechner
vents his anger at the playwright and particularly
Who's Afraid of Virginia Woolf?; he is outraged "at
a theatre and an audience that accepts as a master-
piece an insufferably long play with great preten-
tions that lacks intellectual size, emotional insight,
and dramatic electricity."

_____. "Reality Is Not Enough: An Interview with Alan
Schneider." Tulane Drama Review 9 (Spring 1965):
118-52.
This interview with Schneider, who has directed
nearly all of Albee's plays, provides insight into
the playwright's reputation among others in the
theater world. Schneider indicates that Albee
"builds with words and emotions" and that he is
highly theatrical. There is also discussion of
Who's Afraid of Virginia Woolf? and Schneider's direction of the play. Overall, the director suggests
that "Albee's importance is that he speaks and feels
for the American moment that is now, and he's a talent that has only started."

Schein, Harry. "Vem ar raad for Virginia Woolf." Bonniers Litterara Magasin 30 (1962):706-10. In Swedish.
Schein shows how The Zoo Story and The American
Dream prepared Albee to write Who's Afraid of Virginia Woolf?

Scheller, Bernhard. "Der Figurenaufbau in der Stücken
Edward Albees." In Eberhard Brüning, Klaus Köhler,
and Bernard Scheller, eds. Studien zum amerikanischen
Drama nach dem zweiten Weltkrieg. Berlin: Rütten
and Loening, 1977. Pp. 134-77.
Scheller believes Albee perceived that the
American theatre was stagnating because of its refusal to outgrow bourgeois realism and provide al-
ternatives. Drawing on the French absurdists and

the expressionists, he awakened audiences to the
possibility of shock and excitement. He relies on
the existential philosophers for his depiction of
the angst of modern life. Scheller particularly admires The Zoo Story, Virginia Woolf, and The Death
of Bessie Smith.

_____. "Die Gestalt des Farbigen bei Williams, Albee
und Baldwin und ihre szenische Realisierung in DDR-
Auffuhrungen [The Concept of the Colored Races in
Williams, Albee and Baldwin and Its Scenic Realization in G.D.R.-Productions]." Zeitschrift fur
Anglistik und Amerikanistik 20 (1972):137-57.
　　　All three dramatists express the revolutionary
tendencies inherent in the United States. In The
Death of Bessie Smith, Albee analyzes the exploita-
tion of the masses in the consumer-oriented American
society. In particular, the play reveals the manner
in which Blacks are forced into accepting the norms
of a capitalist society. The "American Dream" for
those in the North is depicted as an illusion allowing little chance for improvement.

Schier, Donald. "Who Cares Who's Afraid of Virginia
　　　Woolf?" Carleton Miscellany 5 (Spring 1964):121-24.
　　　Schier suggests that Albee's implication that
people must face reality in Who's Afraid of Virginia
Woolf? is the play's only contribution, one that is
also quite obvious. He also maintains that this
"elementary idea" is dealt with by a play that is
"long, diffuse, and unsteady."

Schleuter, June. Metafictional Characters in Modern
　　　Drama. New York: Columbia University Press, 1979.
　　　Pp. 79-87.
　　　Examining the relationship of drama in contemporary society along the lines established by Lionel
Abel in Metatheatre, Schleuter considers George and
Martha in Who's Afraid of Virginia Woolf? metafictional characters. George creates and directs his
own story and embodies "a detached representation of
the playwright as artist and director." As such he
is obliged to dispel the illusion of the imaginary
child.

Schneider, Alan. "Why So Afraid?" Tulane Drama Review
　　　7 (Spring 1963):10-13.
　　　Schneider, the director of Who's Afraid of Virginia Woolf?, defends it against the bitter attack
of critics including, in particular, the caustic remarks of Richard Schechner in his "Who's Afraid of
Edward Albee?," pp. 7-10 of the same issue.

Schulz-Seitz, Ruth Eva. Edward Albee-der Dichterphilosoph
　　　der Buhne. Frankfurt: Klostermann, 1966.
　　　In discussing Tiny Alice as an illusion of

68

reality in the context of an artist's drama, Schulz-
Seitz summarizes the plot, comments on each charac-
ter, and comes up with the conclusion that we all
see reality as a combination of reality and illusion
(R = r + i); the two cannot be separated. She sees
Who's Afraid of Virginia Woolf? as a movement on
Albee's part from naturalism to symbolism.

Schwarz, Karl. "Edward Albee's Zoo Story." Die Neueren
Sprachen 18 (June 1969):261-67.
In The Zoo Story, Albee intends to totally involve the audience with his drama. In part he
achieves this by developing "doubly distorted parallels" between Jerry's story concerning the janitoress and the dog and the actual encounter involving
Jerry and Peter. In any case, it is the shock of
Jerry's death scene which draws the spectators emotionally to the stage.

Siegel, Paul N. "The Drama and the Thwarted American
Dream." Lock Haven Review, No. 7 (1965):52-62.
Siegel discusses Albee's The American Dream
among other plays since World War I and determines
it to be representative of the absurdist tradition.

Simpson, Herbert M. "Tiny Alice: Limited Affirmation in
a Conflict Between Theatre and Drama." Forum (Houston) 6 (Fall-Winter 1968):43-46.
Simpson makes the distinction that drama is the
play as it was intended to be performed and theater
is the actual performance of the play. Using this
definition he maintains that theater defeats drama
in Tiny Alice because the "effect of the particular
performance cancels the meaning intended in the
drama." This situation helps to account for the
fact that Albee fails to reach a significant dramatic level; however weak it may be, the play does reveal Albee's potential for dramatic insight.

Skloot, Robert. "The Failure of Tiny Alice." Players
Magazine 43 (February-March 1968):71-81.
In spite of Albee's more recent failures on
Broadway, Tiny Alice remains an important play, "a
work of richness and scope." Nonetheless, a close
analysis reveals that "it is not a very good play"
and its major difficulty is its lack of consistency.
Albee has abrogated the artist's responsibility by
consciously confusing the issues. The "hole at the
center of the play is the sum of its tiny parts ...
imprecise, unclear, slightly dishonest and very pretentious, it might have been written by a hip Plato
smoking pot."

Solomon, Jerry. "Edward Albee: American Absurdist."
Western Speech 28 (Fall 1964):230-36.
Solomon discusses Albee with regard to his con-
nections to the European absurdist tradition.

Spencer, Sharon D. "Edward Albee--The Anger Artist."
     Forum (Houston) 4 (Winter-Spring 1967):25-30.
          Spencer relates Albee to the "sick" comics be-
     cause he uses similar techniques in depicting the
     ever-present anxiety and frustration in society. He
     remains "a shaman providing catharsis but also an
     artist revealing widespread delusions."

Spielberg, Peter. "The Albatross in Albee's Zoo." Col-
     lege English 27 (April 1966):562-65.
          Spielberg argues that "The Rime of the Ancient
     Mariner" is the principal literary source for The
     Zoo Story. Both works begin with a mysterious out-
     cast as the main speaker and there are several other
     similarities. The closest comparison can be made
     regarding the confrontation between the Mariner and
     the albatross and that of Jerry and the dog. It is
     only in the end that Albee significantly differs
     from his source in order to emphasize that modern
     man must always bear an albatross around his neck as
     he remains isolated from his fellow men.

_____. "Reply: The Albatross Strikes Again!" College
     English 28 (October 1966):59.
          Spielberg somewhat testily maintains that his
     comparison of Coleridge's Ancient Mariner with Jerry
     in The Zoo Story is indeed valid.

Stagg, Anne. "House in the Life of a Playwright: Edward
     Albee's Greenwich Village Carriage House." House
     and Garden, December 1967, pp. 160 and 196.
          Stagg takes the reader into the home shared by
     Albee, four cats--Boy, George, Tigger, and Cunégonde
     --and two Pekingese--Spider and Pucci. In the arti-
     cle/interview, Albee expresses his love for Greenwich
     Village, "even though they keep tearing so much of
     it down." The house and its decor stress his appre-
     ciation of darkness and of Chinese art. He used to
     have a marvelous housekeeper "but she went mad."

Stark, John. "Camping Out: Tiny Alice and Susan Sontag."
     Players 41 (April-May 1972):116-69.
          Stark suggests that Tiny Alice implements some
     of Sontag's alternatives for art. Her views on camp
     explain Albee's equivocal treatment of sex and reli-
     gion in the play. Sontag also "believes that inter-
     pretation is not a proper response to art because
     the mimetic theories argue that art is related to
     the world and not self-contained in its own reality,"
     which Stark uses to describe the dramatic method in
     Tiny Alice.

Stavrou, C. N. "Albee in Wonderland." Southwest Review
     60 (Winter 1975):46-61.
          Using four Albee plays to substantiate his
     claim, Stavrou argues that the playwright's alienated

characters "are either attempting to escape reality
or displaying resignation after their illusions have
been shattered." In The American Dream, all except
Grandma live "in a world of delusionary hopes." The
Zoo Story illustrates a dramatic confrontation between the establishment and a nonconformist resulting in a murder that has a significant emotional impact upon the survivor. In Tiny Alice, Albee brings
up the question of how much knowledge is necessary
to sustain life. Finally it is in Who's Afraid of
Virginia Woolf? that Albee explores the illusion/
reality dichotomy to its utmost.

Stenz, Anita M. Edward Albee: Poet of Loss. The Hague:
Mouton, 1978.
Since there has been such a misunderstanding
and misrepresentation by the critics of Albee, Stenz
has endeavored to re-examine his intentions, especially "with respect to the motivation and behavior of
his characters," not only within individual works
but also with regard to one another. Stenz does not
compare his work with that of other playwrights nor
does she relate it to movements of drama; she has attempted "to clarify the meaning of each play in the
light of descriptions of the original performance."
Although she excludes his adaptations because of
their experimental nature, Stenz does treat each
play from The Zoo Story to Seascape in an effort to
"relate the themes of individual works to the oeuvre
as a whole."

Straub, Botho. "Albee, der Broadway und der Tod."
Theater heute 10 (March 1969):45-47. In German.

Stroman, Ben. "Edward Albee's Who's Afraid of Virginia
Woolf?" Vlaamse Gids 48 (May 1964):342-44. In
Flemish.
Stroman sees Albee as a great craftsman who has
developed this play into a significant dramatic
achievement through utterly convincing dialogue. The
central thematic motif is that of impotence and the
play "is a requiem for illusion, a black mass for
the dead."

_____. "Ober de Voorstelling Van Heinar Kipphardts De
Zaak Oppenheimer en van Edward Albee's Kleine Alice."
Vlaamse Gids 49 (December 1965):812-14. In Flemish.
Although the plot is simple in Tiny Alice, nobody can fully understand Albee's intentions. Nonetheless, its brilliant dialogue and its inherent theatricality make the attempt at comprehension worth-
while. Stroman suggests that the characters seem to
represent allegorical abstractions with the Butler
as the voice of the people and therefore the voice
of God.

Sykes, Carol A. "Albee's Beast Fables: The Zoo Story and
     A Delicate Balance." Educational Theatre Journal 25
     (1973):448-55.
          Albee's "beast fables"--the dog story Jerry
     tells and the cat story Tobias relates in their re-
     spective plays--are really about superficial rela-
     tionships between human beings. One critic asserts
     that the two stories function similarly as analogues
     for the plays themselves but Sykes argues that this
     assertion only holds true for A Delicate Balance.
     Only Tobias is forced to realize the total isolation
     of his situation with regard to his wife and friends.
     The encounter in The Zoo Story is different because
     the confrontation with Peter does not leave Jerry as
     indifferent as he was following his meeting with the
     dog.
          •

Szelski, John J. von. "Albee: A Rare Balance." Twentieth
     Century Literature 16 (April 1970):123-30.
          Szelski argues that A Delicate Balance is a
     major work and it deserves more attention both as a
     well-balanced use of Albee's expressed talents and
     as a significant accomplishment in contemporary seri-
     ous drama. Fruitful re-examination of the play cre-
     ates an understanding of its heightened level of il-
     lusion, style, characterization, and theme. Since
     most elements of the work have metaphorical justifi-
     cation it becomes "a quiet and un-paraded vision of
     Albee's honestly felt observations."

Tallmer, Jerry. "Hold That Tiger." Evergreen Review 5
     (May-June 1961):109-13.
          In this "letter" written only a fortnight before
     the opening of The Death of Bessie Smith and ad-
     dressed to Albee, Tallmer challenges the young play-
     wright to make his commitment to the theater. He
     briefly analyzes The Zoo Story and concludes that it
     is "a brilliant act of hostility against the world
     around Albee and nothing more." Finally he exhorts
     Albee to reveal something, anything because in The
     American Dream he sees "no commitment to anything
     except the sheer ferocious pleasures of irony."

Taubman, Howard. The Making of the American Theater.
     New York: Coward-McCann, 1965. Pp. 332-34 et pas-
     sim.
          Without a doubt, Who's Afraid of Virginia Woolf?
     is not a masterpiece, but for other critics and him-
     self "not to recognize that here was a playwright
     with passion and intensity was to be insensate and
     perverse." Taubman also briefly discusses The Bal-
     lad of the Sad Cafe and tries to relate the homosex-
     ual theme predominant in Tiny Alice to other plays
     and playwrights of the fifties and sixties.

Taylor, Charlene M. "Coming of Age in New Carthage:
  Albee's Grown-up Children." Educational Theatre
  Journal 25 (March 1973):53-65.
        Taylor approaches the play through a careful
  analysis of Albee's dialogue, especially with regard
  to his imagery and allusion. She suggests that the
  playwright develops the older couple through a kind
  of rite initiation into full adulthood. Their surviving this experience does not constitute invul-
  nerability but rather it offers the only alternative
  they have. This theme can be seen by studying the
  three ways in which the language of the play is re-
  markable: for its so-called naturalistic quality;
  for its use of childish language and games; and for
  "some highly significant passages of an almost lyri-
  cal nature in which Albee makes heavy use of allusions, metaphor, or both." For George and Martha,
  acceptance of adulthood is a painful necessity because they represent the "spirited parents" of us
  all; the survival of the human race is at stake.

Taylor, Marion A. "Edward Albee and August Strindberg:
  Some Parallels Between The Dance of Death and Who's
  Afraid of Virginia Woolf?" Papers on English Language and Literature 1 (Winter 1965):59-71.
        Taylor indicates some similarities between the
  two plays in the development of a love-hate relationship between the partners of a 23-year-long marriage.
  She suggests the insulting and nagging by the wives
  to be almost identical weapons. The fact that they
  both take lovers who fail to satisfy them and who
  are consequently reduced to abjection only substan-
  tiates her claim. She adds that they both return to
  their husbands and indicates that there are other
  comparisons to be made as well.

_____. "A Note on Strindberg's The Dance of Death and
  Edward Albee's Who's Afraid of Virginia Woolf?"
  Papers on Language and Literature 2 (Spring 1966):
  187-88.
        Taylor suggests that another link between the
  two plays is the similar unfortunate university experiences expressed in Albee's play and in Strindberg's own life as revealed in his attitude toward
  college professors.

Terrien, Samuel. "Demons also Believe: Parodying the
  Eucharist." Christian Century, 9 December 1970,
  pp. 1481-83.
        Along with other recent works, Albee's Who's
  Afraid of Virginia Woolf? "abuses the central mystery of the Christian faith, but at the same time it
  offers--albeit indirectly--a significant lesson for
  our times." Terrien views it as a parody of the Mass
  of Requiem and "the allusions are clear enough." He
  analyzes the play step-by-step in conjunction with

this theme and concludes that a true catharsis takes place in the play. Viewing the final conversation between George and Martha as a positive affirmation of faith, Terrien points to the "genuine biblical fear which is less the product of apprehension than the fruit of grace, the experience of awe at the discovery of love, the outward sign of reconciliation."

Thomas, Michèle. "L'Acceuil de la France au Nouveau Théâtre Anglais [The Reception given to the New English Drama in France], (Avril 1958-Avril 1972)." Recherches Anglaises et Américaines 5 (1972):144-72. In French.

    Thomas suggests that the French performances of Albee's Who's Afraid of Virginia Woolf? in 1964 initiated the assault on French dramatic tradition. Nonetheless, the author points out several of the difficulties encountered in the transfer of drama from one language and cultural background to another. In appendixes, Thomas lists French productions of foreign plays and respective reviews written during the period from 1957 to 1972.

Tolpegin, Dorothy D. "The Two-Petaled Flower: A Commentary on Edward Albee's Play, Tiny Alice." Cimarron Review 14 (January 1977):17-30.

    Tolpegin shows that on a one-dimensional level the characters in Tiny Alice represent limited abstract qualities. For example, Butler represents "technology" and Julian is the symbol for "Obtuse man." But we come to see that each character has the potential for idealized development, or a second dimension. Butler can stand for "service" to mankind and Julian may ultimately become "Aware man." Each man has a choice of two identities and Tiny Alice is a profound and ironic exploration and dramatization of these choices.

Toohey, John L. "A Delicate Balance." In A History of the Pulitzer Prize Plays. New York: Citadel Press, 1967. Pp. 334-39.

    Toohey ends his book with a discussion of Albee's first Pulitzer Prize-winning drama, A Delicate Balance. The article is illustrated with photographs from the production and includes a brief sketch of Albee's life in the theater along with significant reviews of the performances. He concludes that "A Delicate Balance was much the best American play of the season, and far outclassed a remarkably poor field." Toohey also mentions earlier that Who's Afraid of Virginia Woolf? was rejected by the Pulitzer Advisory Board for the 1962 award "in a spectacular display of foolishness and timidity."

Trilling, Diana R. "Who's Afraid of the Culture Elite?"
Esquire, December 1963, pp. 69ff.
She attacks Albee as encouraging elitism in his
supposed social criticism by withholding membership
in an exclusive club from his audiences. Nonetheless, she does mention him in regard to significant
aspects of existential philosophy and modern literature.

Turner, W. L. "Absurdist, Go Home!" Players Magazine 40
(1964):139-40.
Turner reacts adversely to the influence of
European absurdism in Albee's works and calls for a
return to a more traditional American theater.

Valgemae, Mardi. "Albee's Great God Alice." Modern
Drama 10 (1967):267-73.
Valgemae suggests that it is quite possible
that elements in Tiny Alice such as the dream-like
atmosphere, the use of masks, and the reliance upon
stock characters are derived from the early expressionistic plays of O'Neill and in particular from
The Great God Brown.

Vallbona, Rima de. "Edward Albee: el arte y el pueblo."
Indice (Madrid), 1 June 1969, pp. 32-33. In Spanish.

Vos, Nelvin. "The American Dream Turned to Nightmare:
Recent American Drama." Christian Scholar's Review
1 (Spring 1971):195-206.
American history has been highlighted by optimism and hope; material possession usually indicated
the fulfillment of the American dream. The inversion
of these values in the drama of O'Neill, Miller, Williams, and Albee suggests a societal decline. In re-
ducing the dream to ridicule, American dramatists
have depicted a nightmare of debility and impotence.

_____. Eugene Ionesco and Edward Albee: A Critical Es-
say. Grand Rapids: W. B. Eerdmans, 1968.
Vos explores the connection between Albee and
the European absurdist tradition using Ionesco as a
base for comparison.

_____. "The Process of Dying in the Plays of Edward
Albee." Educational Theatre Journal 25 (March 1973):
80-85.
Albee's most recent play, All Over, exemplifies
the participation of both the characters and the
audience in the ritual of dying. Examples of this
phenomenon occur in The Zoo Story, The Death of Bessie Smith, A Delicate Balance, and Everything in the
Garden in which a real or disguised priest usually
presides over the death-watch. This confrontation
with death therefore frequently "becomes the encounter with terror and sometimes the arrival at rest
and peace."

Waldmeir, Joseph J. "Only an Occasional Rutabaga: American Fiction Since 1945." Modern Fiction Studies 15
(1969-70):467-81.
    Five interrelated trends may be identified in
American fiction since 1945: (1) the social critical
trend; (2) the accommodationist trend; (3) the beat-
absurd-black-humorist trend; (4) the quest trend;
and (5) the neo-social critical trend. Waldmeir indicates that Edward Albee, along with B. J. Friedman,
is exemplary of the beat-absurd-black-humorist trend
in modern fiction.

Wallace, Robert S. "The Zoo Story: Albee's Attack on
Fiction." Modern Drama 16 (June 1973):49-54.
    In Albee's plays the characters fail to extri-
cate themselves from sticky situations when they
should because they, like the audience, enjoy vicarious experiences. In this play Jerry's actions indicate how meaningless words have become and how effectively fiction undermines man's conception of
reality.

Way, Brian. Albee and the Absurd: The American Dream and
The Zoo Story. American Theatre. Stratford-upon-
Avon Studies 10. New York: St. Martin's Press,
1967. Pp. 189-207.
    Way provides a very detailed study of Albee's
connection with the theater of the absurd and suggests that the playwright "still believes in the
validity of reason that things can be proved, or that
events can be shown to have definite meanings--and,
unlike Beckett and the others, is scarcely touched
by the sense of living in an absurd universe." Way
suggests that Albee has been attracted to the theatre of the absurd because of the kind of social
criticism in which he engages. In presenting a very
detailed analysis of the two plays, Way delineates
"limitations of scope" but always within the context
of pointing out the playwright's good qualities.

Weales, Gerald. American Drama Since World War II. New
York: Harcourt, Brace, and World, 1962. Pp. 215,
218-21, and 223.
    In his discussion of Off-Broadway productions,
Weales includes brief analyses of Zoo Story, Death
of Bessie Smith, The Sandbox, and The American Dream.
He maintains that the first of these, which was
initially performed in Berlin prior to its New York
production, is "probably the best; certainly it illustrates Albee's wit and his talent for dialogue."

_____. The Jumping-Off Place: American Drama in the
1960's. New York: Macmillan, 1969. Pp. 24-53.
    In this critical survey of drama in the sixties
Weales states that Edward Albee is unequivocally the
American playwright of the era. In spite of the

continuing quarrel between Albee and his critics,
his reputation has expanded into all realms of the
theater. Weales delves into the critical interpretations of others in conjunction with his own analyses
of the plays. In this regard, he suggests that Albee's "subtext" or sub-subject matter regarding homosexuality in the plays has received too much attention. Nonetheless, he feels that all the Albee
plays "insist on suggesting that there is more there
than meets the eye and ear." Weales sees problems
with Albee's forthcoming works because his recent
works reveal a significance which "seems to be im-
posed from the outside instead of meaning from within."

_____. "Off-Broadway: Its Contributions to American
Drama." Drama Survey 2 (June 1962):5-23.
Weales devotes two pages to the four plays Albee
wrote between 1958 and 1960, primarily pointing out
their absurdist overtones and debt to Beckett.

Wellwarth, George E. "Hope Deferred: The New American
Drama. Reflections on Edward Albee, Jack Richardson,
Jack Gelber and Arthur Kopit." Literary Review 7
(1963):8-15. Also in his The Theatre of Protest and
Paradox. New York: New York University Press, 1964.
Pp. 274-84.
Wellwarth suggests that although there have been
plenty of new American dramas, the lack of a "movement," parallel to the English dramatic movement,
"in the U.S. is due to the much greater difficulty
of getting a play produced in the commercial theater
and to the stubborn refusal of the New York drama
critics to get together and form a cheering section
for the American drama." He adds that if a "movement" is recognized, the premiere of The Zoo Story
will be commemorated as its starting point and Albee
will be recognized as its brightest new star. Wellwarth also briefly analyzes Albee's plays through
Who's Afraid of Virginia Woolf?

Wendt, Ernst. "Uber den Dramatiker Edward Albee und sein
Struck Winzige Alice." Theater heute 7 (1966):12-15.
Wendt examines Albee's techniques and themes in
Tiny Alice.

"Wer hat Angst vor Virginia Woolf? von Edward Albee." Der
Spiegel (Hamburg) 43 (June 1963):110-12.
Albee's anger at social injustice and hypocrisy
is noted.

White, James E. "Albee's Tiny Alice, an Exploration of
Paradox." Literatur in Wissenschaft und Unterricht
(Kiel) 6 (1973):247-58.
White disagrees with critics like Brustein and
Dukore who have considered Tiny Alice to be sopho-

moric and argues that the play "probes deeply into
the paradox and irony of man's institutions." Albee
heightens our awareness that man is so subjectively
bound in his quest for the ideal that he may unin-
tentionally mock or pervert it. Julian's actions in
the play are a metaphor for man's search for meaning
and Albee deliberately chooses not to judge the results.

Willeford, William E. "The Mouse in the Model." Modern
Drama 12 (September 1969):135-45.
    Tiny Alice is a serious and original effort by
Albee "to conjure up something that is a genuine
mystery." Alice is the central figure in the drama
and simultaneously portrays a woman, the mouse in
the model, and God. This mouse is a God-metaphor
which reduces "the cosmic to the 'Tiny' of Alice's
name" and it is only through this fusion of identities that she affirms the existence of a transcendent
order.

Winston, Matthew. "Edward Albee: A Delicate Balance."
In Das amerikanische Drama Gegenwart. Ed. Herbert
Grabes. Kronberg: Athenäum, 1976. Pp. 29-43.
    The achievement of A Delicate Balance is re-
evaluated.

Witherington, Paul. "Albee's Gothic: The Resonances of
Cliché." Comparative Drama 4 (Fall 1970):151-65.
    Albee should be examined as part of an emerging
gothic tradition that protests the reason and materialism of society by demysticizing its individuals
and institutions. His plays contain three essential
aspects of this development: reduction, inversion,
and recognition. Thus, Albee exposes society thoroughly but its horrors often lead "to dimensions of
individual possibility beyond the limited circle of
satire."

_____. "Language of Movement in Albee's The Death of
Bessie Smith." Twentieth Century Literature 13
(July 1967):84-88.
    Witherington sees the "conflict between inten-
tion and performance" evident in the language as the
key to the play in the development of a static atmosphere. The imagery and diction dramatize the themes
of purposelessness and the human weakness for misdi-
rected action.

Wolfe, Peter. "The Social Theater of Edward Albee."
Prairie Schooner 39 (Fall 1965): 248-62.
    Wolfe examines eight Albee plays for effective
social criticism. He suggests that The Zoo Story reveals the disasters associated with forming human re-

lationships across class barriers. Social inequality
with racial overtones is evident in The Death of Bessie Smith. The next four plays question three basic
cliché́s: "sugary, home-spun rhetoric of older people,
society's protectiveness of its down-trodden, and the
exalted station of women." In his two most recent
endeavors, Albee has indicated that redemption is at
least sometimes possible.

Woods, Linda L. "Isolation and the Barrier of Language
    in The Zoo Story." Research Studies 36 (September
    1968):224-31.
        The thematic focal point in the play is the
    human isolation which is appropriately dramatized in
    the dialogue. The impotence and barrenness of the
    language serves its purpose by revealing the inabil-
    ity of human beings to communicate.

Wunderlich, Lawrence. "Playwrights at Cross Purposes."
    Works 1 (Winter 1968):14-37.
        The successes of the Albee-Barr-Wilder Play-
    wrights' Unit have been disappointingly few, largely
    because of the unit's eclectic membership and its
    failure to generate a "unified and meaningful aes-
    thetic." It has never fully realized its intention
    to create a cooperative atmosphere in which young
    dramatists could work. Wunderlich includes a chron-
    ological list of all ABW Playwrights' Unit produc-
    tions from 1963 through 1967 to substantiate his
    viewpoint.

_____. "An Early Play by Edward Albee." American Lit-
    erature 42 (March 1970):98-99.
        The one-act play Schism (1946), which Albee
    wrote while a senior at Choate Preparatory School,
    is a very poor play but it reveals his early concern
    for religious and moral themes, and it faintly fore-
    shadows his later works. It certainly serves as a
    basis for measuring the playwright's artistic devel-
    opment and success to date.

_____. "'Santayanian Finesse' in Albee's Tiny Alice."
    Notes on Contemporary Literature 3 (1973):12-13.
        The phrase "Santayanian finesse" in Albee's
    Tiny Alice which had been used by the Lawyer in a
    sonnet written as a schoolboy and criticized as un-
    gainly comes, in fact, from a sonnet entitled "Nihil-
    ist," written by Albee while at Choate.

Wurster, Grace Stewart. "Albee's Festival Chant: Who's
    Afraid of Virginia Woolf?" Michigan Academician 9
    (Summer 1976):61-67.
        Wurster suggests that Who's Afraid of Virginia
    Woolf? can be best understood as "a theme of steril-
    ity played against a countertheme of archetypal fer-
    tility rituals with a statement about truth and

illusion which is developed by association rather
than by logical progression." She analyzes the play
in detail in order to expound upon this thesis.

Wyler, Siegfried. "Zu Edward Albee's Buhnenschaffen."
Reformatio (Zurich) 5 (1967):330-46.

_____. "Zu Edward Albees Buhnenschaffen." In Das
amerikanische Drama. Ed. Hans Itschert. Darmstadt:
Wissenschaftliche Buchgesellschaft, 1972. Pp. 401-
19.
Wyler assesses the stagecraft of Albee's major
plays as impressive, placing the playwright's work
in the tradition of O'Neill, Wilder, Tennessee Williams, and Arthur Miller. He also acknowledges Albee's debt to Absurdism and symbolist drama.

Zimbardo, Rose A. "Symbolism and Naturalism in Edward
Albee's The Zoo Story." Twentieth Century Literature 8 (April 1962):10-17.
Albee's synthesis of symbolism and naturalism
in The Zoo Story helps to usher in a new era in
American theater. Traditional Christian and classic
myth survive in an expertly constructed and viable
dialogue. The central theme of isolation and salvation through sacrifice assist in the creation of a
contemporary morality play.

Zolotow, Sam. "Producing Team Plans Repertory." New
York Times, 5 September 1967, p. 50.
Zolotow reveals the plans of the newly formed
producing agency for the revival of short plays by
Albee, LeRoi Jones, and Pinter along with two new
one-act plays by Albee, Box and Quotations from
Chairman Mao Tse-tung.

II. DISSERTATIONS

Baker, Burton. "Edward Albee's Nihilistic Plays." Dissertation Abstracts International 35:5387A. University of Wisconsin, 1974.
Even in his funniest plays, Baker argues, Albee
evinces a deeply nihilistic view of the world. Baker
examines the philosophical attitudes in all of Albee's
plays and adaptations, and finds that like Beckett,
he denies any value in human potential.

Berger, Jere Schindel. "The Rites of Albee." Carnegie-
Mellon University, 1973. Available only on microfilm.

Blades, Larry Thomas. "Williams, Miller and Albee: A
Comparative Study." Dissertation Abstracts Interna-
tional 32:4600A. St. Louis University, 1971.
Blades compares the thematic relationships

between the three playwrights, devoting separate
chapters to society, the individual, guilt and
atonement, sex and marriage, and the family.

Brand, Patricia Ann. "Decline and Decay in the Plays of
Edward Albee." Dissertation Abstracts International
36:3708A. New York University, 1975.
Brand considers Albee's corpus in the light of
Oswald Spengler's Decline of the West, which "gives
a new perspective to his plays and explains some of
the obscurities in his work, his fascination with
certain recurring themes, and even the technical experimentation." She concludes that Albee, while
not optimistic, expects man to face his chaotic age with
dignity and without illusions.

Burns, Carol Ann. "Seeing Double: Analogies in the Plays
of Edward Albee." Dissertation Abstracts International 39:2268A. State University of New York at
Binghamton, 1978.
In a discussion of most of Albee's plays, Burns
compares pervasive, and successful, use of analogies
and double plots to similar techniques used in the
Renaissance. Following the example of Francis Fergus-
son's explication of Hamlet, Burns traces Albee's own
use of analogous action in The Zoo Story and throughout his work.

Dieb, Ronald. "Patterns of Sacrifice in the Plays of
Arthur Miller, Tennessee Williams, and Edward Albee."
Dissertation Abstracts International 30:5104A. University of Denver, 1969.
Dieb explores the problem of contemporary es-
trangement, and the use of ritual sacrifice by these
three playwrights as a method of resolving this
alienation. After establishing a psychological and
spiritual framework, he devotes a chapter to each
man, arguing that Albee draws upon absurdist techniques but ultimately fails by denying his sacrificial characters the opportunity for change.

Dillon, Perry C. "The Characteristics of the French Theater of the Absurd in the Plays of Edward Albee and
Harold Pinter." Dissertation Abstracts International
29:257A. University of Arkansas, 1968.
After outlining the elements of the French Theater of the Absurd, Dillon demonstrates the extent to
which the plays of Albee and Pinter partake of these
elements, concluding that their closest correspond-
ences to the French lie in their rhythmical but
everyday language and their emphasis on alienation.

Doerry, Karl W. "Edward Albee's Modern Morality Plays."
Dissertation Abstracts International 33:2368A.
University of Oregon, 1972.
Doerry argues that "the meaning of Albee's

plays, The Zoo Story, Who's Afraid of Virginia
Woolf?, Tiny Alice, and A Delicate Balance can best
be explicated by treating them as modern morality
and mystery plays." He outlines major thematic and
formal criteria, opening his discussion of the four
plays with Tiny Alice, his "most complex play," which
most nearly fulfills the criteria.

Dubler, Walter. "O'Neill, Wilder, and Albee: The Use of
Fantasy in Modern American Drama." Harvard University, 1964. Abstract not available.

Ducker, Danny. "Hermeneutics and Literary Criticism: A
Phenomenological Mode of Interpretation with Particular Application of Who's Afraid of Virginia Woolf?"
Dissertation Abstracts International 36:8045A.
University of Wisconsin, 1975.
 Ducker critiques the theories of interpretation
forwarded by Hirsch and Palmer, and shows how they
can be resolved in Cavell's phenomenology of interaction. Then, along the lines of Cavell's approach to
King Lear, Ducker interprets Albee's Virginia Woolf
in order to embody the concepts under discussion.

Fedor, Joan Roberta. "The Importance of the Female in
the Plays of Samuel Beckett, Harold Pinter and Edward Albee." Dissertation Abstracts International
38:1378A. University of Washington, 1976.
 Even if Beckett, Pinter, and Albee are aware of,
and concerned with expressing, the chaos of their
times, Fedor argues, they are unclear as to how to
deal with it. Since women are traditionally linked
with both chaos and redemption, it is through studying their female characters that one senses their
attitudes toward contemporary pessimism. For Albee,
"the female is ... brave and resilient, but she is
finally unable to transcend the reality of modern
chaos."

Fleming, William P., Jr. "Tragedy in American Drama: The
Tragic Views of Eugene O'Neill, Tennessee Williams,
Arthur Miller, and Edward Albee." Dissertation Abstracts International 33:308A. University of Toledo,
1972.
 By analyzing selected works of the four playwrights, Fleming comes to a definition of "a type of
tragedy unique to America, but by its very nature
... universal." Albee is seen as emphasizing man's
search for reality and his understanding of death
and illusion.

Hempel, Peter Andrew. "From 'Survival Kit' to Seascape:
Edward Albee's Revolutionary Drama." Dissertation
Abstracts International 36:6683A. University of
Texas at Austin, 1975.
 Hempel reflects on Albee's moral vision, espe-

cially as seen in <u>Who's Afraid of Virginia Woolf?</u>, <u>Tiny Alice</u>, and <u>Seascape</u>. The playwright projects a broad, humanistic social concern, as opposed to self-interest. His increasing preoccupation with death "suggests both a new rage and a new compassion in his later works."

Hill, Linda Marjenna. "Language as Aggression: Studies in the Postwar Drama." <u>Dissertation Abstracts International</u> 35:4524A. Yale University, 1974.

    In her study of Albee's <u>The American Dream</u> and five postwar European plays, Hill asserts that language itself is seen as pernicious, rather than simply inadequate. Hill discusses what language accomplishes in each play; and takes up the reception and the milieu of each play.

Hull, Elizabeth Anne. "A Transactional Analysis of the Plays of Edward Albee." <u>Dissertation Abstracts International</u> 36:313A. Loyola University of Chicago, 1975.

    Hull examines most of Albee's major works in light of "the relatively new field in psychology, transactional analysis." She concludes that "while TA as a technique of literary analysis ignores many other interesting aspects of the playwright's work, it does account for the psychological realism which is a major factor in the dramatic success of Albee's work."

Jánský, Anne Leah Lauf. "Albee's First Decade: An Evaluation." <u>Dissertation Abstracts International</u> 30:3462A. St. Louis University, 1969.

    As the title implies, Jánský's study provides an overall evaluation of Albee's first decade as a prominent playwright, emphasizing the general qualities of his art. She comments that he "shows all the technical skills which mark a top-flight playwright," but she adds that his plays reflect a "narrowness of vision which, unlike his technical virtuosity, has not developed during the first ten years of his career."

Langdon, Harry. "A Critical Study of <u>Tiny Alice</u> by Edward Albee Focusing on Commanding Image and Ritual Form." <u>Dissertation Abstracts International</u> 31:3080A. University of Iowa, 1970.

    Langdon applies a basically Jungian approach to <u>Tiny Alice</u>, seeing the play's key in its commanding image of enclosure. He discusses the ritualistic actions which enable Julian to move from one level of enclosure to another. The study has implications for almost any investigation of non-realistic drama.

Larner, Daniel. "Self-Conscious Form in Modern American
    Drama." Dissertation Abstracts International 29:
    4494A. University of Wisconsin, 1968.
        Lerner lists three purposes behind his analysis:
    "(1) to describe a new concept, self-conscious form,
    for use in dramatic criticism; (2) to show how Ameri-
    can criticism, mostly of the last thirty years, can
    support a coherent understanding of this concept;
    and (3) to use this concept in criticizing a group
    of American plays written since 1953." Among the
    five plays singled out for extensive study is Albee's
    The American Dream.

Levene, Victoria E. "The House of Albee: A Study of the
    Plays of Edward Albee." Dissertation Abstracts In-
    ternational 33:317A. State University of New York
    at Binghamton, 1972.
        In this comprehensive examination of Albee's
    corpus to date, Levene stresses "reiterated motifs"
    and the progressions from play to play, principally
    from satire to affirmation. She touches on personae
    and archetypes, concluding that "Albee increasingly
    constructs his works as organic forms."

Levy, Valerie Brussel. "Violence as Drama: A Study of
    the Development of the Use of Violence on the Ameri-
    can Stage." Dissertation Abstracts International 31:
    6618A. Claremont Graduate School and University
    Center, 1970.
        Prefacing her study with a review of Elizabethan
    drama and Freudian psychology, Levy concentrates on
    violence as portrayed by O'Neill, Tennessee Williams,
    and Albee. She explores the latter's symbolic use
    of the family in the American tradition of dialogue
    as cruelty.

Leyden, William. "Social Protest and the Absurd: A Read-
    ing of the Plays of Edward Albee." Dissertation Ab-
    stracts International 32:6434A. University of Ore-
    gon, 1971.
        Leyden argues that Albee should be relegated
    neither to the social protest tradition nor to the
    Absurdist tradition since his plays effectively
    blend both strains. The Zoo Story, for example, may
    be influenced by Beckett, but it contains social
    protest. Box-Mao-Box, absurdist in form, offers a
    warning against the stupidity of institutions, which
    places it solidly in the tradition of social realism.

McCants, Sarah Maxine. "The Shade and the Mask: Death
    and Illusion in the Works of Edward Albee." Disser-
    tation Abstracts International 35:6722A. University
    of Southern Mississippi, 1974.
        McCants explores the delusion-illusion syndrome
    "which separates men from each other and from the
    truth." Paradoxically it is by facing death that
    Albee's stronger characters learn to control life.

Martin, Emma Jean. "Edward Albee: Theory, Theme, Technique." Florida State University, 1969. Abstract not available.

Mayberry, Robert Lawrence. "Theatre of Discord: The Dissonance of Language and Light in Selected Plays of Samuel Beckett, Edward Albee and Harold Pinter." Dissertation Abstracts International 40:5440A. University of Rhode Island, 1979.
     Investigating the "disassociation of acoustic and visual space" in certain one-act plays by Beckett, Pinter and Albee, Mayberry asserts that what the audience sees is not synchronous with what it hears; therefore, these plays "constitute a theatre of discord, typified by the opposition of the static visual space and the frenetic deluge of language." The spectators must resolve the dissonance to discover meaning, acting as the protagonists of the play with the playwright as their antagonist. Albee fragments the audience's experience intentionally in Quotations from Chairman Mao Tse-tung, daring each spectator to reorder the play's chaos, a discord which "parallels the jangle of experiences we call living."

Miller, Robert R. "Tragedy in Modern American Drama: The Psychological, Social, and Absurdist Conditions in Historical Perspective." Dissertation Abstracts International 36:3717A. Middle Tennessee State University, 1975.
     Miller examines Albee's American Dream as "an absurdist portrayal of characters whose lives are lived without meaning." He notes that their crisis of identity is "tragic because they are not aware of the problem." In effect, their obstacle to fulfillment is ignorance: "Albee epitomizes in absurdity the meaninglessness of characters' lives in modern tragedy."

Moses, Robbie Jeanette Odom. "The Theme of Death in the Plays of Edward Albee." Dissertation Abstracts International 35:4443A. University of Houston, 1974.
     In tracing the development of the single theme which enfolds all thirteen of Albee's plays to date, Moses underscores "the pervasiveness of death" in the shorter plays, the adaptations, and the long plays. She reaches the conclusion that "for Albee, spiritual death is a far worse fate than physical death" and that in his plays "death is an entrance into renewed life."

Norton, Rictor C. "Studies of the Union of Love and Death: I. Herakles and Hylas: The Homosexual Archetype. II. The Pursuit of Ganymede in Renaissance Pastoral Literature. III. Folklore and Myth in Who's Afraid of Virginia Woolf? IV. The Turn of the Screw: Coincidentia Oppositorum." Dissertation Ab-

stracts _International_ 33:5190A. Florida State University, 1972.
      With the framework of _Dies_ _Irae_, Easter, The
Birthday, and The Exorcism, Norton describes "the
processes of eliminating evil to make way for
growth." Albee's play contains possible fairytale
allusions to the three little pigs and the big bad
wolf, as well as to the Dionysian ritual of purgation and rebirth. Finally, George devours "his
Christlike 'son' in the form of a eucharistic tele-
gram, thus being reborn."

Plunka, Gene Alan. "The Existential Ritual in the Plays
      of Jean Genet, Peter Shaffer, and Edward Albee."
      Dissertation _Abstracts_ _International_ 39:7342A.
      University of Maryland, 1978.
      Plunka comments that Albee is an "innovator,"
who works with ceremonies which are existentially
oriented, yet whose plays are unlike those of Genet
and Shaffer. All three share, however, an affinity
for "the sexual, the ritual and the existential."

Rios, Charlotte Rose. "Violence in Contemporary Drama:
      Antonin Artaud's Theater of Cruelty and Selected
      Drama of Genet, Williams, Albee, Bond, and Pinter."
      Dissertation _Abstracts_ _International_ 41.
      University of Notre Dame, 1981.
      The painful search for reality, the violent
confrontation of characters with each other and society, are traits of Artaud's theatre of cruelty.
Albee is seen as an American playwright who under-
stands the power of cruelty in certain situations,
especially in _The_ _Zoo_ _Story_ and _Who's_ _Afraid_ _of_ _Vir-_
ginia _Woolf?_

Rule, Margaret W. "The Reception of the Plays of Edward
      Albee in Germany." _Dissertation_ _Abstracts_ _Interna-_
      tional 32:983A. University of Arkansas, 1971.
      Presenting a wide spectrum of German critical
reaction to Albee, whose _Zoo_ _Story_ opened in Berlin
in 1959, Rule observes that two major themes emerge
in his plays: the individual's isolation in contemporary society and "a world-wide sickness arising
from a status-symbol society and a complacent middle
class." In addition, German critics have noted his
development of a "composite woman figure" (materialism), and a universal application of the American
dream, suggesting its metaphysical significance.

Sanders, Walter E. "The English Speaking Game Drama."
      Dissertation _Abstracts_ _International_ 30:5001A.
      Northwestern University, 1970.
      In describing Beckett, Pinter, and Albee as
"game-dramatists," Sanders perceives the game as the
central principle in the theme and structure of their
plays. He analyzes _The_ _Zoo_ _Story_ and _Who's_ _Afraid_

86

of Virginia Woolf? in terms of game movement toward
a crisis.

Sapoznik, Ran. "The One-Act Plays of Thornton Wilder,
William Saroyan and Edward Albee." *Dissertation Abstracts International* 37:700A. University of Kansas,
1975.
      Sapoznik provides "a close analysis of the
dramatic and theatrical means used by Wilder, Saroyan
and Albee in their one-act plays." Three major characteristics of this genre are established: economical
treatment of all elements, strong unity, and episodic
form "in which each episode may be self-contained,
but in which all are bound together by a strong line
of dramatic suspense."

Schneider, Ruth Morris. "The Interpolated Narrative in
Modern Drama." *Dissertation Abstracts International*
34:6605A. State University of New York at Albany,
1973.
      Schneider examines *The Zoo Story* in terms of
the narrative which "casts a thematic light on the
play as a whole." The parable which Jerry tells
Peter is the core of the play: "Peter's refusal to
understand the parable and Jerry's refusal to allow
Peter to go on not understanding create the final
enlightenment of the play both for Peter and for the
audience." The narrative technique of Hampton,
Pinter, Beckett, and Ionesco is similarly analyzed.

Schupbach, Deanne Justina. "Edward Albee's America."
Dissertation Abstracts International 32:4022A.
University of Texas at Austin, 1970.
      In considering the character types of Albee's
plays, Schupbach follows a roughly chronological
order, by generations. At the center of Albee's
view of America lie "two antithetical sets of values,
the altruistic and the acquisitive." The progression
of generations, it is suggested, imply the playwright's vision that the latter will dominate in the
future.

Shelton, Lewis Edward. "Alan Schneider's Direction of
Four Plays by Edward Albee: A Study in Form." *Dissertation Abstracts International* 32:4754A. University of Wisconsin, 1971.
      Shelton ponders the directorial perspective in
clarifying the structure, internal and external, of
*Who's Afraid of Virginia Woolf?, The American Dream,
Tiny Alice,* and *A Delicate Balance.* Alan Schneider
has shaped the dramatic form of each, his aim to
translate the playwright's "perceptions of reality
into viable theatrical language."

Smith, Rebecca Louise. "Dissonance as Method in the Plays of Edward Albee." University of Alberta (Canada), 1975. Abstract not available.

Steiner, Donald Lee. "August Strindberq and Edward Albee: The Dance of Death." Dissertation Abstracts International 33:766A. University of Utah, 1972.
    Steiner presents a comparative study of the two playwrights, focusing on their treatment of the theme of death.

Stephens, Suzanne Schaddelee. "The Dual Influence: A Dramaturgical Study of the Plays of Edward Albee and the Specific Dramatic Forms and Themes Which Influence Them." Dissertation Abstracts International 34:342A. Miami University, 1972.
    Viewing Albee's dramaturgy as the way form shapes theme, Stephens scrutinizes his plays in respect to "the appropriateness of the relationship between its theme and the form which gives it substance." In addition, she notes the way both elements have been influenced by realism-expressionism and Absurdism.

Storrer, William Allin. "A Comparison of Edward Albee's Who's Afraid of Virginia Woolf? as Drama and as Film." Dissertation Abstracts International 29:3544A. Ohio University, 1968.
    Storrer contends that although drama and film communicate similar content, the two media draw on a different "primary communicating element." Through both verbal and visual elements Albee presents content based on four levels of response: a view of college life, classic tragedy, truth vs. illusion, and George and Martha as symbols of the decline of the West. The fact that both drama and film successfully communicate the playwright's vision "is a positive comment on the universality of Albee's dramatic expression."

Wagner, Marlene S. "The Game-Play in Twentieth Century Absurdist Drama: Studies in a Dramatic Technique." Dissertation Abstracts International 32:4637A. University of Southern California, 1972.
    This investigation of game-plays includes Albee's Who's Afraid of Virginia Woolf? as a drama with a traditional structure, where "the games in it are a device to reveal plot rather than a strict substitute for it."

Ware, Robert Gordon. "Edward Albee's Early Plays: A Dramaturgical Study." Dissertation Abstracts International 41:1843A. Stanford University, 1979.
    The special qualities of Albee's first plays, their fascinating mixture of absurdist techniques and shocking contemporary dialogue, are analyzed

and the source of Albee's early power as a dramatist is considered.

Wilson, Raymond J. "Transactional Analysis and Literature." Dissertation Abstracts International 34: 7793A. University of Nebraska, 1973.

Transactional analysis, as evolved by Eric Berne, can provide the basis for "creating new categories for thinking about the human actions described in literature." In Chapter Four Wilson examines Who's Afraid of Virginia Woolf? in tems of psychological games, which furnish the key to understanding the central action of the play.

Winchell, Cedric. "An Analysis of the Symbology in the Earlier Plays by Edward Albee." Dissertation Abstracts International 32:6600A. University of California at Los Angeles, 1971.

This exegesis of Albee's symbology attempts to clarify his dramatic intentions and techniques: "The text describes Albee's psychic fixation at the level of the adolescent Eternal-Son who rebels forever against all collective standards or values." Winchell employs the concepts of ego-development, individuation, and centroversion, as derived from Jung and Erich Neumann, to explore the use of the "unconscious" in The Zoo Story, Fam and Yam, The Sandbox, The Death of Bessie Smith, and Albee's adaptation of Melville's Bartleby.

III. REVIEWS AND ANNOUNCEMENTS

ALL OVER

Daily News (New York), 29 March 1971, in New York Theatre Critics' Reviews 32 (1971):320.

National Observer, 29 March 1971, p. 21.

New York Post, 29 March 1971, in New York Theatre Critics' Reviews 32 (1971):320.

New York Times, 29 March 1971, p. 41.

Women's Wear Daily, 29 March 1971, in New York Theatre Critics' Reviews 32 (1971):322.

Times (London), 30 March 1971, p. 10a.

Wall Street Journal, 30 March 1971, in New York Theatre Critics' Reviews 32 (1971):32.

Village Voice, 1 April 1971, pp. 59 and 66.

New York Times, 2 April 1971, p. 32.

New York Times, 4 April 1971, II:1.

Newsweek, 5 April 1971, p. 52.

Time, 5 April 1971, p. 69.

New Yorker, 10 April 1971, p. 95.

Saturday Review, 10 April 1971, p. 54.

Nation, 12 April 1971, pp. 476-77.

New Republic, 17 April 1971, p. 24.

Nation, 3 May 1971, pp. 570-71.

Crinkley, Richmond. "The Development of Edward Al-
    bee." National Review, 1 June 1971, pp. 602-04.
        Crinkley calls All Over, with A Delicate
    Balance, "Albee's most satisfying achievement."
    Albee's hypersensitivity, at once "his central
    virtue and his central fault," lends strength
    to this play, which succeeds in part due to its
    portrayal of the doldrums of modern times, and
    of the death of an obsolescent social milieu.
    Crinkley wishes that Albee could rise above
    bitchy responsiveness to his critics' attacks,
    but finds this stance harmonious with the over-
    all thrust of All Over, which is, finally, "a
    big play about smallness."

Massachusetts Review 12 (Autumn 1971):823.

New York Theatre Critics' Reviews 32 (1971):320-23.

THE AMERICAN DREAM

New York Times, 26 October 1960, p. 40.

New York Times, 25 January 1961, p. 28.

Time, 3 February 1961, pp. 53 and 55.

Balliett, Whitney. "Three Cheers for Albee." New
    Yorker, 4 February 1961, pp. 62 and 64-66.
        Balliett sees Albee as an uncommonly suc-
    cessful practitioner of the difficult art of
    "horror-comedy." The horror of The American
    Dream, "a unique and often brilliant play," is
    merely implied. Balliett provides an extensive

summary of the play's "endless series of sur-
prises," and concludes: "This is a play for the
resilient young and the wise old. All those
paunchy, sluggish targets in between had best
stay away." The review ends with a brief, un-
sympathetic assessment of the concurrently-
produced Bartleby.

Clurman, Harold. Nation, 11 February 1961, pp. 125-
26.
Clurman does not believe that The American
Dream quite lives up to the promise Albee has
shown in The Zoo Story. He calls it "funny and
horrid, a poker-faced grotesque." Commenting
that Ionesco's influence through such plays as
The Bald Soprano is "not altogether helpful,"
Clurman insists Albee's talent "lies closer to
realism than perhaps he knows"--a prophetic
statement considering the later Who's Afraid of
Virginia Woolf?

Saturday Review, 11 February 1961, p. 54.

Theatre Arts 45 (March 1961):68.

Christian Century, 1 March 1961, p. 30.

Educational Theatre Journal 13 (May 1961):109-10.

Hatch, Robert. "Theater: Arise Ye Playgoers of the
World." Horizon 3 (July 1961):116-17.
Hatch groups Albee with the French Absurd-
ists`as "dispassionate chroniclers of humanity's
swift and irreversible decline." He asserts,
"our horror at the statement of an Albee play
comes as an aftertaste; but unlike Beckett, it
comes as an admonition." Hatch finds both
American Dream and Bessie Smith engrossing, and
is disappointed at the audience's misinterpreta-
tion of the violence, especially in the former.

Catholic World, 193 (August 1961):335-36.

Trotta, Geri. "On Stage: Edward Albee." Horizon 4
(September 1961):78-79.

New York Times, 25 October 1961, p. 33.

Gellert, Roger. "Albee et al." New Statesman, 3
November 1961, pp. 667-68.

Popkin, Henry. "Theatre Chronicle." Sewanee Review
69 (1961):342-43.

New York Times, 12 February 1962, p. 27.

New York Times, 25 February 1962, VI:30.

Funke, Lewis. "Theatre: Albee Revivals." New York
    Times, 29 May 1963, p. 39.

Lewis, Theophilus. "Theater: The Zoo Story and The
    American Dream." America, 22 June 1963, pp. 891-
    92.

New York Times, 13 February 1965, p. 10.

New York Times, 3 October 1968, p. 55.

THE BALLAD OF THE SAD CAFE

New York Times, 27 October 1963, II:1.

Daily News (New York), 31 October 1963, in New York
    Theatre Critics' Reviews 24 (1963):214.

New York Herald Tribune, 31 October 1963, in New
    York Theatre Critics' Reviews 24 (1963):212-13.

New York Journal American, 31 October 1963, in New
    York Theatre Critics' Reviews 24 (1963):213-14.

New York Post, 31 October 1963, in New York Theatre
    Critics' Reviews 24 (1963):212.

New York Times, 31 October 1963, p. 27.

New York World-Telegram and The Sun, 31 October
    1963, in New York Theatre Critics' Reviews 24
    (1963):215-16.

Time, 8 November 1963, p. 67.

New Yorker, 9 November 1963, p. 95.

New York Times, 10 November 1963, II:1.

Newsweek, 11 November 1963, p. 76.

New Republic, 16 November 1963, pp. 28-29.

Saturday Review, 16 November 1963, p. 54.

Gilman, Richard. "Albee's Sad 'Ballad.'" Common-
    weal, 22 November 1963, pp. 256-57.
        Gilman summarizes his review in his first
    sentence: "The Ballad of the Sad Cafe is a
    failure for which it is strangely difficult to
    assign responsibility, since its deficiencies
    are spread uniformly throughout its structure

and procedures, nowhere presenting a surface of radical blunder and never suggesting a clear, redeeming alternative." The chief failing, Gilman feels, lies in the impossibility of successfully adapting serious fiction to the stage.

Nation, 23 November 1963, pp. 353-54.

New York Theatre Critics' Reviews 24 (1963):212-16.

Sontag, Susan. "Going to the Theater." Partisan Review 31 (Winter 1964):97-98.
      In a series of reviews thematically linked by Sontag's belief in the bourgeois vacuity of the Broadway stage, the reviewer calls Albee's special talent "sensationalism masking as cultural expose." She finds that The Ballad of the Sad Cafe demonstrates Albee's lack of ability to adapt fiction to the stage and sums up her perception of Albee's shallowness with "phoniness wins the day."

Catholic World 198 (January 1964):263-64.

Vogue, 1 January 1964, p. 20.

America, 4 January 1964, p. 26.

National Review, 14 January 1964, pp. 34-35.

Times Literary Supplement, 27 February 1964, p. 166.

Hudson Review 17 (Spring 1964):81-83.

Players Magazine 40 (1964):138.

Sewanee Review 72 (1964):724-26.

Books and Bookmen 11 (November 1965):459.

Times Literary Supplement, 6 January 1966, p. 13.

BARTLEBY

Taubman, Harold. New York Times, 25 January 1961, p. 28:1.
      Commenting that Bartleby is a "curtain-raiser," to accompany the performance of Albee's American Dream, Taubman remarks that "the operatic treatment stretches out a skimpy theme beyond its tolerance." He adds that James Hinton, Jr., collaborated with Albee on the libretto and the music was written by William Flanagan.

BOX, QUOTATIONS FROM CHAIRMAN MAO TSE-TUNG, BOX

New York Times, 8 March 1968, p. 48.

New York Times, 17 March 1968, II:1.

Hewes, Henry. Saturday Review, 23 March 1968, p. 34.
    Hewes carefully describes the play's
    three-part structure of taped monologue from
    inside a "box," triple monologue from an ocean
    liner, and reiteration of the initial box scene.
    He considers the play a carefully constructed
    and potentially elucidating work of art, but
    feels it suffers from overly self-conscious,
    overly abstract orchestration. He wonders if
    audiences can put up with its boring nature in
    exchange for its artistic value.

Nation, 25 March 1968, p. 420.

Newsweek, 28 March 1968, p. 109.

Times (London), 10 July 1968, p. 8g.

Chapman, John. "Albee's 'Box-Mao-Box' Built with
    Monologues." New York Daily News, 1 October
    1968, in New York Theatre Critics' Reviews 29
    (1968):228.

New York Post, 1 October 1968, in New York Theatre
    Critics' Reviews 29 (1968):229.

New York Times, 1 October 1968, p. 39.

Women's Wear Daily, 1 October 1968, in New York
    Theatre Critics' Reviews 29 (1968):230

Wall Street Journal, 2 October 1968, in New York
    Theatre Critics' Reviews 29 (1968):229.

National Observer, 7 October 1968, p. 22.

Village Voice, 10 October 1968, p. 38.

Time, 11 October 1968, p. 73.

New Yorker, 12 October 1968, pp. 103-04.

New York Times, 13 October 1968, II:5.

Commonweal, 25 October 1968, p. 120.

New York Theatre Critics' Reviews 29 (1968):213 and
    228-30.

Library Journal 94 (July 1969):2635.

Times Literary Supplement, 25 June 1970, p. 687.

COUNTING THE WAYS

Barnes, Clive. New York Times, 4 February 1977,
        III:3.
            Counting the Ways is a satire on the hope
    and inspiration of Elizabeth Barrett Browning's
    poem, Barnes comments, but the "flamboyantly
    dejected" husband and his "defeatedly flamboy-
    ant" wife fail to communicate with the audience.
    The playwright retains the "trappings of real-
    ism while rejecting its substance," creating a
    typical combination of "fun and menace." Like
    Pinter, too, Albee possesses an "unerring gift
    for the way people almost talk." From his be-
    ginnings as a neorealist, Albee has constructed
    a theatre of sound and feeling, "a theatre of
    the heart."

New York Times, 6 February 1977, p. 2.

New York Times, 27 February 1977, p. 17.

THE DEATH OF BESSIE SMITH

New York Times, 2 March 1961, p. 19.

New Yorker, 11 March 1961, p. 114.

Nation, 18 March 1961, p. 242.

New Republic, 27 March 1961, pp. 29-31.

Theatre Arts 45 (May 1961):56.

Hatch, Robert. "Theatre: Arise Ye Playgoers of the
        World." Horizon 3 (July 1961):116-17.
            See annotated review under The American
        Dream above.

Catholic World 193 (August 1961):335-36.

Commonweal, 25 August 1961, pp. 471-72.

New York Times, 25 October 1961, p. 33.

New Statesman, 3 November 1961, pp. 667-68.

New York Times, 11 June 1963, p. 29.

New York Times, 3 October 1968, p. 55.

A DELICATE BALANCE

New York Times, 16 August 1966, p. 35.

Daily News (New York), 23 September 1966, in New
     York Theatre Critics' Reviews 27 (1966):296.

New York Post, 23 September 1966, in New York Thea-
     tre Critics' Reviews 27 (1966):296.

New York Times, 23 September 1966, p. 44.

New York World Journal Tribune, 23 September 1966,
     in New York Theatre Critics' Reviews 27 (1966):
     295.

Women's Wear Daily, 23 September 1966, in New York
     Theatre Critics Reviews 27 (1966):297.

Wall Street Journal, 26 September 1966, p. 18.

Time, 30 September 1966, p. 88.

New Yorker, 1 October 1966, p. 121.

New York Times, 2 October 1966, II:1.

Newsweek, 3 October 1966, p. 98.

Lewis, Theophilus. "Theatre: A Delicate Balance."
     America, 8 October 1966, pp. 432-33.
          Lewis lauds Albee's productivity and con-
     tends that A Delicate Balance, with its complex
     investigation of conflicting loyalties, is his
     most mature work to date. The only flaw lies
     "in the playwright's lack of empathy: when he
     learns to endow his characters with heart as
     well as logical minds, Albee will rise from
     playwright to dramatist." Lewis feels that
     this play will prove to be the best of the
     Broadway season.

New Republic, 8 October 1966, pp. 35-36.

Saturday Review, 8 October 1966, p. 90.

New York Times, 9 October 1966, pp. 10-11.

Nation, 10 October 1966, pp. 261-63.

Publishers Weekly, 10 October 1966, p. 72.

Times (London), 10 October 1966, p. 6.

Manchester Guardian, 13 October 1966, p. 9.

Commonweal, 14 October 1966, pp. 55-56.

New York Review of Books, 20 October 1966, pp. 4-5.

Reporter, 20 October 1966, pp. 52-53.

Life, 28 October 1966, p. 119.

New York Times, 28 October 1966, p. 35.

Vogue, 1 November 1966, p. 150.

New York Times, 13 November 1966, pp. 1 and 3.

Christian Century, 23 November 1966, p. 1447.

Listener, 24 November 1966, pp. 763-64.

Look, 30 (1966):42-48.

New York Theatre Critics' Reviews 27 (1966):294-97.

Tri-Quarterly, No. 5 (1966):182-88.

Hudson Review 19 (Winter 1966-1967):627-29.

National Review, 24 January 1967, pp. 99-100.

Library Journal, 1 February 1967, p. 594.

Books Abroad (Summer 1967):346.

Christian Science Monitor, 6 November 1967, p. 6.

Publishers Weekly, 27 November 1967, p. 45.

Schlocker, Georges. "Albee's 'Empfindliches Gleich-gewicht.'" Theater heute 9 (February 1968):20.

EVERYTHING IN THE GARDEN

New York Times, 24 October 1967, p. 50.

New York Times, 26 November 1967, II:1.

New York Times, 30 November 1967, p. 60.

Village Voice, 7 December 1967, p. 33.

Time, 8 December 1967, p. 96.

New York Times, 10 December 1967, II:5.

Newsweek, 11 December 1967, p. 96.

Brustein, Robert. "Albee at the Crossroads." New Republic, 16 December 1967, pp. 25-27.
    The only constant in Albee's career, ac-cording to Brustein, is his love-hate relation-ship with his audience: "his desire to under-

mine the audience and be applauded for it is
now leading him into the most extraordinary
stratagems and subterfuges. Not the least of
these is his disguising Everything in the Garden as a typically innocuous Broadway hit,
which Brustein feels leads to failure on the
level of both entertainment and artistic event.
Albee's lack of personal vision drives him to
adapt the work of others, but his strident
Americanization adds little to Cooper's "black
comedic attack on the values and prejudices of
the mindless, country-club classes of England."

Saturday Review, 16 December 1967, pp. 25-27.

Nation, 18 December 1967, p. 669.

Reporter, 28 December 1967, pp. 38-39.

New York Theatre Critics' Reviews 28 (1967):204-05
and 211-13.

Lewis, Theophilus. "Everything in the Garden."
America, 6 January 1968, pp. 19-20.

Simon, John. "Albee's Necrosis." Commonweal, 12
January 1968, pp. 444 and 446.

West, Anthony. "Albee's Innocence." Vogue, 15
January 1968, p. 28.

New York Times, 30 January 1968, p. 37.

Prideaux, Tom. "Why Must I Worry About Albee?"
Life, 2 February 1968, p. 16.

FAM AND YAM

Gelb, Arthur. New York Times, 26 October 1960,
p. 44:1.
In this one-act, Albee proves that he
possesses the ability to look at himself objec-
tively and laugh. Gelb rates Richard Barr's
directing as good, if somewhat unsure. He remarks that the play is a "mildly diverting
spoof of playwrights" with Fam as the Famous
American and Yam as the Young American, who
suggests a kind of "avant-garde Pinocchio."

First Stage, 1 (1961-1962):7-9.

LADY FROM DUBUQUE

Christian Science Monitor, 1 February 1980, in New
    York Theatre Critics' Reviews 41 (1980):387.

Daily News (New York), 1 February 1980, in New York
    Theatre Critics' Reviews 41 (1980):385.

New York Post, 1 February 1980, in New York Theatre
    Critics' Reviews 41 (1980):385-86.

Kerr, Walter. New York Times, 1 February 1980,
    C:5:1.
        Albee perhaps is "playing a game within a
    game" in a drama based on the problem of iden-
    tity in the face of the "dark angel," death.
    His characters pose three questions: who am I?,
    who are they?, and who are you?, but in the end
    the audience is left with these questions un-
    answered--and one death, conclusions "which do
    not seem to constitute a play."

Women's Wear Daily, 1 February 1980, in New York
    Theatre Critics' Reviews 41 (1980):386.

Wall Street Journal, 8 February 1980, in New York
    Theatre Critics' Reviews 41 (1980):388-89.

New York, 11 February 1980, pp. 74-75.

New Yorker, 11 February 1980, pp. 63-64.

Newsweek, 11 February 1980, pp. 102-03.

Time, 11 February 1980, p. 69.

Nation, 23 February 1980, p. 221.

New Republic, 8 March 1980, pp. 26-27.

Saturday Review, 15 March 1980, pp. 34-35.

New York Theatre Critics' Reviews 41 (1980):385-89.

LISTENING

Barnes, Clive. New York Times, 4 February 1977,
    III:3.
        Barnes describes Listening as a "chamber
    opera and a symbolic poem about communication
    as a present branch of catatonia." He observes
    that the symbolism is subtle, but ubiquitous,
    and that Albee takes banalities and "transmits
    them into a different form of life, which is
    the entire secret of poetry." The message is
    perhaps too obvious, but the play plays better
    than it reads.

New York Times, 6 February 1977, p. 2.

New York Times, 27 February 1977, p. 17.

New York Times, 3 May 1977, III:2.

Los Angeles Times, 3 October 1977, p. 78.

Los Angeles Times, 31 October 1977, p. 50.

Los Angeles Times, 10 December 1977, p. 32.

LOLITA

New York, 16 March 1981, pp. 35-39.

Daily News (New York), 20 March 1981, in New York
    Theatre Critics' Reviews 42 (1981):312-13.

Barnes, Clive. New York Post, 20 March 1981, in New
    York Theatre Critics' Reviews 42 (1981):314.
        Barnes claims that Albee's adaptation of
    Nabokov's masterpiece is "a picaresque play,
    that at times sounds regrettably like a film
    script abandoned by Stanley Kubrick." The
    original subject matter has become coarsened,
    "vulgar and misbegotten," although the first
    act has some amusing moments. Donald Suther-
    land's performance is lauded.

New York Times, 20 March 1981, C:3:1. .

Women's Wear Daily, 20 March 1981, in New York Thea-
    tre Critics' Reviews 42 (1981):316.

Christian Science Monitor, 25 March 1981, in New
    York Theatre Critics' Reviews 42 (1981):314-15.

Kerr, Walter. "How Albee Avoided Lolita." New York
    Times, 29 March 1981, II:3:1.
        Kerr avers that Lolita is never childlike
    or naive, but begins in the siren phase of her
    relationship with Humbert. It is also a mis-
    take, Kerr believes, to have the narrator on
    stage at all times so that Albee never has "to
    write Lolita at all," playing with his charac-
    ters like toys. There is no real communication,
    interaction, or emotion because the omnipresent
    narrator never lets the play become real or im-
    portant.

New York, 30 March 1981, p. 34.

New Yorker, 30 March 1981, p. 62.

Wall Street Journal, 31 March 1981, in New York
        Theatre Critics' Reviews 42 (1981):314.

Macleans, 6 April 1981, p. 62.

People, 6 April 1981, pp. 44-46.

New Republic, 11 April 1981, pp. 27-28.

Nation, 18 April 1981, pp. 474-76.

New York Theatre Critics' Reviews 42 (1981):312-16.

MALCOLM

New York Times, 7 January 1966, II:1.

Daily News (New York), 12 January 1966, in New York
        Theatre Critics' Reviews 27 (1966):394-95.

New York Journal American, 12 January 1966, in New
        York Theatre Critics' Reviews 27 (1966):395.

New York Post, 12 January 1966, in New York Theatre
        Critics' Reviews 27 (1966):394.

New York Herald Tribune, 12 January 1966, in New
        York Theatre Critics' Reviews 27 (1966):393-94.

New York Times, 12 January 1966, p. 29.

New York World-Telegram and The Sun, 12 January
        1966, in New York Theatre Critics' Reviews 27
        (1966):392-93.

New York Theatre Critics' Reviews, 17 January 1966,
        pp. 392-95.

Time, 21 January 1966, p. 50.

New Yorker, 22 January 1966, p. 74.

Newsweek, 24 January 1966, p. 82.

New Republic, 26 January 1966, pp. 34 and 36.

Corrigan, Robert W. "Theatre: Malcolm 'didn't mean
        very much.'" Vogue, 15 February 1966, p. 56.
            Corrigan accuses Albee of fathering "Pop
        theatre" in Malcolm, referring to its setting
        with "Mondrian-like frames in front of shocking
        orange cyclorama." The playwright has created
        "a kind of medieval Fellini through Tom Wolfe,"
        a version of an adolescent's search for a father
        which "didn't mean very much."

Sheed, Wilfred. "The Stage: Notes on Albee." Common-
    weal, 18 February 1966, pp. 584-85.

Library Journal, 1 June 1966, p. 2868.

Choice: Books for College Libraries, 3 (September
    1966), 534.

Books Abroad (Winter 1966), 90.

World Premières, 15 (1966), 181-82.

"Malcolm Adapted by Edward Albee from the novel by
    James Purdy." Virginia Quarterly Review, 43
    (Winter 1967), xxi.

THE SANDBOX

New York Times, 17 May 1960, p. 42.

New York Times, 12 February 1962, p. 27.

New York Times, 25 February 1962, VI:30.

Show (July 1962), 27.

SEASCAPE

Daily News (New York), 27 January 1975, in New York
    Theatre Critics' Reviews 36 (1975):368.

New York Post, 27 January 1975, in New York Theatre
    Critics' Reviews 36 (1975):368.

New York Times, 27 January 1975, p. 20.

Women's Wear Daily, 27 January 1975, in New York
    Theatre Critics' Reviews 36 (1975):371.

Wall Street Journal, 28 January 1975, in New York
    Theatre Critics' Reviews 36 (1975):372.

Christian Science Monitor, 30 January 1975, in New
    York Theatre Critics' Reviews 36 (1975):370.

New York Times, 2 February 1975, II:5.

Kroll, Jack. "Leapin' Lizards." Newsweek, 10
    February 1975, p. 75.
        Kroll states that in attempting to become
    a playwright of ideas Albee has lost much of the
    vitality and tension that led to the success of
    his earlier works. The ideas expressed in Sea-
    scape are shallow and the central characters are

merely one more typical alienated married couple.
The reptilian friends, who symbolically prep to
inherit the world, are not much better, and "the
second-act confrontation between sapiens and
saurians is an appallingly banal ordeal of
lending-library metaphysics."

Time, 10 February 1975, p. 57.

New York Theatre Critics' Reviews, 36 (1975), 368-73.

TINY ALICE

New York Times, 18 December 1964, p. 38.

New York Times, 27 December 1964, II:1.

Chapman, John. "Edward Albee's 'Tiny Alice,' or The
Temptation of John Gielgud." New York Daily
News, 30 December 1964, in New York Theatre
Critics' Reviews 25 (1964):97.
Chapman compares Albee's play to T. S.
Eliot's The Cocktail Party since "both are
stated in terms of drawing room comedy, and each
has a deep undercurrent of mysticism." The play
is puzzling, but never boring, and the director,
Alan Schneider, is credited with "a sure sense
of theatre."

New York Herald Tribune, 30 December 1964, in New
York Theatre Critics' Reviews 25 (1964):96.

New York Post, 30 December 1964, in New York Theatre
Critics' Reviews 25 (1964):97.

New York Times, 30 December 1964, p. 15.

New York World-Telegram and The Sun, 30 December 1964,
in New York Theatre Critics' Review 25 (1964):95.

New York Times, 31 December 1964, p. 14.

New York Theatre Critics' Reviews, 25 (1964), 95-98.

Christian Science Monitor, 2 January 1965, p. 6.

London Times, 7 January 1965, p. 7.

Time, 8 January 1965, p. 32.

New Yorker, 9 January 1965, p. 84.

New York Times, 10 January 1965, II:1.

Newsweek, 11 January 1965, p. 75.

Village Voice, 14 January 1965, pp. 13 and 17.

Time, 15 January 1965, pp. 68-70.

Saturday Review, 16 January 1965, p. 40.

Nation, 18 January 1965, p. 65.

New York Herald Tribune, 20 January 1965, p. 16.

New York Times, 21 January 1965, p. 22.

Commonweal, 22 January 1965, pp. 543-44.

Brustein, Robert. "Three Plays and a Protest." New
    Republic, 23 January 1965, pp. 32-34 and 36.

Reporter, 28 January 1965, pp. 53-54.

Life, 29 January 1965, p. 14.

Saturday Review, 30 January 1965, pp. 38-39 and 65.

Vogue, 15 February 1965, p. 50.

Lipton, Edward. "The Tiny Alice Enigma." Saturday
    Review, 20 February 1965, p. 21.

New York Review of Books, 25 February 1965.

Catholic World, 200 (March 1965), 383-84.

Educational Theatre Journal, 17 (March 1965), 66-67.

Sign, 44 (March 1965), 27.

America, 6 March 1965, pp. 336-37.

Library Journal, 15 March 1965, p. 1343.

New York Times, 23 March 1965, p. 33.

Simon, John. "Theatre Chronicle." Hudson Review,
    18 (Spring 1965), 81-84.
        In asserting that the mixture of plot and
    symbolism in Tiny Alice is too complex to be
    meaningful, Simon gives a compact and helpful
    exegesis of both. He maintains that the play
    is also a failure on linguistic and dramaturgi-
    cal grounds, bemoaning its "unintegrated" homo-
    sexual undercurrent. For him, the play holds
    only one mystery: "What does Sir John Gielgud
    do for twenty seconds with his head inside
    Irene Worth's deshabille?"

Esquire, April 1965, pp. 58 and 60.

New York Times, 11 April 1965, II:1.

Christian Science Monitor, 27 May 1965, p. 4.

World Theatre, 14 (May-June 1965), 317.

Choice: Books for College Libraries, 2 (July-
    August 1965), 309.

Books Abroad, 39 (Autumn 1965), 459.

Saturday Review, 4 September 1965, p. 43.

Publishers Weekly, 21 February 1966, p. 195.

Arts and Architecture, 83 (April 1966), 34-35.

Times Literary Supplement, 26 May 1966, p. 462.

Theater heute, 7 (July 1966), 43-45.

Commonweal, 16 September 1966, pp. 582-85.

Boston Globe, 3 January 1967, p. 18.

New York Daily News, 30 September 1969, in New York
    Theatre Critics' Reviews 30 (1969):256.

New York Post, 30 September 1969, in New York Theatre
    Critics' Reviews 39 (1969):255.

New York Times Supplement, 30 September 1969, p. 42.

Women's Wear Daily, 30 September 1969, in New York
    Theatre Critics' Review 30 (1969):256.

Wall Street Journal, 1 October 1969, in New York
    Theatre Critics' Review 30 (1969):255.

New York Times, 12 October 1969, II:9.

Newsweek, 13 October 1969, p. 125.

Time, 17 October 1969, p. 72.

Saturday Review, 18 October 1969, p. 20.

Nation, 27 October 1969, p. 451.

New Republic, 1 November 1969, p. 22

Times (London), 17 December 1969, p. 15a.

National Review, 30 December 1969, p. 1334.

New York Theatre Critics' Reviews, 30 (1969), pp. 251, 254-57.

Times (London), 10 January 1970, IIIc, p. 10.

Times (London),16 January 1970, p. 13b.

New York Times, 17 January 1970, p. 24.

Daily Telegraph, 19 January 1970, p. 12.

WHO'S AFRAID OF VIRGINIA WOOLF?

New York Times, 7 October 1962, II:1.

Manchester Guardian, 15 October 1962, p. 7.

Daily News (New York), 15 October 1962, New York Theatre Critics' Reviews 23 (1962):251.

New York Herald Tribune, 15 October 1962, New York Theatre Critics' Reviews 23 (1962):252.

New York Journal American, 15 October 1962, New York Theatre Critics' Reviews 23 (1962):252-53.

New York Mirror, 15 October 1962, New York Theatre Critics' Reviews 23 (1962):254.

New York Post, 15 October 1962, New York Theatre Critics' Reviews 23 (1962):251.

New York Times, 15 October 1962, p. 33.

New York World-Telegram and Sun, 15 October 1962, New York Theatre Critics' Reviews 23 (1962):254.

New York Times, 16 October 1962, p. 79.

New Yorker, 20 October 1962, pp. 85-86.

New York Journal American, 21 October 1962, in New York Theatre Critics' Reviews 23 (1962):253.

Time, 26 October 1962, pp. 84 and 86.

Nation, 27 October 1962, pp. 273-74.

Saturday Review, 27 October 1962, p. 29.

New York Times, 28 October 1962, II:1.

Newsweek, 29 October 1962, pp. 52-53.

Theatre Arts, 46 (November 1962), 10-11.

New Republic, 3 November 1962, pp. 29-30.

Newsweek, 5 November 1962, pp. 74-75.

Times (London), 5 November 1962, p. 14.

Commonweal, 9 November 1962, pp. 175-76.

America, 17 November 1962, pp. 1105-06.

Players Magazine, 39 (December 1962), 85.

Vogue, December 1962, pp. 120-21.

Life, 14 December 1962, pp. 107-08, 110.

New York Theatre Critics' Reviews (1962), pp. 251-54.

Hudson Review, 15 (Winter 1962-63), 571-73.

Catholic World, 196 (January 1963), 263-64.

World Premières, 14 (January 1963), 60.

National Review, 15 January 1963, pp. 35-36.

Jubilee, 10 (February 1963), 55.

Critic, 21 (March 1963), 16-19.

Gassner, John. "Broadway in Review." Educational
     Theatre Journal, 15 (March 1963), 77-80.
          The fact that theatre is experienced
     moment-by-moment contributes much to the suc-
     cess of Who's Afraid of Virginia Woolf?, Albee's
     first Broadway play. Conceding the lack of
     clear message or outcome, Gassner emphasizes
     the play's basis in struggle rather than expla-
     nation. He compares Albee favorably with
     O'Neill, and calls the play "the negative play
     to end all negative plays, yet also a curiously
     compassionate ... and exhilarating one."

Harper's Magazine, 226 (March 1963), 272.

Reporter, 25 April 1963, pp. 48-50.

Saturday Review, 29 June 1963, pp. 39-40.

New York Times, 16 August 1963, p. 15.

New York Times, 6 October 1963, p. 68.

New York Times, 9 November 1963, p. 15.

Esquire, December 1963, p. 69.

Tulane Drama Review, 7 (1963), 7-10.

New York Review of Books, 1 (special issue 1963),
     16.

Times (London), 7 February 1964, p. 15.

New York Times, 8 February 1964, p. 15.

New Statesman, 14 February 1964, p. 262.

Spectator, 14 February 1964, pp. 213-14.

Listener, 20 February 1964, p. 313.

Illustrated London News, 22 February 1964, p. 288.

Atlantic, 213 (April 1964), 122.

Show (May 1964), 112.

New York Times, 26 November 1964, p. 52.

THE ZOO STORY

Darmstadter Echo, 29 September 1959, n.p.
     Review of the German production.

New York Times, 29 September 1959, p. 45.

Die Welt, 29 September 1959, n.p.
     Review of the German production.

Christian Century, 77 (1960), 193-94.

New York Times, 15 January 1960, p. 37.

The New Yorker, 23 January 1960, pp. 72-76.

Saturday Review, 30 January 1960, p. 28.

New York Times, 31 January 1960, II:1.

Saturday Review, 6 February 1960, p. 32.

Nation, 13 February 1960, pp. 153-54.

108

New York Times, 15 February 1960, p. 23.

Brustein, Robert. "Krapp and a Little Claptrap."
New Republic, 22 February 1960, pp. 21-22.
While acknowledging Albee's great dramatic
talent, Brustein confesses that he is "deeply
depressed by the uses to which this talent has
been put." He dismisses the play as beat-
generation "claptrap."

New York Times, 26 August 1960, p. 13.

Players Magazine, 37 (October 1960), 9-10.

Plays and Players (October 1960), 13.

Newsweek, 13 March 1961, p. 91.

Esquire, April 1961, pp. 48-50.

Theatre Arts, 45 (May 1961), 53-58.

New York Times, 29 May 1963, p. 39.

Hudson Review (Summer 1961), 314.

New York Times, 11 June 1963, p. 29.

America, 22 July 1963, pp. 891-92.

Times Literary Supplement, 27 February 1964, p. 166.

New York Times, 13 February 1965, p. 10.

New York Times, 9 June 1965, p. 42.

Commonweal, 9 July 1965, pp. 501-02.

New York Times, 11 October 1968, p. 41.

2 AMIRI BARAKA

Born October 7, 1934, Newark, New Jersey

    A graduate of Harvard and Columbia Universities,
LeRoi Jones belonged in his youth to a group of Greenwich
Village intellectuals of the "beat" generation. His theatrical debut as a playwright when he was thirty changed
the direction of his life. Dutchman, one of four plays
by Jones that opened in New York in 1964, soon became a
classic parable of the Black man's victimization by white
America. Within a short time Jones became thoroughly
politicized, separated from his white wife and his daugh-
ters, and moved to Harlem, where he founded the Black
Arts Repertory Theatre School. His plays became increas-
ingly violent and totally hostile to white society, leav-
ing the critics who had originally praised him mystified
and distrustful. Because he deliberately rejected the
need for approval of his work by white critics, his more
recent works must be evaluated in the context of Black
Nationalism. They are propaganda plays, designed to
hasten Black social and cultural emancipation. He formed
Spirit House Movers in Newark, New Jersey, a group of
Black non-professional actors. In 1968 he founded the
Committee for Unified Newark, which advocated the speaking of Swahili and the adoption of the Kawaida faith, and
he assumed the title Imamu (spiritual leader) and the
name Amiri Baraka.

PRIMARY SOURCES

I. STAGE

Arm Yrself Or Harm Yrself. Staged Newark, 1967. Newark:
    Jihad Publications, 1967.

The Baptism. Staged New York, 1964. In The Baptism and
    the Toilet. New York: Grove Press, 1967.

Ba-Ra-Ka. In Spontaneous Combustion: Eight New American
 Plays. Ed. Rochelle Owens. New York: Winter House,
 1972.

A Black Mass. Staged Newark, 1966. In Four Black Revolutionary Plays. Indianapolis: Bobbs-Merrill, 1969.

_____. London: Calder and Boyars, 1971.

Black Power Chant. In Drama Review 16 (December 1972):53.

Bloodrites. Staged Newark, 1970. In Black Drama Anthology. Ed. Woodie King and Ron Milner. New York:
 New American Library, 1971.

Board of Education. 1968.

Dante. Staged New York, 1961; as The 8th Ditch, New York,
 1964. In The System of Dante's Hell. New York:
 Grove Press, 1965.

_____. London: MacGibbon and Kee, 1966.

The Death of Malcolm X. In New Plays from the Black Theatre. Ed. Ed Bullins. New York: Bantam, 1969.

Dutchman. Staged New York, 1964. In Dutchman and the
 Slave. New York: William Morrow, 1964; London:
 Faber and Faber, 1965.

_____. In Black Theatre. Ed. L. Patterson. New York
 and Toronto: Dodd, Mead, 1971.

_____. In Classic through Modern Drama: An Introduc-
 tory Anthology. Ed. Otto Reinert. Boston: Little,
 Brown, 1970.

_____. In Contemporary Black Drama. Ed. C. F. Oliver
 and S. Sills. New York: Scribners, 1971.

_____. In Introduction to Drama. Ed. P. J. Dolan and
 G. M. Dolan. New York: Wiley, 1974.

_____. Masterpieces of the Drama, fourth edition.
 Ed. A. W. Allison, A. Carr, and A. M. Eastman. New
 York: Macmillan, 1979.

_____. In Theatre in America. Ed. E. Parone. New
 York: Dell, 1965.

_____. In A Treasury of the Theatre, vol. 2, fourth ed.
 Ed. John Gassner and Bernard F. Dukore. New York:
 Simon and Schuster, 1970.

Experimental Death Unit #1. Staged New York, 1965. In
    Four Black Revolutionary Plays. Indianapolis: Bobbs-
    Merrill, 1969.

_____. London: Calder and Boyars, 1971.

A Good Girl is Hard to Find. Staged New York, 1965. In
    Four Black Revolutionary Plays. Indianapolis: Bobbs-
    Merrill, 1969.

_____. London: Calder and Boyars, 1971.

Great Goodness of Life (A Coon Show). Staged New York,
    1969. In Best Short Plays of the World Theatre,
    1958-1967. Ed. Stanley Richards. New York: Crown,
    1968.

_____. In A Black Quartet. Ed. Clayton Riley. New
    York: New American Library, 1970.

_____. In The Disinherited: Plays. Ed. A. C. Ravitz.
    Encino, California: Dickenson Publishers, 1974.

_____. In Four Black Revolutionary Plays. Indianapolis:
    Bobbs-Merrill, 1969.

_____. London: Calder and Boyars, 1971.

_____. In Kuntu Drama: Plays of the African Continuum.
    Ed. P. Carter-Harrison. New York: Grove Press,
    1974.

Home on the Range. Staged Newark and New York, 1968. In
    Drama Review, 12 (Summer 1968): 106-11.

Insurrection. 1968.

Jello. Staged New York, 1965. Chicago: Third World
    Press, 1970.

Junkies Are Full of (SHHH...). Staged Newark, 1970; New
    York, 1970. In Black Drama Anthology. Ed. W. King
    and R. Milner. New York: New American Library, 1971.

The Kid Poeta Tragical. 1969.

Madheart (A Morality Play). Staged San Francisco, 1967.
    In Black Fire. Ed. LeRoi Jones and Larry Neal. New
    York: William Morrow, 1968.

_____. In Four Black Revolutionary Plays. Indianapolis:
    Bobbs-Merrill, 1969.

_____. London: Calder and Boyars, 1971.

_____. In Nommo. Ed. W. H. Robinson. New York: Macmillan, 1972.

The Motion of History and Other Plays. New York: William Morrow, 1978.

Police. In Drama Review 12 (Summer 1968): 112-15.

A Recent Killing. Staged New York, 1973.

S-1 (A Play). Staged New York, 1976.

Sidney Poet Heroical. Staged New York, 1975.

The Slave. Staged New York, 1964. In Drama and Revolution. Ed. Bernard F. Dukore. New York: Henry Holt, 1971.

_____. In Dutchman and the Slave. New York: William Morrow, 1964; London: Faber, 1965.

_____. In Sophocles to Baraka. Ed. Bernard F. Dukore. New York: Crowell, 1976.

_____. In Three Negro Plays. Harmondsworth, England: Penguin Books, 1969.

Slave Ship: A Historical Pageant. Staged Newark, 1967; New York, 1969. Newark: Jihad Publications, 1969.

_____. In The Great American Life Show. Ed. John Lahr and Jonathan Price. New York: Bantam, 1974.

_____. In The Off Off Broadway Book. Ed. Albert Poland and Bruce Mailman. Indianapolis: Bobbs-Merrill, 1972.

The Toilet. Staged New York, 1964. In America's Lost Plays. New York and Toronto: Dodd, Mead, 1965.

_____. In The Baptism and the Toilet. New York: Grove Press, 1967.

_____. In Best American Plays, Sixth Series. Ed. John Gassner and Clive Barnes. New York: Crown, 1971.

_____. In The Best Plays of 1964-1965. New York and Toronto: Dodd, Mead, 1965.

_____. In Grove Press Modern Drama. Ed. John Lahr. New York: Grove Press, 1975.

II. FILM

Black Spring, 1967.   The New Ark, 1969.

Dutchman, 1967.   A Fable, 1971.

III. FICTION

The System of Dante's Hell. New York: Grove Press, 1965.

_____. London: MacGibbon and Kee, 1966.

Tales. New York: Grove Press, 1967.

_____. London: MacGibbon and Kee, 1969.

IV. NONFICTION AND EDITED BOOKS

African Congress: A Documentary of the First Modern Pan-African Congress (editor). New York: William Morrow, 1972.

"The Beat Generation" (with David Fitelson and Norman Podhoretz). Partisan Review 25 (1958):472-79.

"The Black Aesthetic." Negro Digest 18 (September 1969): 5-6.

"Black (Art) Drama Is the Same As Black Life." Ebony 30 (February 1971):74-75, 78, 80-82.

Black Fire: An Anthology of Afro-American Writing (editor, with Larry Neal). New York: William Morrow, 1968.

Black Music. New York: William Morrow, 1967.

"Black Revolutionary Poets Should Also Be Playwrights." Black World 22 (April 1972):4-6.

A Black Value System. Newark: Jihad Publications, 1970.

Blues People: Negro Music in White America. New York: William Morrow, 1963.

_____. London: MacGibbon and Kee, 1965.

"Communications Project." Drama Review 12 (Summer 1968): 53-57.

The Creation of the New Ark. Washington, D.C.: Howard University Press, 1975.

The Cricket: Black Music in Evolution (editor). Newark: Jihad Publications, 1969.

Cuba Libre. New York: Fair Play for Cuba Committee, 1966.

114

Fidel Castro. New York: Totem Press, 1959.

The _Floating Bear: A Newsletter, Numbers 1-37_ (with Diane
    de Prima). La Jolla, California: Laurence McGivery,
    1974.

Four _Young Lady Poets_ (editor). New York: Totem Press,
    1961.

Home: Social Essays. New York: William Morrow, 1966.

_____. London: MacGibbon and Kee, 1968.

In _Our Terribleness: Some Elements and Meaning in Black
    Style_ (with Fundi = Billy Abernethy). Indianapolis:
    Bobbs-Merrill, 1970.

"In Search of the Revolutionary Theatre." _Negro Digest_
    16 (April 1966):20.

Kawaida Studies: The New Nationalism. Chicago: Third
    World Press, 1972.

"LeRoi Jones Speaking." _New York Herald Tribune_, 26 July
    1964, pp. 7-8.

The _Moderns: New Fiction in America_ (editor). New York:
    Corinth Books, 1964.

_____. London: MacGibbon and Kee, 1965.

"Myth of a Negro Literature." _Saturday Review_, 20 April
    1963, pp. 20-21.

"Philistinism and the Negro Writer." In _Anger and Beyond:
    The Negro Writer in the United States_. Ed. Herbert
    Hill. New York: Harper and Row, 1966. Pp. 51-61.

Raise, Race, Rays, Raze: Essays Since 1965. New York:
    Random House, 1971.

"The Revolutionary Theatre." _Liberator_ 5 (July 1965):4.

Selected Plays and Prose. New York: William Morrow,
    1979.

Strategy and Tactics of a Pan-African Nationalist Party.
    Newark: Jihad Publications, 1971.

"Three Modes of History and Culture." _Negro Digest_ 14
    (April 1965):38.

"What the Arts Need Now." _Negro Digest_ 16 (April 1967):
    5-6.

"'Why I Changed My Ideology': Black Nationalism and Socialist Revolution." Black World 24 (July 1975): 30-42.

V. POETRY (Note: Baraka has written so many poems that it seemed expedient here to list his major collections rather than his separate works. For more information, consult Dace, Letitia, listed under "SECONDARY SOURCES.")

Black Art. Newark: Jihad Publications, 1966; second edition, 1967; third edition, 1969.

Black Magic: Collected Poetry 1961-1967. Indianapolis: Bobbs-Merrill, 1969.

_____. London: MacGibbon and Kee, 1969.

The Dead Lecturer. New York: Grove Press, 1964.

Hard Facts. Newark: Peoples War Publications, 1976.

It's Nation Time. Chicago: Third World Press, 1970.

A Poem for Black Hearts. Detroit: Broadside Press, 1967.

Preface to a Twenty Volume Suicide Note. New York: Totem Press, 1961.

Selected Poetry of Amiri Baraka. New York: William Morrow, 1979.

Spirit Reach. Newark: Jihad Publications, 1972.

VI. TRANSLATIONS

DUTCHMAN

    Dutchman. Tr. Ettore Capriolo. Sipario 230 (June 1965):84-89. Italian.

    _____. Tr. Eric Kahane. L'Avant Scène 516 (5 April 1973):19-58. French.

    Dutchman. Tr. Sandra Lucas-Hoch. Frankfurt: Fischer, 1970. German.

    Dutchman. Dorei. Tr. Kunitaka Chuji. Tokyo: Shobunsha, 1969. Japanese.

    Le Métro fantôme. L'Esclave. Tr. Eric Kahane. Paris: Gallimard, 1967. French.

Rättegängen mot LeRoi Jones. Tr. Olor Jouason.
Lund: Studentlitt, 1969. Swedish.

THE SLAVE

Le Métro fantôme. L'Ésclave. Tr. Eric Kahane.
Paris: Gallimard, 1967. French.

FOUR BLACK REVOLUTIONARY PLAYS

Quattro Commedie per la Rivoluzione Nera. Tr. Angela
Terzani. Torino: Einaudi, 1971. Italian.

Théâtre Noir Révolutionnaire: à la gloire de l'homme
noir: Première unité expérimentale de mort. Une
messe noire. Les Joies de la vie. Madheart.
Tr. Nicole Tisserand. Paris: Buchet-Chastel,
1972. French.

VII. INTERVIEWS

Coleman, Michael. "What Is Black Theatre? An Interview
with Imamu Amiri Baraka." Black World 20 (April
1971):32-36.
Baraka explains how the Black theatre movement
is separate from traditional "show business" and
expresses his contempt for Blacks or whites who portray Black life in a way that pleases white bourgeois
audiences.

Lewis, Ida. "LeRoi Jones: Une interview exclusive." Jeune
Afrique (Paris), 1 September 1970, pp. 24-27.
Baraka describes what he hopes his work in the
drama will do to stimulate the Black community to action against their white oppressors. He comments
briefly on the high points and shifts of his own
career and on his growing political awareness and
militancy.

X, Marvin. "Everything's Cool ... An Interview." Black
Theatre 1 (1968):16-23.
Baraka acknowledges that his early works often
used conventional language and allusions to Western
myths, but he claims that he is working toward a more
authentic Black drama with an emphasis on pantomime,
ritual, and Black musical rhythms.

_____, and Faruk. "Islam and Black Art: An Interview
with LeRoi Jones." Negro Digest 18 (January 1969):
4-10, 77-80.
Baraka discusses the influence of Islam on his
work and the spiritual rallying point for Black cultural and political revolution which he believes
Islam will provide.

SECONDARY SOURCES

I. CRITICISM

Adams, George R. "Black Militant Drama." American Imago
     28 (Summer 1972):107-28.
          Adams attempts to explain the use of biblical
     myths in Dutchman.

_____. "'My Christ' in Dutchman." College Language
     Association Journal 15 (1971-1972):54-58.
          Adams again works on imagery in Dutchman. This
     time he explicates the Christian archetypes he sees;
     for example, Lula at the end of the play refers to
     the martyred Clay as "My Christ, my Christ."

Baker, Houston H., Jr. "'These Are the Songs If You Have
     the Music': An Essay on Imamu Baraka." Minority
     Voices (Pennsylvania State University) 1 (1977):1-18.
          "As an alternative to the sickness and death at
     hand" Black writers sought to bring new life to those
     Black and African elements within the cities. Baraka
     reflects this process better than any other Black
     writer.

Baker, John. "Criteria for First Printings of LeRoi
     Jones." Yale University Library Gazette 49(1975):
     297-98.
          Mr. Baker offers some criteria in an attempt to
     clear up some of the confusion surrounding the first
     printings of books by LeRoi Jones.

_____. "LeRoi Jones, Secessionist, and Ambiguous Col-
     lecting." Yale University Library Gazette 46
     (1972):159-66.
          Collecting such a controversial writer is dif-
     ficult. "Can literature written in the ghetto en-
     dure? The more the black writer secedes, the farther
     his work moves from the universal."

Benston, Kimberly W., ed. Imamu Amiri Baraka (LeRoi
     Jones): A Collection of Critical Essays. Englewood
     Cliffs, N.J.: Prentice-Hall, 1978.
          This is an impressive collection of essays on
     Baraka by major critics of his work, written on a
     wide variety of topics. Essays in the drama section,
     "Black Labs of the Heart," are included in this
     bibliography.

_____. The Renegade and the Mask. New Haven: Yale
     University Press, 1976.
          Benston traces both African and Western influ-
     ences on Baraka's political and aesthetic views. The

book also contains a useful bibliography.

_____. "Vision and Form in The Slave Ship." In Imamu
Amiri Baraka (LeRoi Jones): A Collection of Critical
Essays. Ed. Kimberly W. Benston. Englewood Cliffs,
N.J.: Prentice-Hall, 1978. Pp. 174-185.
    Baraka's early plays attempted to awaken Black
audiences to a new self-awareness and anger at their
victimization by white society. In The Slave Ship
the objectives of Baraka's revolutionary theatre
"are fully realized." He transforms the whole audience into passengers on a slave ship. Through the
use of music and myth Baraka calls upon the Black
community's "shared aesthetic--the genius for musical improvisation" and thereby instills in them national pride and purpose.

Bigsby, C. W. E. Confrontation and Commitment: A Study
of Contemporary American Drama. Columbia: University of Missouri Press, 1968.
    Bigsby argues that the thriving new American
theatre is based largely on techniques of confrontation and commitment, with a faith in the human character not found in the absurdists. Section Two,
"Commitment," focuses on Black dramatists and includes a chapter on Baraka, pp. 138-55. Bigsby contrasts Baraka's call for action with Hansberry's
call for compassion. He compares Baraka with Brecht,
discusses Baraka's separatist political views, and
critiques Baraka's plays to date, with particular
emphasis on Dutchman. He calls the plays "revenge
fantasies--public rites of purgation in which the
audience is invited to participate," and says that
Baraka is "one of the few Negro playwrights who has
shown an interest in and an understanding of the nature and problems of drama itself."

Billingsley, R. G. "LeRoi Jones's The Slave: Right Ideas
Stink a Lotta Times." Umoja 2 (1975):72-81.

Brady, Owen E. "Baraka's Experimental Death Unit #1:
Plan for (R)evolution." Negro American Literature
Forum 9 (1975):59-61.
    Baraka's vision is his consciousness of moral
decadence and his belief in the evolution of man
toward a new moral establishment. Experimental
Death Unit #1 describes certain phases of American
decadence.

_____. "Cultural Conflict and Cult Ritual in Leroi
Jones' 'The Toilet.'" Educational Theatre Journal
28 (March 1976):69-77.
    "This work is a metaphor for the explanation of
the hero's double consciousness, his conflict over
his roles as a Negro and as an American. Ora represents the black society close to Africa, Foots the

part of the black community trying to make a bridge
to success in both white and black worlds. Foots'
tragic fate and the play's setting are metaphors for
American life, and the play's action is a ritual
dramatizing the psychic conflict and initiation of
Ray Foots."

_____. "Great Goodness of Life: Baraka's Black Bour-
geoisie Blues." In Imamu Amiri Baraka (LeRoi Jones):
A Collection of Critical Essays. Ed. Kimberly W.
Benston. Englewood Cliffs, N.J.: Prentice-Hall,
1978. Pp. 157-66.
     Brady says: "Baraka's play Great Goodness of
Life: A Coon Show translates the revolutionary potential of E. Franklin Frazier's Black Bourgeoisie
into art through techniques drawn from the blues
and through an invocation of the rational aspects of
minstrelsy." The revolutionary function of the play
is to chastize the Black middle class "for trying to
gain acceptance from white Americans."

_____. "LeRoi Jones's The Slave: A Ritual of Purga-
tion." Obsidian 4 (Spring 1978):5-18.
     Brady maintains that Baraka's Dutchman and The
Slave are companion pieces, The Slave fulfilling
Clay's prophecy that a bloody racial war will destroy
the existing social order in America. He includes a
careful examination of character and symbol in The
Slave. The self-sacrifice of the protagonist "re-
vitalizes the hope for a better life."

Brecht, Stefan. "LeRoi Jones's Slave Ship." Drama Review
14 (1970):212-19.
     Brecht examines the images in the play and its
overall structure. He explains its special appeal to
Black audiences.

Brown, Cecil M. "Black Literature and LeRoi Jones."
Black World (formerly Negro Digest) 19 (1970): 24-31.
     Brown denies Baraka's assertion that only Negro
writers who oppose white society have value, but he
welcomes the author's pride in Black culture and
history and revolutionary fervor. Basically this
article is an answer to Baraka's "The Myth of Negro
Literature."

Brown, Lloyd W. Amiri Baraka. Boston: G. K. Hall, 1980.
     Brown provides the most up-to-date assessment
of Baraka's literary career. In the Twayne format
he offers a chronology and bibliography as well as a
detailed evaluation of Baraka's fiction, poetry, and
drama.

_____. "Comic Strip Heroes: LeRoi Jones and the Myth of American Innocence." *Journal of Popular Culture* 3 (Fall 1969):191-204.
This article focuses on Baraka's poetry but contains a useful description of his favorite myths and cultural stereotypes.

_____. "The Cultural Revolution in Black Theatre." *Negro American Literature Forum* 8 (Spring 1974):159-74.
Baraka's revolutionary doctrines as they are revealed in his plays are categorized and appraised.

_____. "High and Crazy Niggers: Anti-Rationalism in LeRoi Jones." *Journal of Ethnic Studies* 2 (Spring 1974):1-9.
This article is a mostly sympathetic appraisal of Baraka's attacks on aspects of Western culture, which the establishment calls rational or traditional and which Baraka calls racist or exploitative.

_____. "Jones (Baraka) and His Literary Heritage in *The System of Dante's Hell*." *Obsidian* 1 (1975):5-17.
Brown argues that it would be misleading to assume that Baraka's own repudiation of Western heritage automatically negates the importance of Western literature and philosophy in his work.

_____. "LeRoi Jones (Imamu Amiri Baraka) as Novelist: Theme and Structure in *The System of Dante's Hell*." *Negro American Literature Forum* 7 (1973):132-42.
Brown argues that *Dante's Hell*'s themes present a coherent and significant perception of experience, and that any fruitful study of Baraka's meaning must include a closer analysis of his narrative techniques, structure, and vocabulary.

Burford, W. W. "LeRoi Jones: From Existentialism to Apostle of Black Nationalism." *Players* 47 (1972):60-64.
Burford traces the escalating racial emphasis in the artist's works from a more general existentialist viewpoint to a radical Black militancy.

Burns, Glen. "How the Devil Helped LeRoi Jones Turn into Imamu Amiri Baraka." In Alfred Weber and Siegfried Neuverler, eds. *Amerikanisches Drama und Theater um 20. Jahrhundert*. Göttingen: Vandenhoeck, 1975. Pp. 261-88.
Burns describes the transformation of a Black intellectual into a revolutionary and notes the growth of Baraka's messianic purpose as a Black nationalist.

Casimir, Louis J. "Dutchman: The Price of Culture Is a
    Lie." In The Binding of Proteus: Perspectives on
    Myth and the Literary Process. Ed. Marjorie W.
    McCune et al. Lewisburg, Pa.: Bucknell University
    Press, 1980. Pp. 298-310.
        Casimir shows that the Black hero of Dutchman,
    Clay, tries to survive by conforming to white behav-
    ioral and educational norms only to be betrayed and
    destroyed by that same culture.

Coleman, Larry G. "LeRoi Jones' Tales: Sketches of the
    Artist as Young Man Moving toward a Blacker Art."
    Black Lines 1 (Winter 1970):17-26.
        Coleman is primarily concerned with Baraka's
    short stories but the development of his political
    beliefs and racial awareness clarifies issues in his
    plays as well.

Cooke, Michael G. "The Descent Into the Underworld and
    Modern Black Fiction." Iowa Review 5 (1974):72-90.
        Cooke comments on Toomer, Baraka, Ellison,
    Camara Laze, Amos Tutola, and Wilson Harris. One
    way in which Black literature seems pioneering is
    its development of the theme of descent into the
    underworld: "The primary force of [Baraka's] The
    System of Dante's Hell derives from the punishing
    ordinariness of the situation for black people and
    from the fact that there appears no hope of purga-
    tion, let alone salvation."

Costello, Donald P. "LeRoi Jones: Black Man as Victim."
    Commonweal 88 (1968):436-40.
        Baraka, taking his own advice, has cast the
    "emotional history of the black man in this country"
    as that of victim, and Baraka as the Black man's
    chronicler.

Dace, Letitia. LeRoi Jones (Imamu Amiri Baraka): A Check-
    list of Works By and About Him. London: Nether
    Press, 1971.
        Dace provides an invaluable catalogue of
    Baraka's achievements of the sixties. She describes
    primary sources in detail and offers a checklist of
    criticism of his poetry, drama, and political writ-
    ings.

Dennison, George. "The Demagogy of LeRoi Jones." Com-
    mentary 39 (February 1965):67-70.
        "Like every demagogue, Baraka speaks to the
    private and fragmentary wishes of individuals, and
    assures the fragmentary person that he is in reality
    a thundering herd." In this context, Dennison dis-
    cusses The Slave and The Toilet.

Feuser, Willfried. "Alain Ricard, Théâtre et nationalisme: Wole Soyinka et LeRoi Jones." African Literature Today 8 (1976):124-30.
    Alain Ricard compares these two writers by combining the study of structures and themes in two literatures with a thorough investigation of the social and political background from which they emanate.

Fischer, William C. "The Pre-Revolutionary Writings of Imamu Amiri Baraka." Massachusetts Review 14 (Spring 1973):259-305.
    Fischer provides a detailed survey of Baraka's early writings and he notes the development of his racial awareness.

Gaffney, Floyd. "Black Theatre: The Moral Function of Imamu Amiri Baraka." Players 50 (1975):122-31.
    Gaffney applauds the didacticism of Baraka's dramas which never diminishes their force or urgency.

Gallagher, Kathleen. "The Arts of Poetry: Jones and MacLeish." Midwest Quarterly 12 (1971):383-92.
    The suggestion is that Black Art might have been written as a deliberate, forty-years-later response to "Ars Poetica" or that Jones at least wrote with MacLeish in mind.

Grabes, Herbert. "LeRoi Jones (Imamu Amiri Baraka), Dutchman." In Das amerikanische Drama der Gegenwart. Kronberg: Athenäum, 1976. Pp. 185-200.
    Grabes notes the revolutionary fervor of Baraka's work and believes his plays provide insights into flaws of the American system.

Hagopian, John V. "Another Ride on Jones's Subway." College Language Association Journal 21 (1979):269-74.
    The author presents evidence which suggests that Jones "has used the material of the American race war to create a new and strange variation" of Wagner's "The Flying Dutchman."

Hudson, Theodore R. From LeRoi Jones to Amiri Baraka: The Literary Works. Durham: Duke University Press, 1973.
    Hudson chronicles the biographical and artistic changes that shaped Baraka's career. He is favorably impressed with the playwright's increased participation in Black nationalism.

_____. A LeRoi Jones (Amiri Baraka) Bibliography: A Keyed Research Guide to Works by LeRoi Jones and to Writing About Him and His Works. Washington, D.C.: the Author (1816 Varnum St., N.E. 20018), 1972. 18 pages.

A useful checklist, doubtless the result of
Hudson's research for his full-length study (above).

Iannerella, Michael J. "Black and White." Massachusetts
Studies in English 3 (1972):1-6.
Imaginary interview on Jones' Dutchman.
Iannerella simulates a Black-White dialogue on the
racial issues raised in Dutchman.

Jackson, Esther M. "LeRoi Jones (Imamu Amiri Baraka):
Form and the Progression of Consciousness." College
Language Association Journal 17 (1973):33-56.
The importance of Baraka's aesthetic experiments
relates to his revaluation of the symbolism of color,
not only to the impact of his imagery on the forms
and contents of the American arts but on the idea of
race in Western consciousness.

Jouffroy, Alain. "LeRoi Jones, Théâtre de la révolution
noire." Cahiers de la Compagnie Madeleine Renaud-
Jean Louis Barrault (1967):44-53.
Jouffroy believes one of the most significant
dramatic movements after World War II has been the
growth of a Black radical stage tradition.

Klinkowitz, Jerome. "LeRoi Jones (Imamu Amiri Baraka):
Dutchman as Drama." Negro American Literature Forum
7 (1973):123-26.
Baraka's drama argues the same theme as his
most sustained work of prose: "that authentic existence is possible only in the vital act of warring
against its challenges." Dutchman was written at a
time when the author had abandoned his white wife
and is not only good drama, but "cathartic within
Jones's own career."

Knox, George. "The 'Mythology' of LeRoi Jones's Dutchman." In Sy M. Kahn and Martha Raetz, eds.
Interculture: A Collection of Essays and Creative
Writing Commemorating the Twentieth Anniversary of
the Fullbright [sic] Program at the Institute of
Translation and Interpretation, University of Vienna
(1955-1974). Vienna: Braumauller, 1975. Pp. 243-51.
Knox discusses the "Flying Dutchman" myth and
other allusions in Baraka's play.

Köhler, Klaus. "Das Underground Theatre." In Studien zum
amerikanischen Drama nach dem zweiten Weltkrieg. Ed.
Eberhard Brüning, Klaus Köhler, and Bernhard Scheller.
Berlin: Rütten and Loening, 1977.
Köhler cites The Slave, The Toilet, Dutchman,
and Experimental Death Unit #1 as powerful examples
of revolutionary underground theatre in America.

124

Lederer, Richard. "The Language of LeRoi Jones's The
Slave." Studies in Black Literature 4 (1973):14-
16.
Lederer gives a hearing to the all-too-often
neglected dramaturgic language of Jones's The Slave.

Lindberg, John. "Dutchman and The Slave: Companions in
Revolution." Black Academy Review: Quarterly of the
Black World 21 (1972):101-07.
Lindberg shows that taken together Dutchman
provides the causes of the revolution and The Slave
the solution. They offer striking parallels since
"each is the reverse of the other in character and
name."

_____. "Dutchman and The Slave: Companions in Revolu-
tion." Reprinted in Imamu Amiri Baraka (LeRoi Jones):
A Collection of Critical Essays. Ed. Kimberly W.
Benston. Englewood Cliffs, N.J.: Prentice-Hall,
1978. Pp. 141-47.

Lindenberg, Daniel. "Un Théâtre militant." Temps
Modernes 21 (April 1966):1918-20.
Lindenberg claims Baraka oversimplifies American
politics and institutions and notes that other
minorities, such as the Jews, have been repressed in
America; but he praises him for calling attention to
injustice so effectively.

Llorens, David. "Ameer [sic] (LeRoi Jones) Baraka."
Ebony 24 (August 1969):75-83.
Llorens provides a history of Baraka's involve-
ment in drama from the founding of the Black Arts
Repertory Theatre to Spirit House in Newark and his
role as clergyman in the Kawaida faith.

Martin, Thaddeus. "Dutchman Reconsidered." Black American Literature Forum 2 (1977):62.
In this play Baraka's constant concern seems
always to be the poignant predicament in which the
Black bourgeoisie presently finds itself as this
much maligned segment of Black society symbolically
confronts White America.

Menchise, Don D. "LeRoi Jones and a Case of Shifting
Identities." College Language Association Journal
20 (1976-1977):232-34.
Menchise briefly discusses the shifting identities of Baraka: "Beat poet ... exponent of Negritude
... fanatical revolutionist, and Jones as Imamu Amiri
Baraka."

Miller, Jeanne-Marie A. "The Plays of LeRoi Jones."
College Language Association Journal 14 (1971):331-
39.
Miller begins by establishing the moral basis

of Baraka's art and develops her readings of his
plays along ethical lines. A fairly extensive
treatment of Dutchman and The Slave with shorter attention to Baptism, The Toilet, A Black Mass, Great
Goodness of Life, Madheart: A Morality Play, and
Slave Ship. Miller maintains that Jones seeks a
mental revolution, often punishing the audience.

_____. "The Plays of LeRoi Jones." College Language
    Association Journal 20 (1976-1977):232-34.
        Baraka believes that the theatre should be used
    to reform society; the didacticism of his own plays
    is consistent with this principle.

Mitchell, Loften. Black Drama: The Story of the American
    Negro in the Theatre. New York: Hawthorn Books,
    1965.
        Mitchell surveys the history of Blacks in the-
    atre in America. He includes a brief discussion of
    the initial impact of Dutchman and a lengthier
    treatment of Baraka's role in the Black Arts Theatre.
    He calls Baraka "one of the most misunderstood men
    in America," claiming that he is not articulate, but
    pro-Negro. He also discusses Baraka's participation
    at the New School Conferences.

Mootry, Maria K. "Themes and Symbols in Two Plays by
    LeRoi Jones." Negro Digest 21 (1969):42-47.
        Mootry provides an analysis of The Baptism and
    The Toilet.

Munro, C. Lynn. "LeRoi Jones: A Man in Transition."
    College Language Association Journal 17 (1973):
    57-78.
        Munro compares Dante's Inferno with Baraka's
    System of Dante's Hell. This provides insights
    into the philosophy behind Baraka's plays.

Neal, Lawrence. "Development of LeRoi Jones." Liberator
    6 (January 1966):20; (February 1966):18.
        Brief mention of the playwright's increasing
    militancy.

Nelson, Hugh. "LeRoi Jones's Dutchman: A Brief Ride on
    a Doomed Ship." Educational Theatre Journal 20
    (1968):53-59.
        Nelson traces the myth of the "Flying Dutchman"
    from Sir Walter Scott's Rokeby through Baraka's
    play: "Jones has made a complex use of the 'Dutch-
    man' theme in converting it into modern myth."

O'Brien, John. "Racial Nightmares and the Search for
    Self: An Explication of LeRoi Jones's 'A Chase
    (Alighieri's Dream).'" Negro American Literature
    Forum 7 (1973):89-90.

This explication states that Baraka "symbolically identifies his hero's journey through hell with
Dante Alighieri's."

Otten, Charlotte. "LeRoi Jones: Napalm Poet." Concerning
    Poetry (West Washington State College) 3 (1970):5-11.
        "He means poetry to be an irritant, a pain-
    inducer, a shocker, a thought-erupter, a spirit-
    inflamer, a depth charge, an emotional Molotov cock-
    tail." Although she analyzes Baraka's poetry, her
    claims for the poetry apply equally to the drama.

Pearson, Lou Anne. "LeRoi Jones and a Black Aesthetic."
    Paunch 35 (1972):33-66.
        Pearson extensively surveys all of Baraka's
    work to reveal his search for literary and aesthetic
    forms suitable to express his radical philosophy.

Peavy, Charles D. "Myth, Magic, and Manhood in LeRoi
    Jones's Madheart." Studies in Black Literature 1
    (1970):12-20.
        In Baraka's Madheart, the chief impediment to
    the Black male's realization of his identity is the
    White woman.

_____. "Myth, Magic, and Manhood in LeRoi Jones's
    Madheart." Reprinted in Imamu Amiri Baraka (LeRoi
    Jones): A Collection of Critical Essays. Ed.
    Kimberly W. Benston. Englewood Cliffs, N.J.:
    Prentice-Hall, 1978. Pp. 167-73.

Primeau, Ronald. "Imagination as Moral Bulwark and Cre-
    ative Energy in Richard Wright's Black Boy and LeRoi
    Jones's Home." Studies in Black Literature 1 (1970):
    66-88.
        A brief explication of symbols and archetypes
    in Dutchman, a favorite topic which is accorded much
    more extensive treatment elsewhere. See Werner,
    Craig; Hagopian, John V.; Casimir, Louis J.; and
    Knox, George.

Reed, Daphne S. "LeRoi Jones: High Priest of the Black
    Arts Movement." Educational Theatre Journal 22
    (1970):53-59.
        Reed discusses how Jones rebelled against the
    so-called American way of life, substantially altered
    his life-style, and channelled his genius to inter-
    pret the lives, history, culture, and feelings of
    his people.

Ricard, Alain. Théâtre et nationalisme: Wole Soyinka et
    LeRoi Jones. Paris: Présence Africaine, 1972.
        Ricard compares Baraka with Nigerian writer
    Wole Soyinka and shows how each developed from Black
    intellectual into an ardent nationalist artist. This
    allows him to speculate on the nature of racism and

of political protest in Western societies.

Rice, Julian C. "LeRoi Jones's Dutchman: A Reading."
    Contemporary Literature 12 (1971):42-59.
        The explicit thesis of Blues People, the illus-
    tration of "the path the slave took to 'citizenship,'"
    is expressed allegorically in Dutchman, and both
    works view history and the relations between the
    black and white people "within the pattern of Ameri-
    can life."

Rich, Cynthia Jo. "Where's Baraka's Jones?" Black Times
    (Palo Alto) 4 (1972):6-7.
        Baraka has grown more militant but he was al-
    ways sensitive to racial injustice.

Russell, Charlie. "LeRoi Jones Will Get Us All in Trou-
    ble." Liberator 4 (August 1964):18.
        Baraka's anger is a threat to white society.

Savory, Jerold J. "Descent and Baptism in Native Son,
    Invisible Man, and Dutchman." Christian Scholar's
    Review 3 (1972): 33-37.
        Comparing works by Wright, Ellison, and Baraka,
    Savory notes recurrent metaphors involving a visit
    to the underworld and longed for rebirth in modern
    Black literature.

Sollors, Werner. Amiri Baraka/LeRoi Jones: The Quest for
    a Populist Modernism. New York: Columbia University
    Press, 1978.
        Sollors divides Baraka's work into four phases:
    the "aesthetic protest" of his works from 1958 to
    1961, the "political/ethnic protest" of the 1960-
    1965 writings, the decade of Black cultural national-
    ism from 1964 to 1974, and the "Marxist-Leninist, Mao-
    Tse-Tung thought" of the years since 1974.

_____. "LeRoi Jones (Imamu Amiri Baraka)." In
    Martin Christadler, ed. Amerikanische Literatur
    der Gegenwart. Stuttgart: Alfred Kroner, 1973.

Taylor, William P. "The Fall of Man Theme in Imamu Amiri
    Baraka's (LeRoi Jones's) Dutchman." Negro American
    Literature Forum 7 (1973):127-30.
        A close investigation of Dutchman will bear out
    the assertion that Baraka's creations are "far from
    being the racist diatribes" that many of his critics
    have construed them to be.

Tener, Robert L. "The Corrupted Warrior Heroes: Amiri
    Baraka's The Toilet." Modern Drama 17 (1974):
    207-15.
        Tener disputes the simplistic approaches to
    this play. "It is not just the exit from the mater-
    nal world" of the home to the "arena of the gang."

It is the "ideological drift from the sense of what is a boy to the sense of what is a man."

_____. "The Corrupted Warrior Heroes: Amiri Baraka's The Toilet." Reprinted in Imamu Amiri Baraka (LeRoi Jones): A Collection of Critical Essays. Ed. Kimberly W. Benston. Englewood Cliffs, N.J.: Prentice-Hall, 1978. Pp. 148-56.

_____. "Role Playing as a Dutchman." Studies in Black Literature 3 (1972):17-21.
    Tener suggests, after reassessing the meaning of the title--theatrical term meaning a strip of cloth used to cover the cracks between flats--that the theme of the play is anchored to the defects in character and in personality of a Black man and a white woman and to the devices which they use to hide those defects.

Velde, Paul. "LeRoi Jones: Pursued by the Furies." Commonweal 88 (1968):440-41.
    "There is an imaginary battle going on between blacks and whites in this country...." Though Baraka demonstrates, at times, a willingness to cut this Gordian knot, at this stage, his investigations into "blackness" appear to be a militant form of racism.

Werner, Craig. "Brer Rabbit Meets the Underground Man: Simplification of Consciousness in Baraka's Dutchman and Slave Ship." Obsidian 5 (1979):35-40.
    Werner provides what amounts to a Jungian interpretation of the archetypes and symbols in two Baraka plays.

Williams, Shirley Anne. "The Search for Identity in Baraka's Dutchman." In Imamu Amiri Baraka (LeRoi Jones): A Collection of Critical Essays. Ed. Kimberly W. Benston. Englewood Cliffs, N.J.: Prentice-Hall, 1978. Pp. 135-40. Originally printed in Give Birth to Brightness by Shirley Anne Williams. New York: Dial Press, 1977.
    Clay in Dutchman submerges his own nature in order to survive in a white man's world. Ironically, this denial of self only expedites his destruction by Lula and the white power structure. The hopeless folly of denying one's Black identity in America is one of the author's obvious messages.

Willis, Robert T. "Anger and the Contemporary Black Theatre." Negro American Literature Forum 8 (Summer 1974):213-15.
    Willis believes Baraka's militant stance is characteristic of the new Black dramatist, who will continue to use the stage as a medium to facilitate social change.

II. DISSERTATIONS

Brady, Owen E., III. "The Consciousness Epic: LeRoi
    Jones's Use of American Myth and Ritual in The Bap-
    tism, The Toilet, Dutchman, The Slave and A Recent
    Killing." Dissertation Abstracts International 34:
    4243A (Notre Dame, 1974).
        Brady focuses on five plays "written, produced,
    or published in 1964," all of which center on "the
    initiation of a young Black man into the mysteries
    of manhood in America." He presents thematic, myth-
    ic, and archetypal concerns and demonstrates that
    "the structure of American society, according to
    Jones, dictates the structure for his plays." He
    further discusses the use of American history and
    ritual/institutional settings within the plays.

Curb, Rosemary Keefe. "The Idea of the American Dream in
    Afro-American Plays of the Nineteen Sixties." Dis-
    sertation Abstracts International 38:2784A-85A
    (Arkansas, 1977).
        Curb traces the history of the American Dream
    and its dark obverse, the oppression of Blacks. She
    considers the development of this theme in general
    surveys of a dozen or so Black playwrights of the
    sixties, most prominently Baraka and Bullins, who
    "use theater to disseminate political propaganda for
    the Black revolution." Although the American Dream's
    function offers "no prelapsarian innocence, but bat-
    tlegrounds for racial strife," she adds that "ideal-
    istic voices of intelligent, sensitive Black and
    white Americans still champion liberty and justice."

Dippold, Mary D. "LeRoi Jones: Tramp with Connections."
    Dissertation Abstracts International 32:3300A-01A
    (Maryland, 1971).
        Dippold's study is a biographical survey span-
    ning the years 1959-1969 and the playwright's evolu-
    tion from beat poet to Black activist. "It also at-
    tempts to assess Jones's place in Black literature
    and to provide the reader of Jones's work with some
    perspective that may help him to understand that work
    in terms of the Black aesthetic."

Fox, Robert Elliot. "The Mirrors of Caliban: A Study of
    the Fiction of LeRoi Jones (Imamu Amiri Baraka),
    Ishmael Reed, and Samuel R. Delany." Dissertation
    Abstracts International 37:5121A (SUNY, Buffalo, 1977).
        Fox states a dual goal for his study: "to
    demonstrate first, that there is a broad spectrum of
    Black writing that defies the easy categorizations
    which are so often the rule among would-be critics
    of the literature, and to take steps ... toward sup-
    plying serious scholarly analysis of several signifi-
    cant examples of Black fiction...."

Goodman, Gerald Thomas. "The Black Theatre Movement."
Dissertation Abstracts International 36:34A (Pennsylvania, 1974).

Goodman examines various plays whose non-stereotyped nature established them as predecessors to the Black Theatre Movement of the 1960s. He goes on to discuss Baraka and Bullins at some length as "models of the two modes of Black Theatre: revolutionary and experimental." The final chapter describes the place of the Black Theatre Movement within the broader context of American theatre.

Haley, Elsie Galbreath. "The Black Revolutionary Theatre: LeRoi Jones, Ed Bullins, and Minor Playwrights." Dissertation Abstracts International 32:4757A (Denver, 1971).

Haley presents an overview of the revolutionary Black arts movement of the 1960s and its effect on Black theatre. After discussing the development of the movement and the theatres it spawned, Haley devotes individual chapters to Baraka and Bullins, with less detailed attention paid to five other writers of the movement.

Harris, Frances Jeannette Gregory. "The Tragic Dimensions of Modern Black Drama." Dissertation Abstracts International 38:3498A-99A (East Texas State, 1977).

Harris aims to study the often-overlooked topic of Black drama as tragedy; she analyzes the ritual and poetic nature of modern Black drama and judges the plays according to Aristotelian paradigms. She concludes that Black drama is serious literary art, and that many of the plays under study "possess tragic dimensions that transcend the time and place of their setting."

Harris, William J. "Jones/Baraka: The Evolution of a Black Poet." Dissertation Abstracts International 34:7756A (Stanford, 1974).

This study of Baraka's poetry "examines Baraka's attempt to exorcise and escape the intellectual and moral traditions of what he thinks of as Western Civilization and to establish a counter tradition and civilization."

Hicklin, Fannie Ella Frazier. "The American Negro Playwright, 1920-1964." Dissertation Abstracts International 26:542 (Wisconsin, 1965).

Hicklin compiles a historical survey of the development of Black Theater from its pre-twenties roots to its actual inception in the twenties through to the present. She includes both contemporary critical evaluation of the plays discussed and her own evaluations. The study also gives a brief summary of problems that have faced Negro playwrights and an appendix listing 237 plays, with publication and production data.

Hudson, Theodore R. "From LeRoi Jones to Amiri Baraka: The Literary Works." Dissertation Abstracts International 33:313A-14A (Howard, 1972).
Hudson's study "attempts to fill the need for a critical survey of the literary works of LeRoi Jones and, as a corollary, to provide a basis for a better understanding of the content and techniques in his works." Hudson makes a comprehensive survey of Baraka's life and writings; he concludes that "judged as a literary artist by the standards which are still being codified for the so-called 'Black aesthetic,' Jones/Baraka is the exemplary practitioner."

Keyssar-Franke, Helene. "Strategies in Black Drama." Dissertation Abstracts International 35:7909A-10A (Iowa, 1974).
Keyssar-Franke examines seven Black dramas, including Baraka's Dutchman and Bullins' In the Wine Time, in terms of the "pattern and set of devices," or "strategy," used in each one. After a critical discussion of the concept of strategy, she focuses on each play in turn, including brief biographical data on the author, plot summary, and detailed strategic analysis. A lengthy bibliography is included.

Lacey, Henry Clark. "A Study of the Poetry, Drama, and Fiction of Imamu Amiri Baraka (LeRoi Jones)." Dissertation Abstracts International 36:1505A (SUNY at Binghamton, 1975).
Lacey focuses on Baraka's writings between 1960 and 1970 in terms of "autobiographical and socio-political meanings," as well as techniques, reliance on traditions, and "considerable innovations." His study is based around the three phases of Baraka's career: the "schwartz bohemian," the Black writer "in rebellion against his own assimilationist ways as well as the ivory tower aestheticism of his peers," and the committed Black writer.

Ogunbiyi, Yemi. "New Black Playwrghts in America (1960-1975): Essays in Theatrical Criticism." Dissertation Abstracts International 37:1299A (New York, 1976).
Ogunbiyi sees Black activist theatre as a result of the socially turbulent sixties. His essays are "an attempt to evaluate and understand the works of some of the major black playwrights of the period," including Baraka, Bullins, Harrison, Kennedy, Dean, and Wesley. Attention is given to the plays as performance as well as literature.

Singleton, Carole Waters. "Black Theatre as Cultural Communication: An Educative Process." Dissertation Abstracts International 36:3217A-18A (Maryland, 1975).
Singleton's purpose is "to present a critical analysis of the educative role of Black Theatre as

cultural communication and to determine the extent of its impact upon American society." The study investigates the interaction of societal trends and the Black Theatre during three distinct periods from 1920 to 1970. It concludes that "now more than ever, Black Theatre seems to be a viable tool for teaching Blackness as that concept is now perceived."

Smith, Cynthia Janis. "Escape and Quest in the Literature of Black Americans." Dissertation Abstracts International 36:287A (Yale, 1974).
    Smith points out the conflict between biblical imagery and religious experience that has been evident in Black literature from the earliest antebellum slave narratives. She considers the conflict between what is practiced and what is preached in white America to be "a central issue in the work of Jean Toomer, Richard Wright, James Baldwin, and LeRoi Jones."

Tedesco, John L. "The White Image as Second 'Persona' in Black Drama, 1955-1970." Dissertation Abstracts International 35:4742A (Iowa, 1974).
    In addition to the subject indicated by the title, Tedesco speculates on the effect of such an image on the white audience. Several plays are discussed, among them works by Baraka, Bullins, Baldwin, Hansberry, and others. Five different white "personae" emerge, all negative; the overall effect is to suggest changes to the white audience.

Williams, Roosevelt John. "Modes of Alienation of the Black Writer: Problem and Solution in the Evolution of Black Drama and the Contemporary Black Theatre." Dissertation Abstracts International 35:5370A (McGill, Canada, 1974).
    Williams presents a two-part study, opening with a theoretical discussion of the nature of the modes of the Black writer's alienation. This leads to "concrete illustration in the actual historical evolution of Black drama from the eighteenth century to the present time," including the detailed analysis of representative plays.

III. REVIEWS

A BLACK MASS

Gussow, Mel. New York Times, 30 September 1972, p. 18:1.
    Gussow reviews a double bill revival of Madheart and A Black Mass. Neither works as drama, but each play is successful "as exhortation." In Madheart Baraka satirizes black women

who imitate whites; in <u>Black</u> <u>Mass</u>, on the other
hand, Black men create a hideous beast who is
"so hopelessly ugly ... that he could be nothing
but a white man."

DUTCHMAN

<u>New</u> <u>York</u> <u>Times</u>, 25 March 1964, p. 46:2.

<u>New</u> <u>Yorker</u>, 4 April 1964, pp. 78-79.

<u>Newsweek</u>, 13 April 1964, p. 60.
<u>Dutchman</u> is called "the most impressive
work by an American playwright in the past few
years." The theme of racial hatred and violence
is given a mythic setting. Lula is seen as "the
contemporary Flying Dutchman condemned to ride
forever in pursuit of an impossible quarry."

<u>Vogue</u>, July 1964, p. 32.

<u>Ebony</u>, 24 (August 1965):75-78.

<u>New</u> <u>York</u> <u>Times</u>, 17 November 1965, p. 53:7.

GREAT GOODNESS OF LIFE (A COON SHOW)

<u>New</u> <u>York</u> <u>Times</u>, 27 April 1969, p. 92:1.

<u>New</u> <u>York</u> <u>Times</u>, 4 May 1969, II:1:5.

<u>New</u> <u>York</u> <u>Times</u>, 31 July 1969, p. 28:1.
<u>Great</u> <u>Goodness</u> <u>of</u> <u>Life</u> was one of four
plays by Black writers staged at the Gate The-
atre on Second Avenue. It deals with the folly
of Blacks who attempt to win favors in white
society.

<u>New</u> <u>York</u> <u>Times</u>, 3 August 1969, II:1:4.

<u>New</u> <u>York</u> <u>Times</u>, 22 September 1969, p. 36:1.

<u>New</u> <u>York</u> <u>Times</u>, 20 September 1972, p. 41:1.

HOME ON THE RANGE

Sullivan, Dan. <u>New</u> <u>York</u> <u>Times</u>, 21 May 1968, p. 42:1.
"To criticize this poem, or incantation,
or heroique ... as if it were a piece of literature is to miss the point. Jones uses words as
weapons; he is a propagandist."

MADHEART

See review for <u>A</u> <u>Black</u> <u>Mass</u> above.

A RECENT KILLING

New Yorker, 10 February 1973, p. 75.

Nation, 12 February 1973, pp. 218-19.

Kroll, Jack. Newsweek, 19 February 1973, p. 75.
        Kroll praises this play as an autobio-
    graphical recounting of Baraka's own youthful
    stint in the Air Force with an emphasis on the
    racism and brutality of the officers.

S-1

        Gussow, Mel. New York Times, 29 July 1976, p. 18:4.
            Gussow says S-1 is "not just political
        theatre but theatre as politics." The play is
        a protest against a federal crime-wide reform
        bill called Senate Bill 1. Baraka's dialogue
        is "dense with dogma and with isms--and with
        Marxist-Leninist clichés." One sees that "good
        and evil are not a matter of color" in this
        latter day Baraka play, "but of politics."

SIDNEY POET HEROICAL

New York Times, 21 May 1975, p. 54:4.

Saturday Review, 12 July 1975, p. 52.
        This play is a satire of the career of
    Sidney Poitier, a Black film star who appeals
    to white audiences. The hypocrisy of the
    media and its attempted emasculation of the
    Black man are recurrent themes.

THE SLAVE

New York Times, 17 December 1964, p. 51:1.

Time, 25 December 1964, p. 62.
        The play is called a kind of "Greenwich
    Villagey talkfest." War has broken out between
    Blacks and whites, and a Black leader visits
    his former white wife. Jones, like Genet says
    the reviewer, projects his fantasies onto the
    stage. He is hardest on those who would be his
    friends--the white liberal intellectuals.

New Yorker, 26 December 1964, p. 50.

Newsweek, 28 December 1964, p. 56.

Nation, 4 January 1965, p. 16.

Hewes, Henry. "Crossing Lines." Saturday Review, 9 January 1965, p. 46.
   Hewes calls Baraka "less an astute dramatic craftsman than he is a Negro creatively expressing his portion of a total anger that his race has had to suppress...." Though the reviewer feels the unneeded violence of both plays helps to prevent them from succeeding, he sees positive aesthetic elements in both. He points out a seemingly inherent difficulty in theatrically interpreting The Slave script.

New Republic, 23 January 1965, p. 32.

Vogue, February 1965, p. 98.

See Bain's review of The Toilet below.

New York Times, 17 November 1965, p. 53:7.

SLAVE SHIP

New York Times, 22 November 1969, p. 46:1.

Kerr, Walter. New York Times, 23 November 1969, II:1:1.
   Kerr calls Slave Ship "an improvisation from a scenario that can scarcely have covered more than three typewritten pages." The evening is mostly syncopated song and the action involves various acts of brutality on board a slave ship.

Oliver, Edith. New Yorker, 6 December 1969, p. 168.
   Oliver calls the production "more a demonstration of the conditions aboard a slaver than it is an actual play," giving ample evidence to back this conclusion. The dehumanizing events portrayed can evoke only horror and anger in the onlookers.

New York Times, 13 September 1970, II:1:1.

THE TOILET

See Hewes' review of The Slave above.

Bain, Myra. "Everybody's Protest Play." National Review, 23 March 1965, p. 249.
   Bain has little good to say about Black drama; in particular, she comments that The Toilet and The Slave are "anarchic and prurient in tone, language and style." She adds that "these two plays present a nightmare of twisted logic," and she dismisses Baraka as "the latest bombshell among the hip writers."

3 ED BULLINS

Born July 2, 1935, Philadelphia, Pennsylvania

Ed Bullins has been called a Black Nationalist playwright by critics who believe his strength as an artist
lies in his depiction of urban Black people estranged
from mainstream American cultural values. Although soci-
ologists might consider his characters "victims" of racial
prejudice and an unjust economic system, Bullins emphasizes the valor rather than the pathos of American Blacks.
He intends his major work to be a cycle of twenty plays
which will constitute a kind of Black American epic.
Bullins' dramatic method frequently verges on the expressionistic. He uses all white walls and a crimson carpet
in Goin' a Buffalo to suggest the oppressiveness and la-
tent violence of white America, and he introduces different levels of stark flats in The Duplex to portray a society divided into competing social levels. Many of his
works, such as Four Dynamite Plays, have a strong revolutionary bias, but the satirical bent of his recent plays
may signal an interest in reforming, rather than destroy-
ing, the current political and social scene.

PRIMARY SOURCES

I. STAGE

The American Flag Ritual. In The Theme Is Blackness: The
     Corner and Other Plays. New York: Morrow, 1973.

The Black Revolutionary Commercial #2. The Drama Review
     13 (Summer 1969):144-45.

Clara's Ole Man. Staged San Francisco, 1965. In The
     Drama Review 12 (Summer 1968). In Five Plays by Ed
     Bullins. Indianapolis: Bobbs-Merrill, 1969.

The Corner. Staged Boston, 1969. In Black Drama Anthology. Ed. Woodie King and Ron Milner. New York: New American Library, 1972. In The Theme Is Blackness: The Corner and Other Plays. New York: Morrow, 1973. In Black Drama Anthology. Ed. Woodie King and Ron Milner. New York: New American Library, 1971. Pp. 77-88.

Daddy. Staged New York, 1977.

Death List. Staged New York, 1970. In Four Dynamite Plays. New York: Morrow, 1971.

The Devil Catchers. Staged New York, 1970.

Dialect Determinism. Staged San Francisco, 1965. In Spontaneous Combustion: Eight New American Plays. Ed. Rochelle Owens. New York: Winter House, 1972. In The Theme Is Blackness: The Corner and Other Plays. New York: Morrow, 1973.

The Duplex: A Black Love Fable in Four Movements. Staged New York, 1970. New York: Morrow, 1971.

The Electronic Nigger. Staged New York, 1968. In New American Plays, Vol. 3. Ed. William M. Hoffman. New York: Hill and Wang, 1969. In Five Plays by Ed Bullins. Indianapolis: Bobbs-Merrill, 1969. In The Electronic Nigger and Other Plays. London: Faber and Faber, 1970.

The Fabulous Miss Marie. Staged New York, 1971. In The New Lafayette Theatre Presents. Ed. Ed Bullins. New York: Doubleday, 1974.

The Game of Adam and Eve. Staged Los Angeles, 1966.

The Gentleman Caller. Staged New York, 1969. In Illuminations 5 (Mill Valley), 1968. In A Black Quartet. Ed. Clayton Riley. New York: New American Library, 1970.

Goin' a Buffalo: A Tragifantasy. Staged New York, 1968. In New Black Plays. Ed. William Couch. Baton Rouge: Louisiana State University Press, 1969. In Five Plays by Ed Bullins. Indianapolis: Bobbs-Merrill, 1969. In Black Theatre U.S.A.: Forty-five Plays by Black Americans, 1847-1974. Ed. J. V. Hatch. New York: The Free Press, 1974.

The Helper. Staged New York, 1970. In The Theme Is Blackness: The Corner and Other Plays. New York: Morrow, 1973.

Home Boy (lyrics by Ed Bullins, music by Aaron Bell).
    Staged New York, 1976.

House Party (lyrics by Ed Bullins, music by Pat Patrick).
    Staged New York, 1973.

How Do You Do: A Nonsense Drama. Staged San Francisco,
    1965; Boston, 1969. Mill Valley: Illuminations
    Press, 1965.

I am Lucy Terry. Staged New York, 1976.

In New England Winter. Staged New York, 1971. In New
    Plays from the Black Theatre. Ed. Ed Bullins. New
    York: Bantam, 1969.

In the Wine Time. Staged New York, 1968. In Black
    Theatre. Ed. Lindsay Patterson. New York: Dodd,
    Mead, 1971. Pp. 379-406.

It Bees Dat Way. Staged London, 1970. In Four Dynamite
    Plays. New York: Morrow, 1971.

It Has No Choice. Staged San Francisco, 1966; Boston,
    1969.

Jo Anne!!! Staged New York, 1976.

The Man Who Dug Fish. Staged Boston, 1968. In The
    Theme Is Blackness: The Corner and Other Plays.
    New York: Morrow, 1973.

A Minor Scene. Staged San Francisco, 1966. In The Theme
    Is Blackness: The Corner and Other Plays. New York:
    Morrow, 1973.

The Mystery of Phillis Wheatley. Staged New York, 1976.

One-Minute Commercial. In The Theme Is Blackness: The
    Corner and Other Plays. New York: Morrow, 1973.

The Pig Pen. Staged New York, 1970. In Four Dynamite
    Plays. New York: Morrow, 1971.

The Play of the Play. In The Theme Is Blackness: The
    Corner and Other Plays. New York: Morrow, 1973.

The Psychic Pretenders. Staged New York, 1972.

Sepia Star. Staged New York, 1971.

A Short Play for a Small Theatre. In The Theme Is Black-
    ness: The Corner and Other Plays. New York: Morrow,
    1973.

A Son, Come Home. Staged New York, 1968. In The Negro
    Digest 17 (April 1968): 54-73. In Five Plays by Ed
    Bullins. Indianapolis: Bobbs-Merrill, 1968.

State Office Bldg. Curse. In The Theme Is Blackness:
    The Corner and Other Plays. New York: Morrow,
    1973.

A Street Play. In The Theme Is Blackness: The Corner and
    Other Plays. New York: Morrow, 1973.

Street Sounds. Staged New York, 1970. In The Theme Is
    Blackness: The Corner and Other Plays. New York:
    Morrow, 1973.

The Taking of Miss Janie. Staged New York, 1975. In
    Famous Plays of the '70s. New York: Dell, 1980.

The Theme Is Blackness. Staged San Francisco, 1966. In
    The Theme Is Blackness: The Corner and Other Plays.
    New York: Morrow, 1973.

You Gonna Let Me Take You Out Tonight, Baby. Staged New
    York, 1972.

II. FILM

Night of the Beast (screenplay). Included in Four Dyna-
    mite Plays, 1971.

The Ritual Masters (scenario), 1972.

III. FICTION

The Hungered One: Early Writings. New York: Morrow,
    1971.

The Reluctant Rapist. New York: Harper and Row, 1973.

IV. NONFICTION

"Black Theatre Groups: A Directory." Drama Review 12
    (Summer 1968): 172-73.
        Bullins, as guest editor for the special Black
    theatre issue of the Drama Review, lists a number of
    Black community theatre groups active in 1968.

"Black Theatre Notes." Black Theatre 1 (1968):4-7.

"Black Theatre: The 70's--Evolutionary Changes." In The
   Theme Is Blackness: The Corner and Other Plays. New
   York: Morrow, 1973. Pp. 1-15.

"The Electronic Nigger Meets the Golddust Twins." Black
   Theatre 1 (1968):24-29.

"Introduction." Playwright's Journal, 1975. No. 12
   (Spring-Summer 1976):3-19.

"The King Is Dead." Drama Review 12 (Summer 1968):23-25.

"The Polished Protest." Contact (July 1963):67-68.

"A Short Statement on Street Theatre." Drama Review 12
   (Summer 1968):93.

"The So-Called Western Avant Garde Drama." Liberator 7
   (December 1967):16.

"Theatre of Reality." Negro Digest 16 (April 1966):60-66.

V. POETRY

To Raise the Dead and Foretell the Future. New York:
   Lafayette Publications, 1971.

VI. TRANSLATION

GOIN' A BUFFALO

   Irány Buffalo. Tr. István Bart. Budapest: Európa,
      1974. Hungarian.

VII. INTERVIEWS

Bullins, Ed. "Talking of Black Art, Theatre, Revolution
   and Nationhood." Black Theatre 5 (1971):23-24.
         Part I - First Pan African Cultural Festival (18-
   26). Part II - Black Theatre: "A Forum" (27-33). Part
   III - Black Theatre Discovers the New Lafayette (34-37).

O'Brien, John. "Interview with Ed Bullins." Negro
   American Literature Forum 7 (Fall 1973):108-12.
         Bullins considers himself a self-made artist on
   whom few literary influences have acted, and he
   stresses the independence of Black theatre, especially
   his own, from the white theatre establishment.

X, Marvin. "Interview with Ed Bullins." In New Plays
   from the Black Theatre. Ed. Ed Bullins. New York:
   Bantam Books, 1969. Pp. vi-xv.
         Currently editor of the journal Black Theatre,
   Bullins feels that Black drama offers the most vital
   and exciting challenge to contemporary theatre, citing
   as examples the plays of LeRoi Jones, Sonia Sanchez,
   and Sister Salimu.

SECONDARY SOURCES

I. CRITICISM

Anderson, Jervis. "Profiles." New Yorker 49 (16 June 1973): 40-44.
This biographical sketch touches on Bullins' relaxed mannerisms, his past theatre experiences and the New Lafayette Theatre, and his dispute with Lincoln Center over The Duplex.

Andrews, W. D. E. "Theatre of Black Reality: The Black Drama of Ed Bullins." Southwest Review 65 (1980): 178-90.
Unlike Baraka's "Messianic" theatre, Bullins' drama is "Orphic," involving a descent into the depths of the ghetto. The abstract sense of menace in his plays is comparable to Pinter's.

Barley, Peter. "The Electronic Nigger." Ebony 33 (September 1968): 97-98, 100-101.
Barley discusses Bullins' contribution to the new Afro-American drama, his revolutionary message, his special treatment of language and setting.

Bentley, Eric. Theatre of War: Comments on 32 Occasions. New York: Viking, 1972. Pp. 406-07.
Bentley believes Bullins has declared war on white racism in plays which reflect the new Black consciousness.

Blackman, Brandon R., IV. "Black Hope of Broadway." Sepia 24 (December 1975):62-68.
Bullins' career is traced. His message is strong but hopeful.

Brooks, Mary Ellen. "Reactionary Trends in Recent Black Drama." Literature and Ideology 10 (1971):41-48.
Brooks suggests that contemporary "revolutionary" black playwrights are, for the most part, reactionary. Jones's and Bullins' characters are those who have been crushed by oppression. In contrast, the values espoused by Baldwin, Lorraine Hansberry, Douglas Turner Ward, and Lonnie Elder are bourgeois.

Brukenfeld, Dick. "Off-Off-Broadway." In Theatre 4: The American Theatre (1970-1971):49.

Clarke, Sebastian. "Black Theatre in America." Plays and Players 20 (December 1972):34-35.
Clarke notes that the work of Black playwrights, including Bullins, has appeared both on and off Broadway, but that the possible changes such a theatre could bring about in relation to contemporary theatre are not yet clear.

Clayborne, Jon L. "Modern Black Drama and the Gay Image."
    College English 36 (November 1974):381-84.
        Bullins, along with other Black dramatists, has
    an unfortunate anti-gay bias.

Cohn, Ruby. "Theatre in Review." Educational Theatre
    Journal 28 (October 1976):406.
        Cohn notes the continuing contributions of Ed
    Bullins to the off-Broadway scene.

Dace, Letitia, and Wallace Dace. Modern Theatre and Drama.
    New York: Richards Rosen Press, 1973. Pp. 56-58.
        Bullins, along with Baraka and other Black
    dramatists, are described in terms of their contri-
    bution to modern American theatre.

Daughtry, Willa A. "A Quarter Century in the Fine Arts,
    1956-1974." Negro Education Review 27 (January
    1976):27.
        Bullins is credited with helping to raise black
    consciousness in society and in the arts.

Davis, Curt. "People in the News." Encore, 23 May 1977,
    p. 31.
        Brief mention of Bullins as an important Black
    American writer.

Eckstein, George. "The New Black Theatre." Dissent 20
    (Winter 1973):111-13.
        Eckstein admires Bullins' courage as a revolu-
    tionary dramatist.

_____. "Softened Voices in the Black Theatre." Dissent
    23 (Summer 1976):308.
        Three years after the above article Eckstein
    notices that most of the Black voices in the theatre
    are more moderate and optimistic.

Evans, Don. "The Theatre of Confrontation: Ed Bullins,
    Up Against the Wall." Black World 23 (1974):14-18.
        Evans denies that Bullins is pessimistic about
    the Black man's struggle in America, but he must
    reveal the impotence he feels in a society that
    thwarts him.

Gaffney, Floyd. "Is Your Door Really Open?" Drama and
    Theatre 7 (Fall 1968):4-7.
        With respect to the plays of Bullins, LeRoi Jones,
    and Douglas Turner Ward, Gaffney argues that Black
    theatre, in its attempt to articulate a peculiarly
    Black consciousness, social and political, is still
    segregationist in that it depends on Black produc-
    tions by Black producers and acting companies. The
    author feels a more genuinely integrated American
    theatre would have a healthier, humanizing influence

on the divisive and confrontational aspects of a
polarized society.

Gant, Lisbeth. "The New Lafayette Theatre." Drama Review 16 (December 1972):52.
Bullins' contribution to the New Lafayette
Theatre's repertory is discussed. His blues dramas
are an alternative to established Broadway drama.

Geisinger, Marion. Plays, Players and Playwrights: An
Illustrated History of the Theatre. New York: Hart
Publishing, 1975. P. 742.
Bullins' major plays are noted in the context
of modern theatre history.

Gilder, Rosamond. "Theatre as People: Book Report." In
Theatre 4: The American Theatre (1970-1971):187.
Discussion of Bullins' current plays off-
Broadway and their impact on theatre audiences.

Giles, James R. "Tenderness in Brutality: The Plays of
Ed Bullins." Players 47 (October-November 1972): 32-
33.
Giles attempts to show the relationship between
Bullins' characters and their social environment.
Despite the cruelty in their surroundings, they are
capable of dreams and gentleness.

Gottfried, Martin. "The New Ethnic Theatre." New York
Post, 4 October 1975, in News--Performing Arts 68
(September-October 1975):134.
Gottfried likes the idea of an ethnic theatre
but feels ethnic plays are often sloppily executed.

Haslam, Gerald S. "Two Traditions in Afro-American Literature." Research Studies 37 (September 1969):183-
93.
Haslam's thrust is that the best of the Black
writers invent synthetic art forms out of their experiences in conflict with a predominantly white culture, and that these forms follow two main traditional lines: the written and the oral. Representing
the written line is the self-conscious "literariness"
of the Harlem Renaissance, which led through the
broader view of the 1930s into the prototypical expression of Richard Wright, followed by Ellison,
Brooks, and Baldwin. These writers combine naturalism, symbolism, and the Black experience into an or-
ganic "existentialism," as opposed to the "slave
narrative" style Cleaver and Malcolm X use. The oral
line has also influenced Ellison, and the Black
Revolutionary group, led by LeRoi Jones, and the
Black Experience group, led by Bullins.

Hatch, James. "Speak to Me in Those Old Words, You Know, Those La-La Words, Those Tung-Tung Sounds." Yale/ Theatre 8 (Fall 1976):33.
    Hatch claims that "the best plays of Ed Bullins are structured like jazz, with theme line and space for improvisation." He suggests that the "looseness" of Afro-American dramatic structure is a virtue.

Hay, Samuel A. "'What Shape Shapes Shapelessness?': Structural Elements in Ed Bullins' Plays." Black World 23 (June 1974):20-26.
    Believing that critics, such as Clive Barnes, have maligned Bullins for not mastering the subtler techniques of playwrighting, Hay shows that Bullins' works, especially The Duplex, are more complex in structure and theme and are more aesthetically so-phisticated than has been acknowledged.

Houghton, Norris. The Exploding Stage: An Introduction to Twentieth Century Drama. New York: Waybright and Talley, 1971. Pp. 202, 237, 251.
    Bullins' angry Black proletarian dramas are mentioned.

Hughes, Catharine. "Bicentennial Reflections." America, 24 July 1976, p. 31.
    Hughes notes the progress of American drama since World War II in confronting major social and racial issues and regards Bullins as a major Black dramatist.

Jackson, Kennell, Jr. "Notes on the Works of Ed Bullins and The Hungered One (short stories)." CLA Journal 18 (December 1974):292-99.
    Although Jackson discusses Bullins' fiction in detail, he also comments on the revolutionary themes and dramatic power of his plays.

Jeffers, Lance. "Bullins, Baraka, and Elder: The Dawn of Grandeur in Black Drama." CLA Journal 16 (September 1972):32-48.
    Unlike most of their more timid colleagues, these three writers are engaged in generating an honest, moral, conscientious literature, American as well as Black, one that favors humanism and is with-out fear of the hypocrisy of the ruling values. All reject "whiteness."

Kuna, F.M. "Current Literature 1970. II. New Writing: Drama." English Studies 52 (December 1971):565-73.
    The dramatic form reflects the contemporary con-frontation of sensibility with a fragmented world. Drama in the 60s goes in two directions: theatre of "mixed means," that connects drama to other expres-sive forms, and theatre that relies on its ritual aspects for a link to its earlier traditions, to the

146

communal, celebratory theatre of primitive culture.
David Mercer's <u>After Haggerty</u> illustrates the first
type; Bullins' <u>The Electronic Nigger</u> approaches pure
ritual.

Lahr, John. "Black Theatre: The American Tragic Voice."
    <u>Evergreen Review</u> 13 (August 1969):55-63.
        Lahr argues that Black drama, still in its in-
    fancy, presents the sole possible vehicle for a
    tragic theatre in America. The Black's experience
    is a radically holistic struggle for existence or
    identity; the white American has parted with his
    "sense of wholeness." LeRoi Jones, Bullins, Lonnie
    Elder, and James Dolan Tuotte have made a start in
    what to Lahr is the right direction, for the Black
    playwright must exorcise all that is culturally
    emasculating and must resist the easy impulse to
    propagandize.

_____. "The Deli: Off Broadway and Off, 68-69." In
    <u>Theatre 2, the American Theatre</u> (1968-1969):
    50.
        Refers to several Bullins dramatic offerings
    in New York.

Miller, Jeanne-Marie A. "Images of.Black Women in Plays
    by Black Playwrights." <u>CLA Journal</u> 20 (June 1977):
    502-07.
        Miller says "the Black female character . . .
    has faced double discrimination--that of sex and
    race." She traces the treatment of Black women
    characters since the nineteenth century. Bullins
    has created strong parts for black women in some of
    his plays.

Moser, Norman. "A Revolutionary Art: Le Roi Jones, Ed
    Bullins and the Black Revolution." <u>December</u> 12
    (1970):180-90.
        See under Baraka above.

Nordel, Roderick. "Bullins and Black Theatre." <u>Christian
    Science Monitor</u>, 4 June 1969, p. 11.
        Bullins is described as a talented angry young
    playwright.

O'Haire, Patricia. "Bullins: A Philadelphia Story." <u>New
    York Daily News</u>, 7 June 1975, in <u>Newsbank--Performing
    Arts</u> 39 (May-June 1975):68.
        Bullins emerged from a Philadelphia ghetto to
    be a major force in modern American drama.

Oliver, Edith. "Report from 137th St." In <u>Theatre 5:
    The American Theatre</u> (1971-1972):133.

Poland, Albert, and Bruce Mailman. The Off-Off Broadway
    Book. Indianapolis: Bobbs-Merrill, 1972. P. 530.
        Bullins' work with the New Lafayette Theatre is
    described.

Reilly, John N. "Ed Bullins." In James Vinson, ed. Con-
    temporary Dramatists. London: St. Martin's Press,
    1977. Pp. 126-28.
        Reilly provides a brief biography, bibliography,
    and evaluation of Bullins' work.

Riche, James. "The Politics of Black Modernism." Litera-
    ture and Ideology, No. 8, 1971, pp. 85-90.
        Riche sees Black modernism as a reactionary
    movement in contemporary literature. The emphasis
    on unique subculture is divisive, and the return or
    attempt to return to African traditions results in
    counter-modernistic tendencies--a retreat to mysti-
    cism, primitivism, irrationality, and hence to an
    essential affirmation of a good many of the stereo-
    types established in the novels of white racists.
    Ultimately, "Ralph Ellison, LeRoi Jones, Ed Bullins,
    and Gwendolyn Brooks reveal the same class outlook
    as their white modernist counterparts."

Robinson, Le Roy. "Black Theatre: A Need for the Seven-
    ties." Soul Illustrated 2 (February 1970): 57.
        Bullins will continue to present the needs of
    Black people in his disturbing dramas.

Simon, John. Uneasy Stages. A Chronicle of the New York
    Theatre, 1963-1973. New York: Random House, 1975.
    P. 452.
        Simon is generally skeptical about the merits
    of ethnic drama but he grants Bullins a talent for
    evoking strong feelings.

Smitherman, Geneva. "Ed Bullins/Stage One: Everybody
    Wants to Know Why I Sing the Blues." Black World 23
    (June 1974):4-13.
        Smitherman claims Bullins "uses the blues motif
    as the central mechanism for conveying his message."
    Goin' a Buffalo, In the Wine Time, The Corner, and
    The Duplex are plays in Bullins' "Stage One" which
    depict the pain and paradoxes of Black experience.

Stamper, Sam. "Playwright in Residence for One Week."
    Bay State Banner, 30 January 1975, in Newsbank--Per-
    forming Arts (January-February 1975), p. 13:4.

Steele, Shelby. "White Port and Lemon Juices: Notes on
    Ritual in the New Black Theatre." Black World 22
    (June 1973): 4-13, 78-83.
        Steele considers the use of symbol and ceremony

in the plays of Ed Bullins, Ben Caldwell, and others,
asserting the commitment of Black drama to its audience's values.

Tener, Robert L. "Pandora's Box: A Study of Ed Bullins'
   Drama." CLA Journal 19 (June 1976):533-44.
      Tener expands the basic premises of James
   Giles's article (see above). He contends that "the
   elements of the social compass in Bullins' vision
   are the conceptual spatial environment, the nature
   of order within that space, and the operating fictive
   values."

True, Warren R. "Ed Bullins, Anton Chekhov, and the
   'Drama Mood.'" CLA Journal 20 (June 1977):521-32.
      Although he notes that Bullins deliberately
   avoids "Western" literary influences, True compares
   the mood dramas of Chekhov and Bullins, emphasizing
   the naturalism of their settings and the passivity
   of their characters, all trapped by social and en-
   vironmental forces seemingly beyond their control.

Turner, Darwin T. "Afro-American Literary Critics."
   Black World 19 (June 1970): 54.
      Critics of Afro-American literature must not
   judge such works on the basis of traditional Western
   models. Bullins' special contributions to the stage
   are noted.

II. DISSERTATIONS

Haley, Elsie Galbreath. "The Black Revolutionary Theatre:
   LeRoi Jones, Ed Bullins, and Minor Playwrights."
   Dissertation Abstracts International 32: 4757A
   (Denver, 1971).
      In her overview of the revolutionary Black
   theatre movement of the 1960s, Haley discusses
   Bullins and Baraka in separate chapters, with a less
   detailed analysis of five other Black playwrights.

True, Warren Roberts. "Chekhovian Dramaturgy in the Plays
   of Tennessee Williams, Harold Pinter, and Ed Bullins."
   Dissertation Abstracts International 37: 5131A
   (Tennessee, 1976).
      True compares the naturalistic dialogue of these
   three playwrights and shows how each depicts vulner-
   able characters who attempt to survive menacing
   outside forces.

See also Amiri Baraka, Secondary Sources, Dissertations,
   especially the entries under Curb, Goodman, Hicklin,
   Keyssar-Franke, Ogunbiyi, Singleton, Tedesco, and
   Williams. (Pp. 129-32.)

III. REVIEWS

CLARA'S OLE MAN

New York Times, 9 March 1968, p. 23:2.

CORNER

New Yorker, 1 June 1972, p. 53.

DADDY

New Yorker, 20 June 1977, p. 89.

THE DUPLEX

Barnes, Clive. New York Times, 10 March 1972, p. 46:1.
Barnes laments that Bullins himself has
disowned this play, because the current production is so good. Though the characters are
Black, they portray a universal situation: the
eternal triangle, mobster husband, lonely wife,
and student boarder. Though the play could
have been cut, all other aspects of the
production are excellent. Barnes notes that
"Bullins writes so easily and naturally that
you watch his plays and you get the impression
of overhearing them rather than seeing them."

New Yorker, 18 March 1972, p. 85.

Newsweek, 20 March 1972, pp. 98-99.

Nation, 27 March 1972, p. 412.

Time, 27 March 1972, p. 81.

THE ELECTRONIC NIGGER AND OTHERS

Barnes, Clive. "American Place Stages 'Electronic
Nigger.'" New York Times, 9 March 1968, p. 23:2.
After confessing that Black theater as it
evolves is "quite different" from the white
theater, Barnes nevertheless sees the evening of
three short Bullins plays as interesting and well-
produced. The first, "A Son, Come Home," seems
hard to understand; "The Electronic Nigger,"
summarized in some detail, is startling and comic.
The final playlet, "Clara's Ole Man," exhibits
Bullins' range and potential.

New Yorker, 9 March 1968, pp. 33-34.

Newsweek, 18 March 1968, p. 110.

150

Nation, 25 March 1968, pp. 420-21.

Ebony, 23 September 1968, pp. 97-98.

THE FABULOUS MISS MARIE

    Gussow, Mel. New York Times, 12 March 1971, p. 28:1.
        Gussow sees this as the "most composed" of
the four plays of Bullins' projected 20-play
cycle to appear so far. Avoiding melodrama, it
is "on the surface more of a comedy than its
predecessors." Though it focuses on the successful but directionless Miss Marie and her life
of middle-class hedonism, there are excellent
performances throughout the cast. According to
Gussow, "This is intended as a black play for a
black audience."

    New Yorker, 20 March 1971, pp. 94-95.

THE GENTLEMAN CALLER (One of four plays by Black writers
    performed at the Anta Theatre in New York.)

    New York Times, 13 April 1969, II:7:1.

    New York Times, 27 April 1969, p. 92:1.

    New York Times, 4 May 1969, II:1:5.

    Shepard, Richard F. "One Act Plays Arrive at Gate
        Theater." New York Times, 31 July 1969, p. 28:1.
        As one of four very different but equally
effective short plays, The Gentleman Caller by
Ed Bullins "holds the viewer from start to
finish." Shepard sees it as a startling and
revolutionary play in the symbol-charged "advanced modern genre."

    Barnes, Clive. "An Essay on Black Drama." New York
        Times, 22 September 1969, 36:1.
        In a brief notice in a longer overview of
Black drama, Barnes urges all readers to attend
this "totally absorbing if dramatically untidy
evening." He feels, however, in A Black Quartet,
The Gentleman Caller is the least of the four,
well below the playwright's usual dexterity.

GOIN' A BUFFALO

    Gussow, Mel. "W.P.A. Stages Bullins' Play on Young
        Adults." New York Times, 16 February 1972,
        p. 28:1.
        Though "not Bullins's most sustained effort,"

the performance is "stoked by the playwright's
power and insight into human behavior." Strong
acting performances put across the despair and
the W.P.A. Theater's innovative staging is
particularly effective.

New Yorker, 4 March 1972, p. 83.

HOME BOY

New York Times, 27 September 1976, p. 42:1.

New Yorker, 11 October 1976, p. 81.

HOUSE PARTY

New York Times, 30 October 1973, p. 35:1.

New York Times, 4 November 1973, II:7:1.

New Yorker, 5 November 1973, pp. 89-91.

HOW DO YOU DO? (and others)

New York Times, 9 March 1969, p. 23:2.

New York Times, 13 April 1969, II:3:3.

New York Times, 5 March 1972, p. 59:1.

I AM LUCY TERRY

New York Times, 12 February 1976, p. 42:1.

New Yorker, 23 February 1976, p. 82.

IN NEW ENGLAND WINTER

New York Times, 27 January 1971, p. 28:1.

New Yorker, 6 February 1971, p. 72.

New York Times, 7 February 1971, II:3:1,4.

IN THE WINE TIME

Patterson, Lindsay. "New Home, New Troupe, New
Play." New York Times, 22 December 1968,
II:7:1.
Patterson comments that it is "pleasing
to see a play by a young black author that
makes little or no mention of whitey, but
presents a slice of black life as it is

actually lived." Though In the Wine Time has
little plot, it features Bullins' excellent
sense for the language of the ghetto. Bullins'
talent is "the stuff that major writers are
made of." (Also printed in Negro Historical
Bulletin, 32 (April 1969), pp. 68-69.)

New York Times, 30 April 1976, III:4:5.
Gussow focuses on the intricacies of the
plot--the tutelage of 15-year-old Ray by his
shiftless uncle Cliff--and on the sensitive
acting of Robert Christian as Cliff. In contrast
with other plays in Bullins' projected 20-play
cycle, this one is a compact family drama.
Though its opening downtown comes eight years
after its original production in Harlem, Gussow
feels that the current production's merits make
it "well worth the wait."

New Yorker, 10 May 1976, pp. 104-05.

JO ANNE!!!

New York Times, 19 October 1976, p. 53:1.

New Yorker, 25 October 1976, p. 62.

MICHAEL (Man-Wo-man)

New Yorker, 22 May 1978, pp. 91-92.

THE MYSTERY OF PHILLIS WHEATLEY

New York Times, 4 February 1976, p. 42:3.
Bullins presents the character of Phillis
Wheatley, the first Black slave and the second
woman to publish a book of poetry in America,
as a source of both racial and national pride.
He captures a "striking episode in eighteenth-
century American history," which has interest
for both children and adults. The playwright
sees her as a Black woman, "misused by civilization," who has forsaken her African heritage
and has learned "to write verse like a gentle
Englishwoman." Children will especially enjoy
the use of direct address and such forces as
Captain Diabolical and Lord Africa, who vie for
Phillis' soul.

THE PIG PEN

Barnes, Clive. "Night of Malcolm X's Death is
Examined." New York Times, 21 May 1970, p. 47:1.

Not seeing this as one of Bullins' best
plays, Barnes still asserts that the play is
"the most meaningful nothing experience ... of
the season." On the night of Malcolm X's assas-
sination, a young hip couple, racially mixed,
give a strained party at which nothing happens.
Barnes cautions the reader: "Don't go for fun--
just for information."

New Yorker, 30 May 1970, pp. 72-73.

New York Times, 31 May 1970, II:1:6.

Nation, 1 June 1970, p. 668.

SEPIA STAR (with Mildred Kayden)

New York Times, 19 August 1971, III:2:3.

A SON, COME HOME

Barnes, Clive. New York Times, 9 March 1968, p.
23:2.
Bullins' use of narrative flashback is
interesting although the dialogue between mother
and son is perhaps too conventional to make an
impact on the audience.

STREET SOUNDS

Gussow, Mel. New York Times, 23 October 1970,
p. 32:1.
Gussow considers this play "powerful, wise
and informative," with action-packed scenes of
ghetto life, which have a kind of "Spoon River"
movement. The playwright creates characters
who are convincing and often very funny.

THE TAKING OF MISS JANIE

New York Times, 18 March 1975, p. 29:4.

New Yorker, 24 March 1975, pp. 61-63.

Nation, 5 April 1975, p. 414.

New York Times, 5 May 1975, p. 40:1.

New York Times, 11 May 1975, II:5:1.

Hewes, Henry. Saturday Review, 17 May 1975, p. 52.
Bullins' successful play was moved to the
Mitzi Newhouse Theatre of Lincoln Center. Hewes
admires the satirical portrait of white and
black "hip" students in the 1960's.

<u>Time</u>, 19 May 1975, p. 80.

<u>America</u>, 31 May 1975, p. 427.

<u>New Republic</u>, 7 June 1975, p. 20.

4 JACK GELBER

Born April 12, 1932, Chicago, Illinois

When he was only twenty-seven, Jack Gelber wrote The Connection for the Living Theatre. Appearing half a year before Albee's Zoo Story, The Connection heralded a change of pace for American drama in its movement away from the conventional family-centered, middle-class drama associated with Miller, Williams, and O'Neill. Instead, junkies and other street people, the marginal men of an absurd universe, assaulted audiences with verbal abuse, obscene actions, and grotesque, disturbing questions. Gelber is still primarily identified with his first play, a tour de force more popular than any of his subsequent works. Nevertheless, The Apple, Square in the Eye, and more recently Sleep indicate that Gelber continues to use the play-within-a-play device and the illusion and reality theme to expose the tentative adaptation of modern protagonists to an often hostile world. Since 1972 Gelber has been a professor of drama at Brooklyn College.

PRIMARY SOURCES

I. STAGE

The Apple. Staged New York, 1961. New York: Grove Press, 1961.

_____. In The Apple and Square in the Eye. New York: Viking Press, 1974.

_____. In Seven Plays of the Modern Theatre. Ed. Harold Clurman. New York: Grove Press, 1962.

Barbary Shore. Adaptation of the novel by Norman Mailer. Staged New York, 1974.

The Connection. Staged New York, 1959. New York: Grove Press, 1960.

_____. London: Faber and Faber, 1961.

156

The Cuban Thing. Staged New York, 1968. New York: Grove
    Press, 1969.

Farmyard. A translation by Gelber and Michael Roloff of a
    play by Francis Xavier Kroetz. Staged New Haven,
    1975. New York: Urizen Books, 1976.

Rehearsal. Staged New York, 1976.

Sleep. Staged New York, 1972. New York: Hill and Wang,
    1972.

Square in the Eye. Staged New York, 1965. New York:
    Grove Press, 1966.

_____. In The Apple and Square in the Eye. New York:
    Viking Press, 1974.

II. FILM

The Connection, 1962.

III. FICTION

The Connection. 1960.

On Ice. New York: Macmillan, 1964; London: Deutsch,
    1965.

IV. TRANSLATIONS

THE APPLE

    De Apple. Tr. G. K. van het Reve. Amsterdam:
        Bezige Bij., 1963. Dutch.

    Der Apfel. Tr. Andreas Christopf. Frankfurt: S.
        Fischer, 1976. German.

    Il Contratto. La Mela. Tr. Furio Colombo. Milano:
        Fettrinelli, 1963. Italian.

    La mela. In Nuovo Teatro Americano. Tr. Furio
        Colombo. Milano: Bompiani, 1963. Italian.

THE CONNECTION

    Il Contratto. La Mela. Tr. Furio Colombo. Milano:

Fettrinelli, 1963. Italian.

Konnex. Tr. Willi H. Thiem. Frankfurt: S. Fischer, 1976. German.

De Schakel. Tr. Gerard Pijfers. Amsterdam: Bezige Bij., 1961. Dutch.

Spojenie. Tr. Juraj Vojtek. Bratislava: Tatran, 1967. Czech.

THE CUBAN THING

Die Sache mit Kuba. Tr. Alexander Gruber. Frankfurt: S. Fischer, 1970. German.

V. INTERVIEWS

Gelb, Arthur. "Dramatists Deny Nihilistic Trend." New York Times, 15 February 1960, p. 23:1.
    An informal discussion with Albee and Gelber, in which Gelber describes The Connection as "an anti-phony play which hits hard at sentimentality. But there is faith in it."

"Jack Gelber Talks About Surviving in the Theater." Theatre (Yale) 9 (Spring 1978), 46-58.
    Gelber speaks of his experiences with the Living Theatre, the popularity of his work in foreign countries, the future of off-Broadway, and his own disregard for fame.

Keating, John. "Gelber's Apple." New York Times, 26 November 1961, II:3:1.
    Gelber states with emphasis: "I want to bring 'death' out into the open and say, 'Consider this.'"

Taylor, Karen. Peoples Theatre in America. New York: Drama Book Specialists/Publishers, 1973. Pp. 275-79.
    Gelber discusses American political hypocrisy toward Cuba and other countries and his new play, The Cuban Thing.

"Young Playwright." New Yorker, 21 July 1960, pp. 24-25.
    Gelber, author of The Connection, lives an un-complicated life which he does not want to change despite theatrical recognition. "I don't want a whole bunch of aggravation. I'm selfish. I don't need anything except to eat and pay rent." Literary influences have been few--The Book of the Dead, Greek philosophy, Turgenev, Gorki, Rilke, and the German Expressionists of the 1920s.

SECONDARY SOURCES

I. CRITICISM

Abel, Lionel. "Living Theatre." Commentary 33 (April
    1962):331-34.
        Abel's article is decidedly unfavorable, even
    condemnatory. He asserts that The Apple is "an
    authentically unbrilliant play with an authentically
    unbrilliant message. What it says is: Be an im-
    becile."

_____. Metatheatre, A New View of Dramatic Form.
    New York: Hill and Wang, 1963. Pp. 128-34.
        Like many modern dramatists Gelber questions
    the traditional view of man in respect to the uni-
    verse. The universe is an illusion, a projection
    of man's needs. The nightmarish drug world of The
    Connection is as "real" as any other.

_____. "Not Everyone Is in the Fix." Partisan Review
    27 (Winter 1960):131-36.
        Though Abel dislikes The Connection, writing
    that there is "nothing delightful" in it, "little
    poetry, and a degree of pain," he nevertheless can-
    not deny that it has a significant effect on the
    audience: "We are shaken up, disturbed and self-
    questioning when we leave the theater."

"The American Playwright in the Seventies: Some Problems
    and Perspectives." Theatre Quarterly 8 (1978):
    45-58.
        A symposium with Gelber, Jack Richardson,
    Lanford Wilson, and others as they discuss the prob-
    lems which serious playwrights must confront in
    the 1970s.

Bigsby, C. W. E. Confrontation and Commitment: A Study
    of Contemporary American Drama, 1959-1961. Columbia:
    University of Missouri Press, 1960. Pp. xviii, 5,
    10, 20, 50-61, 69, 71, 99-100.
        Bigsby frequently refers to The Connection which
    he associates with a new era of alienated, disturbing,
    innovative playwrights. He analyzes the theme and
    structure of the play at length.

Biner, Pierre. The Living Theater. New York: Avon, 1972.
    Pp. 46-49.
        Biner discusses the productions of The Connec-
    tion and The Apple which first made Julian Beck's
    theatre group famous.

Brook, Peter. "From Zero to Infinite." Encore 7 (November-December 1960):6-11.
  Gelber's The Connection rejects the false in theater and cinema, throwing out many of the old illusions: proscenium, exposition, development, etc. Members of the audience are treated as "independent creative witnesses." The article compares Gelber's play to Brook's new film Moderato Cantabile in its attempt to transcend the surface of reality.

Brustein, Robert. Seasons of Discontent. New York: Simon & Schuster, 1965. Pp. 23-26.
  Essentially the same essay as below.

_____ "The New American Playwrights." In Modern Occasions. Ed. Philip Rahv. New York: Farrar, Straus and Giroux, 1966. Pp. 128-29.
  Brustein claims Gelber is not a born writer but an "instinctive dramatist." He dislikes the playwright's "audience-baiting" in The Connection and The Apple and believes the time scheme in Square in the Eye is ineffective.

Burns, Elizabeth. Theatricality. New York: Harper, 1972. Pp. 117, 228.
  Burns comments on the theatrical aspects of Gelber's plays and speaks of their debt to Pirandello and O'Neill.

Corrigan, Robert W. "The Soulscope of Contemporary American Drama." World Theatre 11 (Winter 1962-63): 316-28.
  Contemporary dramatists are nearly all concerned with the modern human condition, expressing "tremendous concern to find a metaphor for universal modern man as he lives on the brink of disaster." The ordinary linear plot is replaced by a contextual form, expressing condition rather than action. Writers like Edward Albee or Jack Gelber have advanced farther than O'Neill, Williams, or Miller, but are more self-conscious and imitative.

Dommergues, Pierre. Les USA: A la Recherche de Leurs Identités. Paris: Grasset, 1967. Pp. 348-51.
  Dommergues finds a new pessimism in American life, a sense of alienation reflected in the theatre in works such as The Connection.

Donahue, Francis. "Anatomy of the New Drama." Southwest Review 56 (Summer 1971):269-77.
  The 1960s was the era of the "New Drama," characterized by a "rebellious and purposefully chaotic" type of drama which originated in response to the well-made, "finished" play in which the audience is uninvolved, except as invisible on-looker. Gelber's

The Connection represents the Theater of Cruelty,
one of the four major currents in the "New Drama."

Dukore, Bernard F. "The New Dramatists: 5. Jack Gelber."
Drama Survey 2 (October 1962):146-57.
Dukore asserts that "Gelber uses images and
symbols in a manner which includes but goes beyond
traditional means." The audience does not statically
view the play, but becomes placed in the position of
the characters, thereby apprehending the scenic movement directly, and becoming involved in it.

_____. "The Noncommercial Theatre in New York Today."
In The American Theatre Today. Ed. Alan S. Downer.
New York: Basic Books, 1967. Pp. 158-62.
Dukore discusses Gelber's techniques and his
relationship with the Living Theatre.

Eskin, Stanley G. "Theatricality in the Avant-Garde
Drama: A Reconsideration of a Theme in the Light of
The Balcony and The Connection." Modern Drama 7
(September 1964):213-22.
Eskin believes that The Connection involves
audiences and players in a common production by means
of theatricality, whereas ordinary Avant-Garde
theater indicates the hollowness of life using artificial theater consciousness.

Gilman, Richard. Introduction to The Apple and Square in
the Eye. New York: Viking Press, 1974. Pp. i-iv.
Gilman enthusiastically introduces Gelber as a
prophetic new voice in the theater who can express
anger and despair in honest terms.

Hentoff, Nat. "Who Else Can Make So Much out of Passing
Out?: The Surprising Survival of an Anti-Play."
Evergreen Review 4 (January-February 1960):170-77.
Hentoff details both favorable and unfavorable
early reactions to The Connection, while asserting
that the play is one of the first to use jazz "organi-
cally and dynamically."

Hurley, Paul J. "France and America: Visions of the Absurd." College English 26 (1965):634-40.
Hurley generally finds the American "absurdists"
inferior to their French counterparts. In Gelber's
one attempt to abandon social realism, The Apple,
the playwright depends on "gimmicks" rather than
"wittily irrational dialogue"as Beckett or Ionesco
would have done.

Jeffrey, David K. "Genet and Gelber: Studies in Addic-
tion." Modern Drama 2 (September 1968):151-56.
Genet's The Balcony and Gelber's The Connection
both employ the device of the play-within-a-play

to contrast unspontaneous characters who hide behind the masks of acting and ritual and spontaneous ones who reject this "hall of mirrors."

Kerr, Walter. The Theatre in Spite of Itself. New York: Simon & Schuster, 1963. Pp. 178-82.
    Kerr discusses Gelber's anti-traditional plays and his ambiguous attitude toward his audience.

Kostelanetz, Richard C. "The Connection: Heroin as Existential Choice." Texas Quarterly 5 (Winter 1962): 159-62.
    Because the play as acted requires the audience's full identification with the characters, its full effect cannot be experienced on the printed page. Consequently, it is much more successful when experienced as an acted play.

_____. "Jack Gelber." Contemporary Dramatists. London: St. Martin's Press, 1977. Pp. 294-96.
    Kostelanetz believes American drama changed radically with the production of Gelber's The Connection and Albee's The Zoo Story, and that Gelber and Albee replaced Tennessee Williams and Arthur Miller in the forefront of theatrical consciousness. Kostelanetz believes that The Connection is Gelber's best play, and that the rest of his theatrical activity, as well as his novel, is uneven. The article includes short, though useful, treatments of The Connection, The Apple, Square in the Eye, The Cuban Thing, and Sleep, and concludes that Gelber is in certain respects, including authentic adventurousness, a more interesting playwright than Albee.

_____. "The New American Theatre." In Richard Kostelanetz, The New American Arts. New York: Horizon Press, 1965. Pp. 62-66.
    Similar to the general essay above.

Lawson, John Howard. "Modern U.S. Dramaturgy." Inostrannaya Literatura, 8 (August 1962):186-96. (In Russian)
    Details the influence of Beckett, Ionesco, and Genet on Edward Albee and Jack Gelber, noting their similar attempts to combine a rejection of bourgeois society with a destruction of the canonic forms of the play. (The article also treats Arthur Miller, William Gibson, Lorraine Hansberry, and Tennessee Williams.)

Lewis, Allan. American Plays and Playwrights of the Contemporary Theatre. New York: Crown, 1965. Pp. 202-04.
    Lewis briefly discusses Gelber as a modern American writer who shocks audiences with his subject matter and contemporary theatricality.

162

Little, Stuart. *Off Broadway*. New York: Coward-McCann,
    1972. Pp. 205-09.
        Mention is made of the Living Theatre and of
    various productions of Gelber's controversial plays.

Mee, Charles L., Jr. "The Beck's Living Theatre."
    Tulane Drama Review 7 (Winter 1962):194-205.
        Mee praises the vitality of *The Connection* and
    believes it is the "perfect wedding of style and
    play." The basic metaphor of dope addiction is
    well suited to dramatize the pointlessness and self-
    destruction of modern existence. Although Mee ad-
    mires the opening scene of *The Apple* in which an
    artist paints a canvas which the audience later bids
    on, he feels the play is far less effective than *The
    Connection*. Mee emphasizes the Living Theatre's
    interpretation and production of Gelber's work.

Mottram, Eric. "The New American Wave." *Encore* 11
    (January-February 1964):22-41.
        After World War II, most social problems were
    treated and solved as simply personal problems.
    Rejecting this treatment, writers such as Lionel
    Abel, Edward Albee, Kenneth Brown, Jack Gelber,
    Arthur Kopit, and Jack Richardson produce plays
    dealing with problems of order, law, and justice in
    plots about the nature of punishment "when old grand
    designs of moral stability have collapsed."

Tallmer, Jerry. "Applejack." *Evergreen Review* 6 (May-
    June 1962):95-106.
        The Apple represents a further development from
    The Connection in the direction of breaking down
    "the window-wall of the proscenium." Gelber's con-
    cern with the individual--both as member of the audi-
    ence and as player--leads him to experimentations
    reminiscent of Pirandello.

Tynan, Kenneth. *Tynan Left and Right: Plays, Films,
    People, Places and Events*. New York: Atheneum,
    1967. Pp. 71-73.
        Tynan admires Gelber's audacity but sees flaws
    in the execution of his ideas.

Weales, Gerald. "Off-Broadway: Its Contribution to
    American Drama." *Drama Survey* 2 (June 1962):16-18.
        Weales notes that controversial plays like *The
    Connection*, while not always commercially viable,
    serve as a spur and inspiration to more established
    playwrights.

Wellwarth, George E. "Hope Deferred: The New American
    Drama." *Literary Review* 7 (Autumn 1963):7-26.
        An evaluation of the work of Edward Albee, Jack
    Richardson, Jack Gelber, and Arthur Kopit. Wellwarth

reviews favorably the work of all but Gelber,
asserting that their work will have a more lasting
influence than "the highly touted English Dramatists
movement."

II. REVIEWS

THE APPLE

New York Times, 8 December 1961, p. 44:1.

New Yorker, 16 December 1961, pp. 97-98.

Newsweek, 18 December 1961, p. 72.

New Republic, 25 December 1961, p. 20.

Commonweal, 29 December 1961, pp. 364-65.

National Review, 30 January 1962, p. 68.

Simon, John. Theatre Arts 46 (February 1962):13-14.
        Simon asserts this obscene burlesque attack
    on the establishment "confuses revolt with re-
    voltingness" and does not know "what it is fight-
    ing for."

Christian Century, 21 February 1962, pp. 233-34.

Commentary,33 (April 1962):331-34.

New York Times, 20 April 1962, p. 22:1.

New York Times, 23 April 1962, p. 33:3.

BARBARY SHORE

New York Times, 11 January 1974, p. 16:1.

New York Times, 20 January 1974, II:4:1.

New Yorker, 21 January 1974, pp. 61-62.

THE CONNECTION

New York Times, 16 July 1959, p. 30:2.
Nation, 15 August 1959, p. 80.

Saturday Review, 26 September 1959, p. 27.

New Republic, 28 September 1959, pp. 29-30.

New Yorker, 10 October 1959, pp. 126-29.

Time, 25 January 1960, p. 61.

New York Times, 7 February 1960, II:1:1.

Tynan, Kenneth. Harper's 220 (April 1960):26-28.
    Calling The Connection "a cultural must,"
    Tynan claims its atmosphere evokes Gorki's Lower
    Depths, its theme of futility Beckett's Waiting
    for Godot.

New York Times, 23 February 1961, p. 30:2.

Esquire, April 1961, pp. 45-47.

New York Times, 16 June 1961, p. 29:1.

New Yorker, 10 November 1980, pp. 174-75.

THE CUBAN THING

New York Times, 25 September 1968, p. 36:2.

New Yorker, 15 October 1968, pp. 95-96.

New Republic, 19 October 1968, p. 36.

REHEARSAL

New York Times, 8 October 1976, III:4:1.

New York Times, 17 October 1976, II:3:1.

SLEEP

New York Times, 23 February 1972, p. 30:2.

New York Times, 27 February 1972, II:3:1.

New Yorker, 4 March 1972, p. 82.

Nation, 6 March 1972, p. 316.

Newsweek, 6 March 1972, p. 66.

SQUARE IN THE EYE

Taubman, Howard. New York Times, 20 May 1965, p. 54:1.
    Taubman summarizes the plot and characters
    of this "domestic tragedy," but finds little
    value in the play beyond the merits of its sets
    and staging.

New Yorker, 20 May 1965, p. 56.

Time, 28 May 1965, p. 83.

Newsweek, 31 May 1965, p. 76.

New York Times, 6 June 1965, II:1:1.

New Republic, 26 June 1965, p. 30.

Vogue, July 1965, p. 38.

Reporter, 1 July 1965, p. 42.

Commonweal, 2 July 1965, p. 474.

5 ARTHUR KOPIT

Born May 10, 1937, New York City

    Since he began his playwrighting career as a sopho-
more at Harvard, Arthur Kopit has amazed his audiences
with dramatic techniques that have alternated between
realism and near fantasy. Like O'Neill, Kopit started
writing for a theatre workshop and his first prize-winning
play, The Questioning of Nick, was in the realistic tradition. In Oh Dad, Poor Dad, Mama's Hung You in the Closet
and I'm Feelin' So Sad he parodied the Gothic dramas of
Tennessee Williams and other plays with strong Freudian
overtones. The Day the Whores Came Out to Play Tennis,
in which Kopit examines the country club set, revealed him
as a perceptive analyst of American social mores. Later,
in Indians he was able to treat the historical reality of
Buffalo Bill and the American West with humor and insight,
and to explore man's need to create myths. Most recently,
in Wings he entered the deeply subjective world of a
stroke victim to investigate problems of personal identity
and communication. The quest for meaning which motivates
all of his characters often ends in disappointment and
frustration, but the playwright himself appears committed
to a search for highly inventive dramatic forms for portraying human experience.

PRIMARY SOURCES

I. STAGE

Across the River and Into the Jungle. Staged Cambridge,
    1958.

And As for the Ladies (as Chamber Music). Staged London,
    1971. In The Day the Whores Came Out to Play Tennis.
    New York: Hill and Wang, 1965.

_____. In Chamber Music and Other Plays. London:
    Methuen, 1969.

Asylum: or, What the Gentlemen Are Up To and And As for
the Ladies. Staged New York, 1963.

Aubade. Staged Cambridge, 1959.

Chamber Music. Staged New York, 1963. In The Day the
Whores Came Out to Play Tennis and Other Plays. New
York: Hill and Wang, 1965.

_____. In Chamber Music and Other Plays. London:
Methuen, 1969.

The Conquest of Everest. Staged New York, 1964. In The
Day the Whores Came Out to Play Tennis and Other
Plays. New York: Hill and Wang, 1965.

_____. In Mademoiselle, November 1964, pp. 207-09.

The Day the Whores Came Out to Play Tennis. Staged New
York, 1965. In The Day the Whores Came Out to Play
Tennis and Other Plays. New York: Hill and Wang,
1965.

Don Juan in Texas. Staged Cambridge, 1957.

Gemini. Staged Cambridge, 1957.

The Hero. Staged New York, 1964. In The Day the Whores
Came Out to Play Tennis and Other Plays. New York:
Hill and Wang, 1965.

An Incident in the Park. In Pardon Me, Sir, But Is My
Eye Hurting Your Elbow? Ed. Bob Booker and George
Foster. New York: Geis, 1968.

Indians. Staged London, 1968; Washington, D.C., and New
York, 1969. New York: Hill and Wang, 1969.

_____. In Clive Barnes and John Gassner, eds. Best
American Plays, 7th Series, 1967-1973. New York:
Crown, 1975.

Louisiana Territory; or, Lewis and Clark--Lost and Found.
Staged Middletown, Conn., 1965.

Mhil' daim. Staged New York, 1963.

Oh Dad, Poor Dad, Mama's Hung You in the Closet and I'm
Feelin' So Sad: A Pseudo-classical Tragifarce in a
Bastard French Tradition. Staged Cambridge, 1960;
London, 1961; New York, 1962. New York: Hill and
Wang, 1960.

_____. London: Methuen, 1962.

_____. In Clive Barnes, ed. Fifty Best Plays of the
American Theatre. Vol. IV. New York: Crown, 1969.

_____. In Norman M. Small, ed. The Making of the Drama:
    Idea and Performance. Boston: Holbrook Press, 1972.

On the Runway of Life, You Never Know What's Coming Off
    Next. Staged Cambridge, 1957.

The Questioning of Nick. Staged Cambridge, Mass., 1957;
    New York, 1974. In The Day the Whores Came Out to
    Play Tennis and Other Plays. New York: Hill and
    Wang, 1965.

Secrets of the Rich. Staged New York, 1977. New York:
    Hill and Wang, 1978.

Sing to Me Through Open Windows. Staged Cambridge, 1959;
    New York, 1965. In The Day the Whores Came Out to
    Play Tennis and Other Plays. New York: Hill and
    Wang, 1965.

To Dwell in a Place of Strangers. Act I was published in
    the Harvard Advocate, May 1958, n.p.

What's Happened to the Thorne's House. Staged Peru,
    Vermont, 1972.

Wings. Staged New Haven and New York, 1978. New York:
    Hill and Wang, 1978.

II. FILM

Oh Dad, Poor Dad. Paramount Pictures, 1966.

III. TRANSLATIONS

THE CONQUEST OF EVEREST

    Tr. Luciano Codignola, in Sipario 21 (January 1965):
        62-64. Italian.

    La Conquête de L'Everest. Tr. Renée Rosenthal, in
        L'Avant Scène, 1 June 1968, pp. 40-43. French.

INDIANS

    Indianer. Tr. Hans Sahl. Frankfurt: S. Fischer,
        1970. German.

    Indianok. Amikor a szajhak teniszezni mentek. Tr.
        Geyza Banyy and Tharia Borbas. Budapest: Europe,
        1973. Hungarian.

Indians. Tr. Mario Maffi. In Sipario 25 (August-September 1970):68-85. Italian.

OH DAD, POOR DAD, MAMA'S HUNG YOU IN THE CLOSET AND I'M FEELIN' SO SAD

Oh Pa, Arme Pa, jij hangt in de kast van ma en het huilen stant me na. Tr. Bert Voeten. Amsterdam: Bezige Bij, 1963. Dutch.

Oh papa, povero papa, la mammo ti ha appeso bell' armadio e io mi sento tanto triste. Tr. Furio Colombo. In Nuovo Teatro Americano. Milano: Bompiani, 1963. Italian.

COLLECTIONS

El Interrogatorio de Nick. El dia que todas las p ... salieron a jugar al tenis. La Conquista del Everest. Indios. Tr. M. Luisa Balseiro. Madrid: Edicusa, 1972. Spanish. (The Questioning of Nick; The Day the Whores Came Out to Play Tennis; The Conquest of Everest; Indians)

O Vater, armer Vater, Mutter hängt dich in den Schrank, und ich bin ganz krank. Sing zu mir durch offene Fenster. Kammermusik. Als die Huren auzogen, um Tennis zu spielen. Tr. Hans Sahl. Frankfurt: S. Fischer, 1965. German. (Oh Dad; Sing to Me Through Open Windows; Chamber Music; The Day the Whores Came Out to Play Tennis)

IV. INTERVIEW

Hennessey, Brendan. "Interview with Arthur Kopit." Transatlantic Review 30 (Autumn 1968):68-73.
    Kopit claims that Indians has Vietnam parallels and that Oh, Dad is analogous to America's position in the world (Rosepetal is America, her beleaguered child, Vietnam).

SECONDARY SOURCES

I. CRITICISM

Asahina, Robert. "The Basic Training of American Playwrights: Theatre and the Vietnam War." Theatre (Yale) 9 (Spring 1978):30-37.

Asahina notes that ideological disgust with the Vietnam war motivated many young playwrights in the 1960s, including Kopit, whose Indians reflects many counterculture themes.

Billman, Carol S. "Illusions of Grandeur: Altman, Kopit, and the Legends of the Wild West." Literature/Film Quarterly 6 (1978):253-61.
    Altman the filmmaker and Kopit the playwright both examine American myths and analyze fundamental American assumptions about "manifest destiny," freedom, and the dream of success.

Brustein, Robert. "The New American Playwrights" (on Albee, Gelber, Richardson, Schisgal, Kopit, LeRoi Jones). In Modern Occasions. Ed. Philip Rahv. New York: Farrar, Straus, and Giroux, 1966. Pp. 123-218.

Cohn, Ruby. "Camp, Cruelty, Colloquialism." In Sarah B. Cohen, ed. Comic Relief: Humor in Contemporary American Literature. Urbana: University of Illinois Press, 1978. Pp. 281-303.
    In her discussion of Albee, Kopit, Guare, Bullins, Shepard, and other young American playwrights, Cohn explicates the satirical techniques, especially related to language, which these new wave dramatists share.

Curtis, Bruce. "The Use and Abuse of the Past in American Studies: Arthur Kopit's Indians, a Case Study." The American Examiner: A Forum of Ideas (Michigan State University) 1 (1969):4-5.
    Kopit has taken certain liberties with history, but his basic study of exploitation is valid.

Deneche, Uta. "Mythos and Rollenkonflect in Arthur Kopits Indians." In Lohnner, Edgar and Rudolf Haas, eds. Theatre and Drama in Amerika: Aspekte and Interpretation. Berlin: Schmidt, 1978. Pp. 375-87.
    Deneche provides a thorough analysis of the myths and symbols Kopit employs in Indians, admiring the playwright's sophisticated understanding of history and culture.

Downer, Alan S. "Experience of Heroes: Notes on the New York Theatre, 1961-1962." QJS 48:261-70.
    A thoughtful survey of the 1961-62 New York theater season discussing Bolt's A Man for All Seasons, Williams' The Night of the Iguana, Pinter's The Caretaker, Genet's The Blacks, Kanin's Gift of Time, Gardner's A Thousand Clowns, Vidal's Romulus, and Kopit's Oh Dad, Poor Dad.... Of the last Downer says that Kopit has "a vitality ... an enthusiasm for the audacious the contemporary theater can ill

spare." However, he also says that "Absurdity is
a theatrical dead end, at the foot of which stand
such ramshackle edifices as 'Oh, Dad, Poor Dad'...."
He concludes that "its being taken even half-seriously
by critics and the audience indicates the general
starvation for theatrical display and real action in
a play."

Harrell, Barbara. "Oh, Say, Can You See?" The American
Examiner: A Forum of Ideas 1 (1969):1-3.
Harrell believes that Kopit stretches some of
his historical metaphors in his attempt to depict
American values in Indians.

Hughes, Catharine. American Playwrights 1945-1975. New
York: Pittman, 1976. Pp. 99-100.
Hughes in 1976 felt that Indians was Kopit's
first worthy successor to Oh Dad. She liked its
"neo-Brechtian" quality but felt the Indian characters were stereotypes.

Hurley, Paul J. "France and America: Versions of the
Absurd." College English 26 (1965):634-40.
Hurley objects to Kopit's literal "equational
symbolism" (which is close to Albee's in its lack of
subtlety) and his moralizing on the evils of "preda-
tory feminism." American absurdists are generally
inferior to the French, Hurley believes.

Jones, John Bush. "Impersonation and Authenticity: The
Theatre as Metaphor in Kopit's Indians." Quarterly
Journal of Speech 59 (1973):443-51.
The play's major theme of mythmaking (which consists of impersonation insofar as a mythic representation is a personification or a cosmic plane of a
natural characteristic) is related to the question of
impersonation versus authenticity: this theme is in
large part communicated by the play's formal aspects
or "shape," and Jones thinks it "hardly accidental"
that the action is constructed out of a complicated
series of impersonations within a framework of the
theatre itself as a metaphor for the mythmaking process. The brilliance of Indians is a direct result
of a unity of structure and theme, form and content.

Jys, Vera M. "Indians: A Mosaic of Memories and Methodol-
ogies." Players 47 (June-July 1972):230-36.
Jys treats the play as a patchwork mosaic of 13
scenes at odds with 4 disconnected stage conventions:
theatre of fact, of alienation, expressionist, and
naturalist theatre. She concludes that one play is
ultimately a failure--interpreted as a history les-
son--owing to inadequacy of language, independence
of 4 separate themes in conflict with each other,

and the impediment presented to action of the plot by
the alternation of scenes.

Köhler, Klaus. "Das Underground Theatre." In Eberhard
Brüning, Klaus Köhler, and Bernard Scheller, eds.
Studien züm amerikanischen Drama nach dem zweiten
Weltkrieg. Berlin: Rütten and Loening, 1977.
Pp. 178-213.
 Köhler notes that Oh Dad was a parody of
Williams' Suddenly Last Summer. He finds that the
themes of hypocrisy and snobbery in American society
are deftly treated in The Whores and studies the
playwright's use of allegory in Chamber Music.

Lahr, John. "Arthur Kopit's Indians: Dramatizing National
Amnesia." Evergreen Review 13 (October 1969):19-21,
63-67.
 Indians exposes the exploitative "democratic"
mythologizing of the American western experience: the
West had the potential of the democratic ideal as an
idea, but in actual fact, and contrary to received
notions, its real use represented a betrayal of that
ideal; Buffalo Bill's ambiguous career becomes the
vehicle for this re-interpretation.

_____. "Indians: A Dialogue between Arthur Kopit and
John Lahr, Edited by Arthur Lahr." Unpaginated insert
in Bantam edition of Indians. New York: Bantam,1971.
 The play's purpose, says Kopit, was to explore
the confused "amorphousness" of history and attempt
to locate the madness of Vietnam in its proper
American context, with respect to that history, and
with respect to the usual American way of conducting
national affairs, including the mythic rationaliza-
tion of our self-interest. The distortion in the
play deliberately emulates the nightmare distortion
of American sensibilities during the Vietnam era.

_____. "In Search of a New Mythology." Evergreen Re-
view, 13 (January 1969):55-58, 84-87.
 Indians is currently the American theatre's most
successful attempt to address the "contemporary void"
with respect to myths, finding in them still-active
and viable sources of imaginative energy.

_____. "Mystery on Stage." Evergreen Review 13 (Decem-
ber 1969):53-57.
 Lahr compares Coover's The Kid, Kopit's Indians,
and Noonan's The Year Boston Won the Pennant as attempts by the playwrights to reintroduce negative
capability to contemporary theatre, so to speak:
plays that present mystery and insoluble irrational-
ism to audiences raised on the paradoxical need for
ambiguity and its simultaneous annihilation by tech-
nology.

Lumley, Frederick. New Trends in Twentieth Century Drama.
London: Barrie and Rockliff, 1967. Pp. 3, 331-32.
Lumley admires Kopit's humor, sense of parody,
and the bizarre flavor of his work.

Mottram, Eric. "The New American Wave." Encore 11
(January-February 1964):22-41.
On Lionel Abel, Albee, Kenneth Brown, Jack Gelber, Kopit, and Jack Richardson: their treatment of
law and order, justice and the nature of punishment
in a post-moral cultural climate.

Murch, A. C. "Genet--Triana--Kopit: Ritual as Danse
Macabre." Modern Drama 15 (March 1973):369-81.
Murch explores the dramatic properties and cultural significance of ritual action (as opposed to
the inaction of the absurdist theatre) in Genet's
The Maids, Triana's The Night of the Assassins, and
Kopit's Chamber Music. Murch considers that the
analogous relationship of the three plays is illus-
trative of the use of a global culture, the common
note of which, in its Western incarnation, is the
alienation of the individual.

Oestreicher, Pamela H. "On Indians." The American Ex-
aminer: A Forum of Ideas 1, iv (1969):3-5.
Oestreicher discusses parallels between the
Indian wars and the situation in Vietnam.

Pardi, Francesca. (Rev.-art). "Bernard Malamud, A New
Life." Nuova Antologia, no. 1964 (August 1964):
554-56. (In Italian)
In a discussion of "obscurantism, selfish petti-
ness, and blind conformism inimical to humanism on
the campus," Pardi contrasts Salinger's and Kopit's
treatment of college life "from the outside" with
Albee's and Malamud's interior view, concluding that
humanism survives in a highly resilient American culture.

Raidy, W. A. "Now Running in New York." Plays and Players 25 (August 1978):36.
In a brief review, William Raidy praises Kopit's
"intensely moving drama," Wings, and the electrifying
performance of Constance Cummings in the lead role.
He finds the play works on two levels: "on one level,
the play is a moving portrait of a woman humiliated
by the ravages of age, but still aware of a half-
forgotten life behind her. Beyond this, there is
another dimension to the drama that tries to tell us
that all mankind is trapped by the confines of mere
language." He also points out but does not elaborate
on the playwright's use of metaphoric allusions and
Joycean devices.

Rinear, D. L. "The Day the Whores Came Out to Play
    Tennis: Kopit's Debt to Chekhov." Today's Speech 22
    (Spring 1974):19-23.
        Rinear suggests that The Day the Whores Came Out
    to Play Tennis may be a conscious, even conscien-
    tious, aping of The Cherry Orchard. The parallels
    are carefully noted, well substantiated, and not
    without interest, but Rinear does not explain why
    Kopit has done what Rinear believes he has done.

Rutledge, Frank C. "Kopit's Indians." The American Ex-
    aminer: A Forum of Ideas 1 (1969):5-6.
        Indians is Kopit's most mature and complex work
    to date.

Szilassy, Zoltan. "Yankee Burlesque or Metaphysical
    Farce? (Kopit's Oh Dad, Poor Dad ... Reconsidered)."
    Hungarian Studies in English 2 (1977):143-47.
        Szilassy argues that Oh Dad is more than the
    satire and tour de force that most early critics per-
    ceived, that it asks important existential questions.

Weales, Gerald. American Drama since World War II. New
    York: Harcourt, Brace and World, 1962. Pp. 222-23.
        Weales notes that Oh, Dad, modeled on Ionesco,
    uses a familiar American theme: the emasculating fe-
    male as both dominating mother and frigid sex image.
    Kopit also is making an irrelevant joke-parody of
    Tennessee Williams' Suddenly Last Summer and Rose
    Tattoo.

Weiher, Carol. "American History on Stage in the 1960s:
    Something Old, Something New." Quarterly Journal of
    Speech 63 (December 1977):405-12.
        Weiher uses Duberman's In White America and
    Kopit's Indians to show the role of the stage in the
    1960s in the demythologization of American history.

Wellwarth, George E. "Hope Deferred: The New American
    Drama. Reflections on Edward Albee, Jack Richard-
    son, Jack Gelber, and Arthur Kopit." Literary Review
    7 (Autumn 1963):7-26.
        In an attempt to find an American counterpart to
    the "New English Dramatists" movement, Wellwarth
    surveys the early work of Albee, Richardson, Gelber,
    and Kopit. With the exception of Gelber, Wellwarth
    finds the playwrights to be of great promise and
    feels that he has found the nucleus of a movement
    which may outlast the much-touted British movement.
    His discussion of Kopit centers on his (then) only
    professionally produced play, Oh Dad, Poor Dad ...
    which he views as "a huge practical joke" and "a
    brilliant satire on the conventions of avant-garde
    drama." He attributes Kopit's success to his ability
    to appeal to sophisticated as well as uncomplicated

senses of humor, and looks forward to Kopit's future achievements.

_____. The Theatre of Protest and Paradox. New York: New York University Press, 1974. Pp. 291-93, 711.
   Wellwarth briefly refers to Oh Dad, which he finds highly original, and the youthful Kopit who is a potential new wave American dramatist.

Wily, Hans-Werner. "Arthur Kopit: Indians." In Herbert Grabes, ed. Das amerikanische Drama der Gegenwart. Kronberg: Athenäum, 1976. Pp. 44-64.
   Hans-Werner Wily discusses Indians as an example of the mature Kopit's work and its relevancy to current American political and social problems.

II. REVIEWS

THE DAY THE WHORES CAME OUT TO PLAY TENNIS

New York Times, 16 March 1965, p. 45:1.

Time, 26 March 1965, p. 58.

Oliver, Edith. New Yorker, 27 March 1965, pp. 146-47.
   Despite some funny lines, Oliver feels this production "just rattles along, without ever taking off."

Newsweek, 29 March 1965, p. 82.

Nation, 5 April 1965, p. 374.

New Republic, 10 April 1965, p. 24.

Vogue, May 1965, p. 142.

INDIANS

Barnes, Clive. New York Times, 9 July 1968, p. 30:2.
   Barnes reviews the world premiere in London commenting that "the play is at its best at its most serious."

New York Times, 21 July 1968, II:12:1.

Newsweek, 29 July 1968, p. 97.

New York Times, 18 May 1969, II:3:5.

New York Times, 27 May 1969, p. 43:1.

Time, 6 June 1969, p. 96.

Saturday Review, 7 June 1969, p. 24.

New York Times, 14 October 1969, p. 51:1.

New Yorker, 18 October 1969, pp. 149-50.

New York Times, 19 October 1969, II:1:1.

Time, 24 October 1969, p. 68.

Newsweek, 27 October 1969, pp. 137-38.

Vogue, November 1969, p. 88.

Nation, 3 November 1969, pp. 485-86.

Commonweal, 7 November 1969, pp. 185-86.

America, 8 November 1969, p. 432.

New Republic, 8 November 1969, p. 24.

Dance Magazine, December 1969, pp. 30-31.

OH DAD, POOR DAD, MAMA'S HUNG YOU IN
THE CLOSET AND I'M FEELIN' SO SAD

New York Times, 6 July 1961, p. 19:2.

New Statesman, 14 July 1961, p. 64.

Spectator, 14 July 1961, p. 60.

Time, 14 July 1961, p. 72.

New York Times, 27 February 1962, p. 28:1.

New Yorker, 10 March 1962, pp. 84-85.

New York Times, 11 March 1962, II:1:1.

Saturday Review, 17 March 1962, p. 35.

New Republic, 19 March 1962, p. 31.

Nation, 31 March 1962, p. 289.

Commonweal, 6 April 1962, p. 41.

New York Times, 29 April 1962, II:3:1.

Educational Theatre Journal 14 (May 1962):169-71.
        John Gassner describes this absurdist play
    as simultaneously "an affront to the playgoer"
    and "a priceless pearl."

Theatre Arts 46 (May 1962):63.

National Review, 5 June 1962, pp. 416-17.

Hudson Review 15 (Summer 1962):267-68.

New York Times, 28 August 1963, p. 28:2.

New Statesman, 15 October 1965, p. 576.

SING TO ME THROUGH OPEN WINDOWS

New York Times, 16 March 1965, p. 45:2.

Newsweek, 29 March 1965, p. 82.

Clurman, Harold. Nation, 5 April 1965, p. 373.
        Clurman comments that Sing to Me is redeemed
    from banality by "a touch of unexpected color."

New Republic, 10 April 1965, p. 24.

WINGS

New York Times, 8 March 1978, III:16:1.

New York Times, 4 June 1978, II:1:1.

New York Times, 22 June 1978, III:20:5.

New York Times, 2 July 1978, II:1:1.

New Yorker, 3 July 1978, p. 70.

Time, 3 July 1978, p. 86.

New York, 10 July 1978, pp. 66-67.

Commonweal, 15 September 1978, p. 594.

New Yorker, 5 February 1979, p. 98.

Nation, 17 February 1979, p. 189.

New York Times, 18 February 1979, II:2:1.

New Leader, 26 February 1979, pp. 19-20.

New Yorker, 9 April 1979, pp. 33-35.

Gruen, John. "Wings on Broadway." Horizon 22, No. 5
        (May 1979), pp. 50-55.
            Gruen has great praise for actress Constance
    Cummings' tour-de-force portrayal of Kopit's
    elderly stroke victim, and interviews Cummings
    on her approach to the role as well as her entire
    theatrical career. Some mention is made ini-
    tially of how Kopit came to create the complex
    and demanding parts based on his own father's
    illness and death.

6 DAVID MAMET

Born November 30, 1947, Chicago, Illinois

David Mamet is one of America's most promising young playwrights. He draws heavily on his Chicago background to write bitter urban comedies, often with overtones of ethnicity or violence. Like England's Harold Pinter, Mamet has an uncanny ear for contemporary speech patterns. He selects exactly the word or phrase that will reveal a character's hidden personality traits or social background. In American Buffalo a junk dealer and his cronies involve the audience in a world of petty crime, gambling, and betrayal. Sexual Perversity in Chicago satirizes male masculinity myths as two Chicago bachelors swap stories of their real and imagined sexual conquests. A Life in the Theatre draws on the playwright's experiences in show business to explore the familiar stage-as-life metaphor but creates actor-characters who are both complex and believable. In another vein, Duck Variations is a classic two-man show in which two elderly Jewish men meet for chats in a city park and philosophize about the wonder of life and the inevitability of their own impending deaths. Mamet has taught at the University of Chicago, Marlboro College, and Goddard College in Vermont and has been connected with both the Goodman Theatre Company and the St. Nicholas Theatre Company in Chicago.

PRIMARY SOURCES

I. STAGE

American Buffalo. Staged Chicago, 1975; New York, 1976. New York: Samuel French, 1977.

_____. New York: Grove Press, 1977.

_____ (condensed). Best Plays of 1976-1977. Ed. Otis Guernsey. New York: Dodd, Mead, 1977.

Dark Pony. Staged New Haven, 1977; New York, 1979.

Duck Variations. Staged Plainfield, Vt., 1972; New York, 1975. In Sexual Perversity in Chicago and Duck Variations. New York: Grove Press, 1978.

_____. In Best Short Plays. Ed. Stanley Richards. New York: Chilton Book Company, 1977.

Lakeboat. Staged Marlboro, Vt., 1970.

A Life in the Theatre. Staged New York, 1977. New York: Grove Press, 1978.

Lone Canoe. Staged Chicago, 1979.

Mackinac (children's play). Staged New York, 1977.

Marranos. Staged New York, 1972.

Mr. Happiness. Staged New York, 1978. In The Water Engine and Mr. Happiness: Two Plays. New York: Grove Press, 1978.

The Poet and the Rent. Staged New York, 1974.

Reunion. Staged Chicago, 1976; New York, 1979.

The Revenge of the Space Panda.... Staged Chicago, 1977.

The Sanctity of Marriage. Staged New York, 1979.

A Sermon. Staged New York, 1981.

Sexual Perversity in Chicago. Staged Chicago, 1974; New York, 1975. In Sexual Perversity in Chicago and Duck Variations. New York: Grove Press, 1978.

Shoeshine. Staged New York, 1979.

Squirrels. Staged New York, 1972.

The Water Engine. Staged Chicago, 1977; New York, 1978. In The Water Engine and Mr. Happiness: Two Plays. New York: Grove Press, 1978.

The Woods. Staged Chicago, 1977; New York, 1977. New York: Grove Press, 1979.

II. FILM

The Postman Always Rings Twice, 1981.

III. NONFICTION

"David Mamet on His Play, A Life in the Theatre." New York Times, 16 October 1977, II:7:4.
          It is "a play about and in praise of actors." Mamet eulogizes the passing generation of actors and

initiates the new in his microcosm of a theater "that is always dying."

"Learn to Love the Theater." Horizon, October 1978, p. 96.
The task and responsibilities of actors and critics alike are the subject of Mamet's article. He demands an informed love and respect for the theater from both parties.

"Playwrights on Resident Theatres: What Is to Be Done?" Theater 10 (Summer 1979):82.
Mamet urges the unification of regional theaters: "It isn't sufficient anymore to see ourselves as the tools of the commercial stage; we have to get over our feeling of powerlessness."

IV. INTERVIEWS

Fraser, Gerald. "David Mamet (On His Career)." New York Times, 5 July 1976, 7:1.
Gerald Fraser's informal interview reveals some of the primary sources and influences for Mamet's plays--sexual myths and writing at Goddard.

Gottlieb, Richard. "The Engine That Drives Playwright David Mamet." New York Times, 15 January 1978, II:1.
An interview which reveals Mamet's perception of the theater's role in America, where "a play which doesn't soothe or reinforce certain preconceived notions in an audience, simply baffles them."

SECONDARY SOURCES

I. CRITICISM

"CBS Fellowships in Creative Writing" (at Yale School of Drama, awards go to David Mamet, Eric Bentley, William Hauptman and Arthur Kopit). New York Times, 27 October 1976, 55:2.

"David Mamet Weds Lindsay Crouse, Daughter of Late Playwright Russel Crouse." New York Times, 22 December 1977, II, 6:4.
Announcement of the playwright's marriage.

Eder, Richard. "David Mamet's New Realism." New York Times Magazine, 12 March 1978, pp. 40-43.
The author traces Mamet's movement away from the absurd. Structure, language, and character begin to demonstrate an increase in action, a release from isolation, and a celebration of life.

Gussow, Mel. "New American Playwrights: David Mamet, Albert Innaurato, Christopher Durang and Michael Cristofer." New York Times, 13 February 1977, II:1:4.
Mel Gussow's article cites the similar characteristics of these new playwrights--"comic impulse,

sense of moral dismay, and heightened social consciousness"--and reviews the development of their
individual careers.

Kalem, T. E. "Pinter Patter." Time, 12 July 1976, p. 68.
    Kalem compares Mamet's naturalistic speech to
    Pinter's.

Kroll, J. "Musak Man." Newsweek, 28 February 1977,
    p. 79.
        The author calls Mamet a "language playwright."
    "Mamet's ear is tuned to an American frequency."
    His reproduction of what he hears is not mere dupli-
    cation but "a kind of verbal cubism."

Lawson, S. "Language Equals Action." Horizon, November
    1977, pp. 40-45.
        Though Lawson's article is primarily concerned
    with the language in Mamet's plays, he also treats
    other salient characteristics: veering from the
    predictable, talking-as-action, predominant usage of
    animal names in titles, and small casts. All under-
    score his great "economy of means."

"New American Playwrights of the 70's: The Way They Are
    Shaping Theater." New York Times, 21 August 1977,
    II:1:3.
        Mamet is called a strong new voice in the
    theatre.

"Producer Jane Harmon Interviewed on A Life in the
    Theater." New York Times, 4 December 1977, 23, 2:1.
        Harmon discusses her faith in Mamet's talent
    and in A Life in the Theatre in particular.

"Star Ellis Rabb Interviewed on A Life in the Theater."
    New York Times, 20 November 1977, II:6:1.
        Rabb discusses his first meeting with Mamet and
    his acceptance of the leading role in the play.

Storey, Robert. "The Masking of David Mamet." Hollins
    Critic 16 (1979):1-11.
        Storey offers one of the more complete assess-
    ments of Mamet's impact on the stage thus far. His
    major themes are analyzed, along with his character-
    izations and dialogue, and he is placed in the con-
    text of the last decade of American drama.

Valleley, J. "David Mamet Makes a Play for Hollywood."
    Rolling Stone, 3 April 1970, p. 44.

Witt, L. "David Mamet." People, 12 November 1979, p. 58.
        This provides brief biography of Mamet and dis-
    cussion of his high output and critical success in
    the last half of the seventies.

II. REVIEWS

AMERICAN BUFFALO

New York Times, 28 January 1976, p. 30:4.

New Yorker, 9 February 1976, p. 81.

New Yorker, 28 February 1977, pp. 54-56.

Time, 28 February 1977, pp. 54-57.

Nation, 12 March 1977, p. 313.

Saturday Review, 2 April 1977, p. 37.

America, 16 April 1977, p. 364.

Plays and Players 24 (June 1977):37.

Simon, John. "American Buffalo." Hudson Review 30
(Summer 1977):259-60.
Simon comments: "I think that when language is used truly poetically it becomes a
legitimate kind of action; the sense of inaction here is proof that the language of American Buffalo is not all that poetic. Moreover,
though I believe that gutter poetry is possible,
it can't be something that fails to move us in-
tellectually and emotionally." The reviewer
adds that the play fails to do this and simply
marks time with mildly funny verbalizations and
petty gripes, as "it retreats deeper and deeper
under the cover of a sheltering affectlessness."

Plays and Players 25 (August 1978):31.

Drama 130 (Autumn 1978):53.

DARK PONY

Fleckenstein, J. "Dark Pony." Educational Theatre
Journal 30 (October 1978):417-18.
Dark Pony is a successful curtain raiser
to Reunion, a loving father's bedtime story to
his daughter.

DUCK VARIATIONS

New York Times, 1 November 1975, p. 15:3.
Mamet tells a touching story of youth and
age in the context of an "unglamorous view of
the show business world."

New York Times, 30 November 1975, II:1-4.

New York Times, 17 June 1976, p. 29:1.

Time, 12 July 1976, p. 68.

New York Times, 15 August 1976, II:1:5.

A LIFE IN THE THEATRE

New York Times, 5 February 1977, p. 10:1.

New York Times, 21 October 1977, III:3:4.

New York Times, 30 October 1977, II:5:3.

New Yorker, 31 October 1977, pp. 115-16.
    Mamet's story of an aging actor being re-
    placed by his protegé is seen as a kind of
    "love letter to the theatre."

Time, 31 October 1977, p. 94.

Nation, 12 November 1977, p. 504.

America, 10 December 1977, p. 423.

Hudson Review 31 (Spring 1978):154-55.

Sultanik, Aaron. "Death and David Mamet." Midstream
    24 (1978):56-57.
    Mamet has captured "the inflections of the
    face behind the mask, but without revealing the
    face underneath the mask."

Plays and Players 26 (August 1979):25.

REUNION

Fleckenstein, J. "Reunion." Educational Theatre
    Journal 30 (October 1978):417-18.
    Reunion touchingly describes a lonely
    daughter's reconciliation with her once alco-
    holic father.

New York Times, 19 October 1979, III:3:4.

New Yorker, 29 October 1979, p. 81.

New York, 5 November 1979, p. 87.

Nation, 1 December 1979, p. 572.

SEXUAL PERVERSITY IN CHICAGO

New York Times, 1 November 1975, p. 15:3.
    The play deals with the mating habits of
    young people, describing male and female "bond-
    ings." More specifically male masculinity
    myths are satirized as is the mindless life-
    style of young single urbanites.

New Yorker, 10 November 1975, pp. 135-36.

New York Times, 17 June 1976, p. 29:1.

Time, 12 July 1976, p. 68.

New York Times, 15 August 1976, II:5:1.

Plays and Players 23 (September 1976):37.

Strothard, P. Plays and Players 25 (February 1978):
       30-31.
            After the original voice in Duck Varia-
       tions, Strothard finds the use of repetition,
       abbreviation, and total grammatical anarchy in
       Sexual Perversity in Chicago "a retrograde
       step, a move towards the devouring standards of
       writing for television and film."

WATER ENGINE

New York Times, 6 January 1978, III:3:1.

New York Times, 15 January 1978, II:3:4.

New Yorker, 16 January 1978, p. 69.

Newsweek, 16 January 1978, p. 69.

Nation, 28 January 1978, p. 92.

New York, 30 January 1978, p. 60.

New York Times, 19 February 1978, II:3:1.

Saturday Review, 4 March 1978, p. 41.

Time, 20 March 1978, p. 84.

America, 8 April 1978, p. 286.

New York Times, 9 April 1978, II:6:6.

Commonweal, 14 April 1978, p. 244.

Harpers, May 1978, pp. 86-87.
            This is generally a negative review of the
       play suggesting that the playwright has devel-
       oped "an allegory of the emptiness of our cul-
       ture," which tends to produce anger in the au-
       dience.

THE WOODS

New Yorker, 7 May 1979, p. 130.

New York, 14 May 1979, p. 75.

Nation, 19 May 1979, pp. 581-82.
　　　Harold Clurman finds at fault the language
and behavior of the characters, saying that
they are "too concrete and superficially recognizable to take wing."　He adds that the audience fails "to learn anything beyond their immediate and unexceptional situation."　The
playwright creates no new insight, psychological or intuitive, and the symbolism evokes
nothing.

7 DAVID RABE

Born March 10, 1940, Dubuque, Iowa

Following the production of his first two plays,
David Rabe was recognized as a major new playwright. Both
Sticks and Bones and The Basic Training of Pavlo Hummel
dealt with issues of war, although Rabe, believing war to
be a permanent human ritual, has objected to being labeled
an "anti-war" dramatist. It is safer to say that he is
opposed to societal manipulation of individuals, whether
it takes the form of basic training exercises which pre-
pare Pavlo Hummel to accept a pointless death or the disturbing effects of mass television on the blinded veteran
and his family in Sticks and Bones. Rabe's later plays
have also concentrated on man's bellicose nature and his
susceptibility to destructive cultural myths. In this
sense there is a strong determinism in his works, and his
characters resemble classical tragic figures as they are
swept up in hostile forces; but Rabe has replaced the
ancient God with tyrannical, man-made institutions. Rabe
is not a "Broadway" writer and his works have mostly been
produced in subsidized public theatres. A master of
classical stage techniques, Rabe also has a fine ear for
dialogue, which occasionally raises his stage language to
the level of poetry. The anger and sense of loneliness
of his principal characters resulted in powerful theatre
in the early 1970s. A younger generation of theatregoers
is sometimes alienated by the implication that only those
who were young during the Vietnam years can understand
such rage and frustration. It remains to be seen if Rabe
can explore new materials and capture the imaginations of
theatre audiences of the 1980s and beyond.

PRIMARY SOURCES

I. STAGE

The Basic Training of Pavlo Hummel. Staged New York,
     1971. New York: French, 1972.

_____. _Scripts_ 1 (November 1971):56-92.

_____. In _The Off Off Broadway Book._ Ed. Albert Poland
and Bruce Mailman. Indianapolis: Bobbs-Merrill,
1972.

_____. In _The Basic Training of Pavlo Hummel, and
Sticks and Bones: Two Plays._ New York: Viking, 1973.

Boom Boom Room. See _In the Boom Boom Room._

Burning. Staged New York, 1974.

In the Boom Boom Room. Staged as _Boom Boom Room_, New York,
1973; revised version as _In the Boom Boom Room_, New
York, 1974. New York: Knopf, 1975; New York: French,
1975.

The Orphan. Staged New York, 1973. New York: French,
1975 (rewritten and revised).

Sticks and Bones. Staged Villanova, Pa., 1969; New York,
1971. New York: French, 1972 (rewritten and revised).

_____. In _The Basic Training of Pavlo Hummel, and
Sticks and Bones: Two Plays._ New York: Viking,
1973.

_____ (condensation). In _The Best Plays of 1971-1972:
The Burns Mantle Yearbook._ Ed. Otis L. Guernsey, Jr.
New York: Dodd, Mead, 1972.

_____. In _Best American Plays; 7th series 1967-1973._
Ed. Clive Barnes and John Gassner. New York: Crown,
1975.

_____. In Stanley Richards, ed. _The Tony Winners._
New York: Dodd, Mead, 1977.

_____. New York: French, 1979 (revised and rewritten).

Streamers. Staged New Haven and New York, 1976. New
York: Knopf, 1977.

_____ (condensation). In _The Best Plays of 1975-1976:
The Burns Mantle Yearbook._ Ed. Otis L. Guernsey,
Jr. New York: Dodd, Mead, 1976.

II. TRANSLATION

STICKS AND BONES

I Blinde. Tr. Bjørn Endreson. Oslo, 1972. Norwegian.

III. INTERVIEWS

Berkvist, Robert. "How Nichols and Rabe Shaped Streamers."
New York Times, 25 April 1976, II:1:1; p. 12:2-4.
    In a series of separate, condensed interviews
with Berkvist, director Mike Nichols and playwright
David Rabe discuss the long history of their association, leading up to Nichols' direction of
Streamers. Nichols analyzes the way he works as a
director and explains why the violence of Streamers
does not conflict with the usual lightheartedness of
his plays. Rabe comments on the effects of the "noncommercial violence" of his plays.

Gussow, Mel. "Rabe Is Compelled to Keep Trying." New
York Times, 12 May 1976, p. 34:1-4.
    Gussow reports that Streamers has just been named
play of the year by the New York Drama Critics Circle.
Rabe discusses his feelings toward playwrighting and
his brief departure from the theatre in 1975. He
explains the steps that went into writing Streamers
and mentions his own obsession with dehumanization.

_____. "Second David Rabe Play to Join Pavlo Hummel at
Public Theater." New York Times, 3 November 1971,
p. 43:1-5.
    Rabe is the only playwright besides Shakespeare
whose works Joseph Papp has produced simultaneously.
Papp speaks highly of Rabe, comparing him to O'Neill.
Rabe himself discusses his service in Vietnam and its
aftermath, which led to the writing of both Sticks
and Bones and Pavlo Hummel.

"Talk of the Town." New Yorker, 20 November 1979, pp. 48-49.
    Rabe describes his experiences as a G.I. in
Vietnam and his frustrations on returning home to
see how the war was misunderstood. He briefly mentions some of his views on language and on his personal life, and he praises producer Joseph Papp.

SECONDARY SOURCES

I. CRITICISM

Adler, T. P. "Blind Leading the Blind: Rabe's Sticks and
Bones and Shakespeare's King Lear." Pennsylvania
Language and Literature 15 (Spring 1979):203-06.
    Cited in Humanities Index, 1980. Not available
for annotation.

190

Asahina, Robert. "The Basic Training of American Play-
    wrights: Theater and the Vietnam War." Theatre
    Yearbook 9 (Spring 1978):30-37.
        Asahina recalls the theatre of the 1960s in a
    broad context of the arts in America and evaluates
    the "link between aesthetic and political radical-
    ism." From this viewpoint he looks at The Basic
    Training of Pavlo Hummel, Sticks and Bones, and
    Streamers, which comprise Rabe's trilogy of plays on
    Vietnam.

Bernstein, Samuel J. The Strands Entwined: A New Direc-
    tion in American Drama. Boston: Northeastern Uni-
    versity Press, 1980. Pp. 17-34.
        Bernstein believes a new wave of important
    drama begins in the 1970s, which blends the American
    naturalistic tradition with European absurdism. He
    is particularly drawn to Rabe's Sticks and Bones,
    which he compares to Arthur Miller's All My Sons.
    In both plays veterans return home to tragedy, but
    Rabe goes beyond Miller's realism in his depiction
    of Vietnam's aftermath.

Brown, Janet. Feminist Drama: Definition and Critical
    Analysis. Metuchen, N.J.: Scarecrow Press, 1979.
    Pp. 37-55.
        Brown devotes a chapter to Rabe, giving a brief
    biography of his life and discussing the audience's
    acceptance and rejection of his work. Primarily,
    she analyzes the character of Chrissy, the go-go
    dancer in In the Boom Boom Room. She considers the
    play "feminist drama because the pattern of the sym-
    bolic action is one of the agent, Chrissy, struggling
    for autonomy."

Brustein, Robert. "The Crack in the Chimney: Reflections
    on Contemporary American Playwrighting." Theater 9
    (1978):21-29.
        Rabe, among other American playwrights, does
    not follow the Ibsenite tradition in its departure
    from the law of cause and effect. America's stage
    is social, domestic, psychological, and realistic,
    hence causal. Rabe, a social dramatist, sketches a
    semi-surrealist portrait of middle-class guilt in
    Sticks and Bones.

Donohue, J. W. "Sticks and Bones on TV." America, 1
    September 1973, p. 120.
        The author defends the virtue of broadcasting
    Rabe's satire on war--its instructiveness.

"Experience Thing." Newsweek, 20 December 1971, p. 58.
        "Faithfulness to experience" is seen as the pre-
    eminent impulse of Rabe's creativity.

"First E. Hulk-K. Warriner Award Goes to Playwright David
Rabe." New York Times, 4 December 1971, p. 23:1.
Announcement of Rabe's selection for the award.

Gottfried, Martin. "David Rabe." In Contemporary Drama-
tists, 2nd ed. New York: St. Martin's Press, 1977.
Gottfried discusses the seminal works of Rabe--
Sticks and Bones and The Basic Training of Pavlo
Hummel--placing them "at a stylistic point between
naturalism and absurdism."

Kauffmann, S. "Sunshine Boys." New Republic, 26 May
1973, p. 22.
Kaufmann scorns theatre critics, "Sunshine Boys,"
who create an inflated estimation of certain playwrights' creative capacities. He views the career
of David Rabe as one example.

Kellman, Barnet. "David Rabe's 'The Orphan': A Peripatet-
ic Work in Progress." Theatre Quarterly 7 (Spring
1977):72-93.
Barnet Kellman directed The Orphan as it
reached its final form, and here he describes the
creative process through which this reworking of
Aeschylus' Oresteia was linked with the seventies
through the analogous horrors of My Lai and the Man-
son murders. An extremely detailed article working
both from the playwright's point of view and the
director's imagination.

Köhler, Klaus. "Das Underground Theatre." In Eberhard
Brüning, Klaus Köhler, and Bernhard Scheeler. Studien
zum amerikanischen Drama nach den zweiten Weltkrieg.
Berlin: Rütten and Loening, 1977. Pp. 178-213.
Like other recent critics (see Bernstein, S. J.),
Köhler sees a blending of realistic and surrealistic
elements in Rabe's work. He compares the returning
veteran's disillusioned middle-class parents in
Sticks and Bones with Miller's tragic Willy Loman.
They have all been destroyed by the false promises
of a materialistic culture.

Marranca, Bonnie. "David Rabe's Viet Nam Trilogy."
Canadian Theater Review 5 (Spring 1977):86-92.
Cited by Carpenter, Charles, "Annual Checklist."
Modern Drama 20 (June 1980):81. Not available for
annotation.

"Prince of the City." New York Times, 13 July 1978, III:
22:1.
Article containing historical basis for Robert
Daley's "Prince of the City" which likens the corrupt network of cops to "Renaissance Princes." Brian
DePalma is to direct the film, Rabe will write the
script, and John Travolta is being sought to play
leading character. [Film was later made, directed
by Sidney Lumet, with screenplay by Lumet and Jay
Presson Allen, starring Treat Williams.]

"Tony Award to Sticks and Bones." New York Times, 24
    April 1972, p. 40:1.
            Sticks and Bones is named "Best Dramatic Play."

"Vietnam." New York Times, 7, 9, 11, 18, 20 March; 1, 9,
    12 April; 24 May; 14 July; 12 August; 2, 26 September,
    1973.
            Articles discussing controversy over showing
    Sticks and Bones on TV when POWs were returning.
    Show postponed by CBS' Paley, then ultimately shown.

Weales, Gerald. Commonweal, 10 March 1972, pp. 14-15.
            In this article-review, Weales discusses new
    versions of plays which Rabe, "fresh from Vietnam,
    wrote as a student at Villanova." Weales calls Rabe
    "the most successful serious playwright to turn up
    in American theatre in recent years." Still he be-
    lieves the title character of Pavlo Hummel is a mix-
    ture of two pacifist stereotypes, the Falstaffian
    clown victim-hero and the sentimental sacrificial
    innocent. He prefers Sticks and Bones, which while
    equally overstated with clichés, has a dramatic in-
    tensity, especially in the final wrist-cutting sui-
    cide. Weales notes: "Rabe is using the obvious
    fakery of television to question the reality of mid-
    dle-class America, the behavioral empty shell which
    leads not simply to high Nielsen ratings but to My
    Lai."

Werner, Craig. "Primal Screams and Nonsense Rhymes:
    David Rabe's Revolt." Educational Theatre Journal
    30 (December 1978):517-29.
            Werner says Rabe is like many classic American
    writers in that he is trapped between irreconcilable
    forces of transcendence and reality. Problems of
    language are at the center of his Vietnam trilogy.
    In Pavlo Hummel Rabe explores the alienating effect
    of the "debased American language." In Sticks and
    Bones this debasement is linked to "the characteris-
    tic American refusal to accept reality." In Streamers
    he reveals the "insurmountable barriers to human com-
    munication."

II. REVIEWS

THE BASIC TRAINING OF PAVLO HUMMEL

    New York Times, 21 May 1971, p. 25:1.

    New Yorker, 29 May 1971, p. 55.

    New York Times, 30 May 1971, II:3:4.

Clurman, Harold. Nation, 7 June 1971, p. 733.
    Clurman says that Pavlo Hummel is "the
first play provoked by the Viet Nam disaster
which has made a real impression on me," and
notes that Hummel's murder by a fellow G.I. in
a brothel "has nothing to do with the issues of
war, but much to do with war itself."

Newsweek, 14 June 1971, p. 70.

Saturday Review, 10 July 1971, p. 36.

New York Times, 11 July 1971, II:1:1.

New York Times, 14 November 1971, II:1:5.

New York Times, 7 December 1971, p. 55:1.

Saturday Review, 26 February 1972, 43-44.

Commonweal, 10 March 1972, pp. 14-15.

Time, 24 April 1972, p. 66.

New Yorker, 2 May 1977, p. 91.

Time, 9 May 1977, p. 50.

Nation, 14 May 1977, p. 602.

IN THE BOOM BOOM ROOM

New York Times, 9 November 1973, p. 31:1.
        Women are seen as victims in American
    society.

New York Times, 18 November 1973, II:3:1.

New Yorker, 19 November 1973, p. 84.

Newsweek, 19 November 1973, p. 96.

Time, 19 November 1973, p. 96.

Nation, 26 November 1973, p. 572.

New Republic, 1 December 1973, p. 22.

Washington Post, 2 December 1973, K:1:4.

Nation, 3 December 1973, p. 603.

Commonweal, 14 December 1973, pp. 294-95.

America, 22 December 1973, p. 485.

Williams, Gary Jay. <u>National</u> <u>Review</u>, 26 January
1974, pp. 90-91.
Williams calls <u>In</u> <u>The</u> <u>Boom</u> <u>Boom</u> <u>Room</u> a
"static coarse play about an unstable go-go
girl with no place to go."

<u>Hudson</u> <u>Review</u> 27 (Spring 1974):85-90.

<u>New</u> <u>York</u> <u>Times</u>, 5 December 1974, p. 55:1.

<u>New</u> <u>Yorker</u>, 9 December 1974, p. 69.

<u>Newsweek</u>, 16 December 1974, p. 105.

<u>Nation</u>, 28 December 1974, p. 701.

<u>Drama</u> 124 (Spring 1977):61.

THE ORPHAN

<u>New</u> <u>York</u> <u>Times</u>, 19 April 1973, p. 51:1.

<u>New</u> <u>Yorker</u>, 28 April 1973, p. 105.
Edith Oliver dislikes this play, arguing
that "it is possible to be overwhelmed by the
Greek dramatists, but it does seem a mistake to
reshape their subject matter into handy 'rele-
vance' to current events."

<u>New</u> <u>York</u> <u>Times</u>, 29 April 1973, II:1:1.

<u>Newsweek</u>, 30 April 1973, p. 87.

<u>Time</u>, 30 April 1973, p. 90.

<u>America</u>, 12 May 1973, pp. 444-45.

STICKS AND BONES

<u>New</u> <u>York</u> <u>Times</u>, 8 November 1971, p. 53:1.

<u>New</u> <u>Yorker</u>, 20 November 1971, p. 114.

<u>Nation</u>, 22 November 1971, p. 539.

<u>Time</u>, 22 November 1971, p. 93.

<u>Saturday</u> <u>Review</u>, 27 November 1971, pp. 70-71.

<u>Newsweek</u>, 29 November 1971, p. 110.

Kauffmann, Stanley. <u>New</u> <u>Republic</u>, 4 December 1971,
p. 22.
Kauffmann says of <u>Sticks</u> <u>and</u> <u>Bones</u>: "When
the dialogue is deliberately wrong, it's appropriately grotesque. When it tries to be 'fine,'

it's corny." He claims that Rabe's "vision is
insufficient," and that "he has seen little that
every member of the audience hasn't seen for
himself."

New York Times, 2 March 1972, p. 33:2.

New Yorker, 11 March 1972, p. 82.

New York Times, 12 March 1972, II:3:4.

America, 18 March 1972, p. 295.

New York Times, 12 March 1973, p. 36:2.

Washington Post, 26 August 1973, C:3:1.

Strothard, P. Plays and Players 25 (April 1978):24-
25.
    Unfavorable review of Sticks and Bones and
Streamers, citing political naiveté as the flaw
--"Can Rabe really be suggesting that American
blood lust did not begin with the Vietnam war?"
Also Strothard discounts the fact that Streamers
is a continuation of the Vietnam trilogy--The
Basic Training of Pavlo Hummel, The Orphan,
and Sticks and Bones.

STREAMERS

New York Times, 22 February 1976, II:1:7.

Newsweek, 23 February 1976, p. 89.

Saturday Review, 17 April 1976, p. 48.

New York Times, 22 April 1976, p. 38:5.

New York Times, 2 May 1976, II:5:1.

New Yorker, 3 May 1976, pp. 76-77.

Time, 3 May 1976, p. 75.

Nation, 8 May 1976, p. 574.

America, 15 May 1976, p. 432.

Commonweal, 21 May 1976, pp. 334-35.

New Republic, 12 June 1976, p. 20.

196

Richardson, J. Commentary 62 (July 1976):61-63.
    Richardson declares: "In Streamers, Rabe
    presents a social microcosm that has achieved
    neither spiritual nor practical goals of the
    old war dramas."

Fleckenstein, Joan S. Educational Theatre Journal
    28 (October 1976):408-09.
        Although Fleckenstein praises Rabe's "mar-
    velous ear for dialogue and his ability to
    evoke unexpected laughter," she finds the first
    act, which introduces characters waiting in a
    barracks before leaving for Vietnam, static.
    The violence of the second act is gratuitous,
    however, and the homosexual theme undeveloped.
    Fleckenstein notes that "Streamers" refers to
    the faulty unopened parachutes of soldiers who
    tumble to their deaths.

Atlantic, December 1976, pp. 108-09.

"David Rabe's Streamers at the Arena Stage." Wash-
    ington Post, 13 January 1977, C:1:6.

Drama, 128 (Spring 1978):69-70.

Aaron, J. Educational Theatre Journal 30 (May 1978):
    271.

8 SAM SHEPARD

Born Samuel Shepard Rogers VII, November 5, 1943,
Sheridan, Illinois

    Having written more than thirty plays in a decade
and a half, Sam Shepard is one of this country's most inventive and prolific playwrights. Television, old movies,
and romantic American myths provide him with characters
and settings. He has a fine ear for the sixties vernacu-
lar, especially apparent in the conversations of characters who belong to the drug or rock music cultures, and
his outrageously funny protagonists deliver monologues of
absurd but entertaining complexity. Frequently the playwright hints that he is nostalgic for an age when simple
heroes could be praised for honest values. Anachronisms
of time and setting, such as his linking of Mae West and
Marlene Dietrich with Paul Bunyan and Jesse James in Mad
Dog Blues, allow him to mix fantasy and folklore with
social commentary. Other plays combine pop music and
biography to produce a media event like Seduced, which
presents the haunting story of a man who resembles Howard
Hughes. Critics of Shepard sometimes lament his loose
plot construction, his occasionally improbable dialogue,
and his extravagant use of symbols or dream elements, but
they cannot overlook this wild new talent which is both
comical and disturbing. Winner of an Obie Award for "sustained achievement" in the theatre, he also received in
1979 a Pulitzer Prize for Buried Child.

PRIMARY SOURCES

I.   STAGE

Action. Staged London, 1974; New York, 1975. In Action
    and The Unseen Hand. London: Faber and Faber,
    1975.

Angel City. Staged San Francisco, 1976. In Angel City
    and Other Plays. New York: Urizen Press, 1976.

Back Bog Beast Bait. Staged New York, 1971. In The Un-
    seen Hand and Other Plays. Indianapolis: Bobbs-
    Merrill, 1971.

Blue Bitch. Staged New York, 1973.

Buried Child. Staged New Haven and New York, 1978. Pulitzer
    Prize. In Buried Child and Seduced and Suicide in
    B Flat. New York: Urizen Books, 1979.

Chicago. Staged New York, 1965. In Eight Plays from
    Off-Off Broadway. Ed. Nick Orzel and Michael T.
    Smith. Indianapolis: Bobbs-Merrill, 1966.

_____. In Five Plays. Indianapolis: Bobbs-Merrill,
    1967.

_____. In Five Plays. London: Faber and Faber, 1969.

Cowboy Mouth (with Patti Smith). Staged New York, 1971.
    In Mad Dog Blues and Other Plays. New York: Winter
    House, 1971.

_____. In Winter Repertory 4 (1972).

Cowboys. Staged New York, 1964.

Cowboys #2. Staged Los Angeles, 1967. In Collision
    Course. Ed. Edward Parone. New York: Random House,
    1968.

_____. In Mad Dog Blues and Other Plays. New York:
    Winter House, 1971.

_____. In Winter Repertory 4 (1972).

Curse of the Starving Class. Staged London, 1977; New
    York, 1978. In Angel City and Other Plays. New
    York: Urizen Press, 1976.

Dog. Staged New York, 1965.

Florence Nightingale Sings. Staged London, 1969.

4-H Club. Staged New York, 1965. In Mad Dog Blues and
    Other Plays. New York: Winter House, 1971.

Forensic and the Navigators. Staged New York, 1967. In
    The Best of Off-Off Broadway. Ed. Michael T. Smith.
    New York: Dutton, 1969.

_____. In The Unseen Hand and Other Plays. Indianapolis: Bobbs-Merrill, 1971.

Fourteen Hundred Thousand. Staged Minneapolis, c. 1966. In Five Plays. Indianapolis: Bobbs-Merrill, 1967.

_____. Included in Five Plays. London: Faber and Faber, 1969.

Geography of a Horse Dreamer. Staged New Haven, 1974. In The Tooth of Crime, and Geography of a Horse Dreamer. New York: Grove Press, 1974; London: Faber and Faber, 1974.

_____. In Four Two Act Plays. London: Faber, 1974.

Holy Ghostly. Staged New York, 1970. In The Unseen Hand and Other Plays. Indianapolis: Bobbs-Merrill, 1971.

_____. In Best Short Plays of the World Theatre 1968-1973. Ed. Stanley Richards. New York: Crown, 1973.

Icarus's Mother. Staged New York, 1965. In Five Plays. Indianapolis: Bobbs-Merrill, 1967.

_____. In Five Plays. London: Faber and Faber, 1969.

Inacoma. Staged San Francisco, 1977.

Killer's Head. Staged New York, 1975.

La Turista. Staged New York, 1967. Indianapolis: Bobbs-Merrill, 1968.

_____. London: Faber and Faber, 1969.

_____. In Four Two Act Plays. Indianapolis: Bobbs-Merrill, 1980.

Little Ocean. Staged London, 1974.

Mad Dog Blues. Staged New York, 1971. In Mad Dog Blues and Other Plays. New York: Winter House, 1971.

Melodrama Play. Staged New York, 1966. In Five Plays. Indianapolis: Bobbs-Merrill, 1967.

_____. In Five Plays. London: Faber and Faber, 1969.

Nightwalk (with Megan Terry and Jean-Claude van Itallie). Staged New York, 1973.

Operation Sidewinder. Staged New York, 1970. In Esquire, May 1969, pp. 152 et passim.

_____. Indianapolis: Bobbs-Merrill, 1970.

_____. In The Great American Life Show. Ed. John Lahr and J. Price. New York: Bantam, 1976.

_____. In Four Two Act Plays. Indianapolis: Bobbs-Merrill, 1980.

Red Cross. Staged New York, 1966. In Five Plays. Indianapolis: Bobbs-Merrill, 1967.

_____. In Five Plays. London: Faber and Faber, 1969.

Rock Garden. Staged New York, 1964; excerpt in Oh! Calcutta!; New York, 1969.

_____. In The Unseen Hand and Other Plays. Indianapolis: Bobbs-Merrill, 1971.

_____. In Scripts, 1 (January 1972):24-30.

_____. In Winter Repertory 4 (1972).

Rocking Chair. Staged New York, 1964.

Savage Love. Staged San Francisco, 1978; New York, 1979.

Seduced. Staged Providence, 1978; New York, 1979. In Buried Child and Seduced and Suicide in B Flat. New York: Urizen Press, 1979.

Shaved Splits. Staged New York, 1969. In The Unseen Hand and Other Plays. Indianapolis: Bobbs-Merrill, 1971.

Suicide in B Flat. Staged New York, 1976. In Buried Child and Seduced and Suicide in B Flat. New York: Urizen Press, 1979.

Tongues (with Joseph Chaikin). Staged San Francisco, 1978; New York, 1979.

The Tooth of Crime. Staged London, 1972; Oswego, N.Y., and New York, 1973. In Performance 5 (March-April 1973):67-91.

_____. In The Tooth of Crime, and Geography of a Horse Dreamer. New York: Grove Press, 1974.

_____. In Four Two Act Plays. Indianapolis: Bobbs-Merrill, 1980.

_____. In Four Two Act Plays. London: Faber and Faber, 1974.

<u>True</u> <u>West</u>. Staged New York, 1980.

<u>The</u> <u>Unseen</u> <u>Hand</u>. Staged New York, 1970. In <u>The</u> <u>Unseen</u>
<u>Hand</u> <u>and</u> <u>Other</u> <u>Plays</u>. Indianapolis: Bobbs-Merrill,
1971.

_____. In <u>Plays</u> <u>and</u> <u>Players</u> 20 (May 1973):i-xi.

_____. In <u>Action</u> <u>and</u> <u>The</u> <u>Unseen</u> <u>Hand</u>. London: Faber
and Faber, 1975.

<u>Up</u> <u>to</u> <u>Thursday</u>. Staged New York, 1965.

II. FILM

<u>Me</u> <u>and</u> <u>My</u> <u>Brother</u>, with Robert Frank, 1967.

<u>Ringaleevio</u>, with Murray Mednick, 1971.

<u>Zabriskie</u> <u>Point</u>, with others, 1970.

III. FICTION

<u>Hawk</u> <u>Moon</u>. Los Angeles: Black Sparrow Press, 1972.

IV. NON-FICTION

"Metaphors, Mad Dogs and Old-Time Cowboys." <u>Theater</u>
<u>Quarterly</u> 4 (August-October 1974):3-16.
Tracing his careers as playwright and director,
Shepard pleads for spontaneity in the theatre, arguing that he never conducts elaborate research on
his plays nor rewrites. All of his writing derives
from "mental pictures" which result from his personal
experiences.

(With Tom Sankly). "OOB and the Playwright: Two Commentaries." <u>Works</u> 1 (Winter 1968):70-73.
OOB stands for Off-Off Broadway. While Shepard
admits that the OOB theatre generally makes a
counter-establishment statement, he is more concerned with gaining exposure for his plays in any
arena than he is with expressing his contempt for
Broadway.

<u>Rolling</u> <u>Thunder</u> <u>Logbook</u>. Illustrated. New York:
Viking Press, 1977.
A collection of folk songs, primarily for
children.

"Sam Shepard, Playwright." Performing Arts Journal 26
(Fall 1977):13-24.
Shepard discusses the impact of drugs on himself and his friends and of the Vietnam war on
American life. Speaking of experimental theatre,
he complains that critics remain devoted to traditional plays, but there is a growing audience for
experimental theatre.

"Time." Theater (New Haven) 9 (Spring 1978):9.
Shepard argues that a playwright alone has the
right to decide if a one-act or two-act play is
better suited to his thematic purposes. He laments
the commercial pressure on writers and audiences to
equate a "major" work with a longer one.

"Visualization, Language and the Inner Library." Drama
Review 21 (December 1977):49-58.
Shepard discusses his approach to playwrighting.
He believes "ideas emerge from plays not the other
way around." He writes for the audience--himself.
At first he refused to rewrite plays since their
faults were "part and parcel of the original process" but now he does some limited rewriting to ac-
commodate differences between the spoken and written
word.

V.   TRANSLATION

LA TURISTA

La Turista. Tr. by Elena Reina. Siparo 25 (February
1970):50-64. Italian.

VI. INTERVIEW

Goldberg, Robert. "Sam Shepard, Off-Broadway's Street
Cowboy." College Papers (Winter 1980):43-45.
Introduced by a brief biographical summary, including Shepard's comment on his actress-wife
Olan and his son Jesse Mojo: "I dreamed about this
family, and it's come true," this extensive interview, given on the California set of Resurrection,
covers all the usual questions about background,
work, and friends. Shepard's answers include some
interesting sidelights on drugs and the '60s, the
role of music, especially jazz, on his work, and
Patti Smith's influence on his writing. There are
some excerpts from her "Sam Shepard--9 Random
Years (7+2)." LeRoi Jones is called the greatest
American playwright and Peter Handke "the best in
the world," after Beckett. Of his craft, Shepard
says: "I write because it's thrilling."

SECONDARY SOURCES

I. CRITICISM

Aaron, J. "Angel City." Educational Theatre Journal 29
     (October 1977):415-16.
          Aaron analyzes three plays which emphasize the
     surrender of America to cinematic dreams. Merton
     of the Movies by George S. Kaufman and Marc Connelly
     and A History of the American Film by Christopher
     Durang are compared to Shepard's Angel City. In all
     three the socialization and corruption of America by
     Hollywood are subjects for disturbing satire.

Bachman, Charles R. "Defusion of Menace in the Plays of
     Sam Shepard." Modern Drama 19 (December 1976):405-
     16.
          Bachman has written one of the most sustained
     and perceptive analyses of Shepard's work, praising
     his transformation of "the original stereotyped
     characters and situations into an imaginative, lin-
     guistically brilliant, quasi-surrealistic chemistry
     of text and stage presentation which is original and
     authentically his own." Bachman considers Chicago,
     Cowboy Mouth, Tooth of Crime, and Forensic and the
     Navigators Shepard's best plays because the theme of
     menace in each is undiluted by the force of surrealism
     that mars many of his works.

Chubb, K. "Fruitful Difficulties of Directing Shepard."
     Theatre Quarterly 4 (August 1974):17-25.
          Chubb, director of the Wakefield Tricycle
     Theatre Company, claims success in directing
     Shepard's plays, noting that he respected the play-
     wright's theatricality and sincerity. Shepard's
     sense of what is theatrically effective "goes beyond
     rules and preconceptions." The lack of traditional
     structure in his plays has frustrated many directors,
     including Charles Marowitz and Richard Schechner.
     Chubb suggests one must intuit Shepard's intentions.

Coe, Robert. "Saga of Sam Shepard." New York Times
     Magazine, 23 November 1980, pp. 56-58, 118, 120,
     122, 124.
          Coe characterizes the playwright-actor turned
     cow-puncher and rodeo rider as a recluse from the
     theatrical mainstream. He comments on Shepard's
     fascination with myth, his original voice, his ver-
     nacular rhythms, and his preoccupation with family
     plays. True West, a play about two brothers, ex-
     tends one of Shepard's persistent themes, "the dis-
     location and impermanence which has characterized
     the American experience since World War II." The

latter part of the article includes biographical data: the English years, Off Off Broadway, and now San Francisco's Magic Theater. In all his work Shepard reflects "his experience of a wilderness where America has always hidden its promise and its dream."

Cohn, Ruby. "Sam Shepard." In Contemporary Dramatists. Ed. James Vinson. London: St. James Press; New York: St. Martin's Press, 1973. Pp. 722-23.
    According to Cohn, Shepard has absorbed American pop art, media myths, and the Southwestern Scene, "and has created image-focused plays in which the characters speak inventive idioms in vivid rhythms." She singles out The Tooth of Crime, La Turista, and Mad Dog Blues for special praise. Shepard's language, particularly his command of slang, is his most distinctive attribute.

Davis, R. A. "'Get up Out a' Your Homemade Beds': The Plays of Sam Shepard." Players 47 (1972):12-19.
    Davis laments the thematic poverty of Shepard's plays. All of his plays deal monotonously with the need for the individual to find a temporary shelter in a harsh world. Nevertheless, Davis comments on Shepard's brilliant theatricality.

Fennell, P. J. "Angel City." Educational Theatre Journal 29 (March 1977):112-13.
    Fennell offers more than a review of Angel City. He discusses Shepard's ability to work with mixed media, in this case film and music, as well as stage action. He notes the recurrent theme of the artist destroyed by success, also apparent in The Tooth of Crime and Suicide in B Flat.

Frutkin, Ren. "Sam Shepard: Paired Existence Meets the Monster." Yale/Theater 2 (Spring 1969):22-30.
    Long discussions of Cowboys #2 and La Turista appear in this article. The central subject of theatre in 1969, Frutkin believes, is the "value of performance." By "performance" he means "the shared style of a generation, the theatricalization of everyday life." In Shepard's plays actors play characters playing actors. But Frutkin believes Shepard is trying to save his audiences from confusing "role-playing" with life by "theatrically rescuing the imagination from total theatricalization."

Gelber, Jack. "Sam Shepard: The Playwright as Shaman." Introduction to Angel City and Other Plays, by Sam Shepard. New York: Urizen Books, 1976. Pp. 1-4.
    Gelber holds that Shepard's plays are dramatic "trips," that his characters are "on trips," and that the plays themselves "are in the form of trips, quests, adventures." Saying Shepard is as American

as peyote, magic mushrooms, rock and roll, Gelber insists that he is the modern equivalent of a primitive Shaman who "directly confronts the supernatural for purposes of cures."

Kleb, William. "Shepard and Chaikin Speaking in Tongues." Theater (New Haven) 10 (February 1978):66-69.
Kleb praises the performance of Tongues at San Francisco's Magic Theatre by Shepard and Joseph Chaikin. A short play of supposed dream sequences, Kleb believes it is "an obvious declaration of aesthetic principles." Actor and playwright function as one in the play so that the staging emphasizes the "shared vision of the role of the artist."

Lawson, Carol. "Two Shepard Plays Opening Tuesday at the Other Stage." New York Times, 31 October 1979, p. C28.
Lawson quotes Joseph Papp as saying that he will produce any of Shepard's plays "whether I like them or not." In this case forthcoming productions of Savage Love and Tongues are discussed. Both had been performed the previous summer at the Eureka Theatre Festival in California. Neither play is discussed in detail.

Marranca, Bonnie. "Alphabetical Shepard." Performing Arts Journal 5 (1981):9-25.
Marranca says Shepard holds the "radical ideal of an authorless work and the denial of the Author as Myth." He substitutes myth for history and experience for theory. Marranca defines certain terms which characterize Shepard's approach to theater, such as "geographies of the spirit" and "the rhythm of imagery." She offers a kind of lexicon to his works.

Rosen, C. "Sam Shepard's Angel City: A Movie for the Stage." Modern Drama 22 (March 1979):39-46.
Rosen calls Shepard a "playwright of zap-pop-pow action" and of "comic book verbs." Like other critics, she notes his obsession with power but her real interest here is with his translation of film techniques--jump-cuts, splicing, etc.--to the stage, all quite appropriate in Angel City which is set in a movie studio. Shepard's plays often depict movies as the ultimate drug, dulling the ethical and moral values of the public.

"Sam Shepard." New York Times, 12 November 1969, p. 42:1.

"Sam Shepard: Biographical Sketch and Portrait." New York Times, 17 April 1979, II:8:5.

"Sam Shepard Wins Pulitzer Prize for Drama (for Buried
    Child)." New York Times, 17 April 1979, p. 1:2.
        An announcement of the Pulitzer committee de-
    cision.

Schechner, Richard. "Drama, Script, Theatre, Performance."
    Drama Review 17 (September 1973):5-36.
        Schechner uses Shepard's The Tooth of Crime as
    an example of the breakdown of barriers between illu-
    sion and reality in the theatre. Until recently
    drama in the Western world preceded the script. The
    reversal of this process limits the effectiveness of
    theatre. "The drama is the domain of the author ...
    the script ... of the teacher."

Shayon, R. L. "T.V. and Radio: Plays Broadcast on WRVR."
    Saturday Review, 9 April 1966, p. 52.
        Shayon briefly comments on Shepard's radio
    plays, Icarus and 4-H Club, both produced when the
    author was 22 years old. Shayon notes "ominous
    overtones of violence and horror in the works" and
    believes their meaning is veiled and abstract.

Simon, John. "Theatre Chronicle: Kopit, Norman, and
    Shepard." Hudson Review 32 (Spring 1979):77-88.
        Simon brilliantly connects these three very
    different plays by showing that in each "language is
    the learnt important element" and that the characters
    in all these plays have split personalities. He
    asks, "has the recession of the word caused the loss
    of a sense of full unified selfhood? Or is it the
    other way around?" Kopit's Wings reveals a new
    maturity in the playwright. Simon praises Kopit's
    skillful handling of multiple perspectives. He finds
    the meaning of Shepard's Buried Child elusive but
    records the disturbing power of the playwright's
    symbols and images. Marsha Norman's Getting Out is
    called "an astonishing first play."

Smith, Patti. "Sam Shepard: 9 Random Years [7 + 2]."
    Poem in Angel City and Other Plays. New York:
    Urizen Press, 1976. Pp. 241-45.
        Smith has written a "biographical" poem which
    recounts Shepard's love-life experiences. It cap-
    tures the spirit that inhabits many of Shepard's
    plays.

Stambolian, George. "Shepard's Mad Dog Blues: A Trip
    Through Popular Culture." Journal of Popular Cul-
    ture 7, pp. 777-86.
        Stambolian believes that Shepard in all of his
    plays is searching for "a new mythology," which will
    be "based on the heart's truth." Shepard perceives
    the destructiveness of myths based on popular cul-
    ture and the particular vulnerability of the artist
    to these myths. Stambolian suggests Shepard's

wild satire of false values indicates his search for truer, more realistic life goals.

Taëni, Rainer. Tendenzen des "neueren Theaters." II: Theater brief aus London. Merkur 24 (October 1970):971-78.
Taëni briefly mentions Shepard's plays Red Cross and Florence Nightingale Sings as examples of exciting new theatre being performed in London during the 1969-1970 theatre season.

Valgemae, Mardi. "Expressionism and the New American Drama." Twentieth Century Literature 17 (October 1971):227-34.
Valgemae briefly discusses Shepard's La Turista as an example of Off-Off Broadway expressionism. He suggests an allegorical interpretation of the play, that slavery turned Americans into monsters.

Ver Meulen, M. "Sam Shepard: Yes, Yes, Yes." Esquire, February 1980, pp. 79-81.
Ver Meulen provides a current biographical sketch of Shepard whom he calls "the hottest young playwright around." He speaks of the inscrutable qualities of his plays but notes their originality and magnetism, commenting as most critics do on the impact of visual and auditory images.

Weales, Gerald. "American Theatre Watch, 1978-1979." Georgia Review 33 (Fall 1979):569-81.
Calling Shepard "the most visible, the most successful, the most impressive representative of the unhousebroken avant-garde," Weales discusses Buried Child, Seduced, and Negrin's Jacaranda in detail. He believes Shepard's acting role in Malick's film Days of Heaven contributed to the movie's strong visual image and compares Days of Heaven's visual impact with the dramatic impact of Shepard's Buried Child. A sequence like Tilden's corn-shucking scene "may imply a dimly remembered sense of family, now broken" --as the clearing of the corn suggests vocation divorced from reality. Usually Shepard's themes defy paraphrase. In Seduced, however, "the multiple seductions of power and money" are clear themes; Jacaranda deals with the self-pity of a failed macho stud.

_____. "American Theatre Watch, 1977-1978." Georgia Review 33 (Fall 1979):515-27.
Weales in discussing the 1978 theatre season makes some perceptive comments about playwrights Ribman, Mamet, Kopit, and Shepard, among others. Ribman's Cold Storage which presents two terminally ill men in a cancer ward is praised for its avoidance of sentimentality. Mamet's Life in the Theatre is seen primarily as a "fragile theatre piece," but nevertheless his protagonist-actors are "metaphors

for all men." Kopit's <u>Wings</u> indicates his growth as a playwright in that the unlikely story of a stroke victim's progress becomes a theatrical tour de force. Shepard's <u>Curse of the Starving Class</u> brings the playwright out of the fantasy world and into realism.

II. DISSERTATION

Fennell, Patrick J. "Sam Shepard: The Flesh and Blood of Theatre." <u>Dissertation Abstracts</u> 38 (1977):3145A.
    Fennell's dissertation devotes a chapter each to Shepard's theatricalism, his use of the "transformations situation," his use of magic (including ritual and trance), his varied language (various forms of slang, Pinteresque ellipses, and futuristic jargon) and his reliance on the media. Fennell covers twenty-seven plays in the most wide-ranging study of the playwright to date.

III. REVIEWS

ACTION

Coveney, M. "Action." <u>Plays and Players</u> 22 (November 1974):29.

<u>New York Times</u>, 16 April 1975, p. 54:1.

<u>Nation</u>, 3 May 1975, p. 542.

<u>New Yorker</u>, 5 May 1975, p. 81.

Schechter,J. "Action." <u>Educational Theatre Journal</u> 27 (October 1975):421-22.

BACK BOG BEAST BAIT

<u>New York Times</u>, 15 January 1974, p. 29:1.

BURIED CHILD

<u>Newsweek</u>, 30 October 1978, p. 106.

<u>New Yorker</u>, 6 November 1978, pp. 151-52.

<u>New Yorker</u>, 27 November 1978, pp. 117-18.

<u>Nation</u>, 2 December 1978, pp. 621-22.

<u>Time</u>, 18 December 1978, p. 76.

<u>America</u>, 30 December 1978, p. 500.

Raidy, W. A. "Buried Child." _Plays_ and _Players_ 26
    (February 1979):36-37.
        Buried Child, "written in almost cartoon-
    like pen strokes," describes the disintegration
    of the American family. Raidy claims Shepard's
    "surrealism intertwined with anthropological
    symbolism of fecundity and sacrifice sometimes
    obscures his message of America's desecration."

CHICAGO

Nation, 4 April 1966, p. 405.

New York Times, 13 April 1966, p. 36:1.

Craig, R. "Chicago." _Drama_ 121 (Summer 1976):75-76.

COWBOY MOUTH/LITTLE OCEAN

Ansarge, P. "Cowboy Mouth/Little Ocean." _Plays_ and
    Players 21 (May 1974):45.

CURSE OF THE STARVING CLASS

Lahr, J. "Curse of the Starving Class." _Plays_ and
    Players 24 (June 1977):24-25.

Curtis, A. "Curse of the Starving Class." _Drama_
    125 (Summer 1977):60-61.

Adler, T. P. "Curse of the Starving Class." _Educa-
    tional Theatre Journal_ 29 (October 1977):409-10.
        The Curse, which had its premiere in London
    at the Royal Court, is an "old fashioned, evi-
    dently autobiographical" work. A family dis-
    pute over the ownership of an avocado farm is
    more successful on a symbolic than on a literal
    level. Images of characters staring into an
    empty refrigerator or descriptions of predatory
    animals devouring each other intensify this
    symbolism. In addition, the protagonist uri-
    nates on stage and covered in sheep's blood
    proceeds to gorge himself on salad.

New Yorker, 13 March 1978, pp. 57-58.

Time, 20 March 1978, pp. 84-85.

Nation, 25 March 1978, pp. 348-49.

America, 8 April 1978, p. 286.

New Republic, 8 April 1978, pp. 24-25.

FORENSIC AND THE NAVIGATORS

New York Times, 20 January 1968, p. 22:2.

New York Times, 2 April 1970, p. 43:1.

New Yorker, 11 April 1970, p. 83.

GEOGRAPHY OF A HORSE DREAMER

New York Times, 18 March 1974, p. 42:1.

Lahr, J. "Geography of a Horse Dreamer." Plays and Players 21 (April 1974):46-47.

Schechter, J. "Geography of a Horse Dreamer." Educational Theatre Journal 26 (October 1974):401-03.

Gussow, Mel. New York Times, 13 December 1975, p. 21:1.
Gussow feels that the New York production of Geography of a Horse Dreamer, unlike the comic strip emphasis of the earlier Yale version, stresses the horror engendered by thought control, as well as the predicament of the entrapped artist. The hero, Cody (but not Wild Bill), is a "lonesome cowboy trapped in a gangster movie"; he represents a search for forgotten values, "the corruption of innocence by civilization, the perversion of an American dream."

New Yorker, 22 December 1975, pp. 60+.

Nation, 3 January 1976, p. 27.

ICARUS'S MOTHER

Albee, Edward. "Icarus's Mother." Village Voice, 25 November 1965, p. 19.
Albee believes in Shepard's talent but has mixed feelings about his craftsmanship.

INACOMA

Kleb, William. "Sam Shepard's Inacoma at the Magic Theatre." Theatre 9 (1977):59-64.

KILLER'S HEAD

New York Times, 16 April 1975, p. 54:1.

Nation, 3 May 1975, p. 542.

LA TURISTA

New York Times, 26 March 1967, II:1:2.

Marowitz, Charles. New York Times, 13 April 1969,
    II:3:3.
        Marowitz considers Shepard "flip, frenetic,
    and anti-ideological," a playwright who "dis-
    penses verbal and visual images ... about as
    accessible as Fort Knox." He complains that
    La Turista, the story of two American tourists
    in need of medical attention, baffles and per-
    plexes the audience, leaving them with a frag-
    mented sense of corruption and spiritual ma-
    laise. Naming Beckett, Ionesco, and Pinter as
    forerunners of such baffling theatre, Marowitz
    asserts that in Shepard's play "there is noth-
    ing to hold on to," yet there is a "richness of
    texture" and a "cool, idiosyncratic style,"
    which suggests future promise.

Commonweal, 2 May 1969, p. 204.

MAD DOG BLUES

Gussow, Mel. New York Times, 9 March 1971, p. 25:1.
        Gussow considers Mad Dog Blues good en-
    tertainment, with the author playing the role
    of on-stage guitarist, tambourinist, and sound
    effects man and with two actresses respectively
    evoking visions of Mae West-Janis Joplin and
    Marlene Dietrich. Legendary American heroes--
    Paul Bunyan, Jesse James, and Captain Kidd--
    are part of the "epic canvas," where the plot
    is loosely centered around a treasure hunt.
    The direction shows a "deep affection for
    America's landscape and mythology," with a
    touch of Pirandello in the key theme: "You are
    who you think you are."

America, 17 April 1971, p. 408.

MELODRAMA PLAY

New York Times, 28 June 1971, p. 37:2.

NIGHTWALK

New York Times, 11 September 1973, p. 52:1.

OH! CALCUTTA!

New York Times, 18 June 1969, p. 33:1.

New York Times, 29 June 1969, II:1:7.

New York Times, 26 October 1976, p. 46:1.

OPERATION SIDEWINDER

New York Times, 13 March 1970, p. 33:1.

New Yorker, 21 March 1970, p. 115.

New York Times, 22 March 1970, II:1.

Newsweek, 23 March 1970, p. 69.

Time, 23 March 1970, p. 49.

Saturday Review, 28 March 1970, p. 24.

Nation, 30 March 1970, pp. 380-81.

America, 11 April 1970, p. 398.

Commonweal, 8 May 1970, pp. 193-94.

RED CROSS

Nation, 21 February 1966, p. 224.

Craig, R. "Red Cross." Drama 121 (Summer 1976):75-76.

New York Times, 29 April 1968, p. 47:2.

New Yorker, 11 May 1968, p. 91.

Commonweal, 14 June 1968, p. 384.

SAVAGE LOVE

New York Times, 16 November 1979, III:6:5.

New York Times, 9 December 1979, I:3:1.

SEDUCED

Kroll, Jack. Newsweek, 8 May 1978, p. 94.
Jack Kroll believes "the real force of Seduced is in its view of the madness of the drive for power." Shepard sees his Howard Hughes figure, Henry Hackamore, as a "perversion of the American individualist genius, breeding laziness and death instead of society and life," and he calls Shepard "the most American" of our playwrights.

Kleb, W. "Tongues." Theater 10 (Fall 1978):66-69.

New Yorker, 12 February 1979, p. 46.

Nation, 24 February 1979, p. 221.

Plays and Players 26 (April 1979):36-37.

SUICIDE IN B FLAT

New York Times, 25 October 1976, p. 42:1.

New York Times, 7 November 1976, II:3:1.

Newsweek, 8 November 1976, p. 109.

THE TOOTH OF CRIME

New York Times, 12 November 1972, p. 77:4.

Newsweek, 27 November 1972, p. 77.

Time, 27 November 1972, p. 73.

New York Times, 8 March 1973, p. 34:1.

New Yorker, 17 March 1973, pp. 92+.

New York Times, 18 March 1973, II:3:5.

New Republic, 24 March 1973, pp. 22+.

Nation, 26 March 1973, pp. 411-12.

America, 31 March 1973, p. 290.

Burgess, J. "The Tooth of Crime." Plays and Players
    21 (July 1974):36-39.

Lambert, J. W. "The Tooth of Crime." Drama 114
    (Autumn 1974):45-46.
        J. W. Lambert finds The Tooth of Crime
    pretentious and slow-moving although the themes
    are strongly American in this story of a pop
    singer, supplanted by a younger one. The play
    draws on images of the Old West, gangsters, and
    old movies.

THE UNSEEN HAND

New York Times, 2 April 1970, p. 43:1.

New Yorker, 11 April 1970, pp. 82-83.

New Republic, 21 April 1973, p. 23.

UP TO THURSDAY

New York Times, 11 February 1965, p. 45:1.

9 NEIL SIMON

Born July 4, 1927, New York City

Although he is not a literary dramatist, and would
probably not wish to become one, Marvin (Neil) Simon is
the most famous and most commercially successful playwright in America. Known to the majority of Americans
for his screenplays, which are often adaptations of his
own stage plays, he is admired for the wit and energy of
his warm-hearted characters. Often Simon's sophisticated,
urban humor is quite naturalistic; he perceives and re-
cords the hilarious composition of everyday conversations.
More frequently, his style is identified with the caustic,
flashy "one-liner" joke, possibly because the instant
gratification provided by a self-contained, humorous line
seems ideally suited to the pace of contemporary life.
Scholars have largely ignored Simon's literary contributions, but observers of popular culture consider his
plays documents of Middle American experience. There is
genuine satire in his studies of material snares, which
tempt basically likeable people to pursue success obses-
sively, and in his stories of the frantic quest for personal fulfillment that makes people insensitive to the
needs of others. Simon, however, rejecting the didacti-
cism of the American Puritan tradition, avoids making controversial statements. The potential irony in his work
remains muted, and dramatic conflicts tend to be revealed
in sentimental good humor.

PRIMARY SOURCES

I. STAGE

Adventures of Marco Polo: A Musical Fantasy (with William
     Friedberg). Staged New York, 1958. New York:
     Samuel French, 1959.

Barefoot in the Park. Staged New York, 1963. New York:
Random House, 1964.

_____. New York: Samuel French, 1964.

_____. In America's Lost Plays. New York and Toronto:
Dodd, Mead, 1964.

_____. In Best Plays of 1963/64: The Burns Mantle
Yearbook. New York and Toronto: Dodd, Mead, 1964.

_____. In The Comedy of Neil Simon. Ed. Neil Simon.
New York: Random House, 1971.

California Suite ("Visitor from New York"; "Visitor from
Philadelphia"; "Visitors from Chicago"; "Visitors
from London"). Staged Los Angeles and New York,
1976. New York: Random House, 1977.

_____. New York: Samuel French, 1977.

Chapter Two. Staged New York, 1977. New York: Random
House, 1979.

Come Blow Your Horn. Staged New York, 1961. London and
New York: Samuel French, 1961.

_____. In The Comedy of Neil Simon. Ed. Neil Simon.
New York: Random House, 1971.

Fools. Staged New York, 1981.

The Gingerbread Lady. Staged New York, 1970. New York:
Random House, 1971.

_____. New York: Samuel French, 1971.

_____ (condensed). In The Best Plays of 1970-1971: The
Burns Mantle Yearbook. Ed. Otis L. Guernsey, Jr.
New York and Toronto: Dodd, Mead, 1971.

God's Favorite. Staged New York, 1974. New York: Random
House, 1975.

_____. New York: Samuel French, 1975.

The Good Doctor (adaptation of Chekhov materials).
Staged New York, 1973. New York: Random House,
1974.

_____. New York: Samuel French, 1974.

_____ (condensed). In The Best Plays of 1973-1974:
The Burns Mantle Yearbook. Ed. Otis L. Guernsey, Jr. New York and Toronto: Dodd, Mead,
1974.

Heidi (with William Friedberg). New York: Samuel French,
1959.

I Ought to Be in Pictures. Staged New York, 1980. New
York: Random House, 1981.

Last of the Red Hot Lovers. Staged New York, 1969. New
York: Random House, 1970.

_____. New York: Samuel French, 1970.

_____ (condensed). In The Best Plays of 1969-1970:
The Burns Mantle Yearbook. Ed. Otis L. Guernsey,
Jr. New York and Toronto: Dodd, Mead, 1970.

_____. In The Comedy of Neil Simon. Ed. Neil Simon.
New York: Random House, 1971.

Little Me. Staged New York, 1962.

Nobody Loves Me (later to become Barefoot in the Park).
Staged New Hope, Pennsylvania, 1962.

No, No, Nanette. Staged New York, 1971.

The Odd Couple. Staged New York, 1965. New York: Random
House, 1966.

_____. New York: Samuel French, 1966.

_____. In Best American Plays, Sixth Series, 1963-1967.
Ed. John Gassner. New York: Crown, 1971.

_____ (condensed). In The Best Plays of 1964-1965: The
Burns Mantle Yearbook. Ed. Otis L. Guernsey, Jr.
New York and Toronto: Dodd, Mead, 1965.

_____. In Best Plays of the Sixties. Ed. Stanley
Richards. Garden City, N.Y.: Doubleday, 1970.

_____. In The Comedy of Neil Simon. Ed. Neil Simon.
New York: Random House, 1971.

_____. In Comedy Tonight! Ed. Mary Sherwin. New
York: Doubleday, 1977.

_____. In 50 Best Plays of the American Theater. Eds. John Gassner and Clive Barnes. Vol. 4. New York: Crown, 1969.

Plaza Suite ("Visitor from Forest Hills"; "Visitor from Hollywood"; "Visitor from Mamaroneck"). Staged New York, 1968. New York: Random House, 1969. House,

_____. New York: Samuel French, 1969.

_____ (condensed). In The Best Plays of 1967-1968: The Burns Mantle Yearbook. Ed. Otis L. Guernsey, Jr. New York and Toronto: Dodd, Mead, 1968.

_____. In The Comedy of Neil Simon. Ed. Neil Simon. New York: Random House, 1971.

The Prisoner of Second Avenue. Staged New York, 1971. New York: Random House, 1972.

_____. New York: Samuel French, 1972.

_____. In Best American Plays, Seventh Series, 1967-1973. Ed. Clive Barnes. New York: Crown, 1974.

_____ (condensed). In The Best Plays of 1971-1972: The Burns Mantle Yearbook. Ed. Otis L. Guernsey, Jr. New York and Toronto: Dodd, Mead, 1972.

Promises, Promises. Staged New York, 1968. New York: Random House, 1969.

_____. In The Comedy of Neil Simon. Ed. Neil Simon. New York: Random House, 1971.

Sketches. Staged Tamiment, Pennsylvania, 1952.

_____ (with Danny Simon). In Catch a Star; staged New York, 1955.

_____ (with Danny Simon). In New Faces of 1956; staged New York, 1956.

The Star-Spangled Girl. Staged New York, 1966. New York: Random House, 1967.

_____. In The Comedy of Neil Simon. Ed. Neil Simon. New York: Random House, 1971.

The Sunshine Boys. Staged New York, 1972. New York: Random House, 1973.

_____. New York: Samuel French, 1974.

_____ (condensed). In The Best Plays of 1972-1973: The Burns Mantle Yearbook. Ed. Otis L. Guernsey, Jr. New York and Toronto: Dodd, Mead, 1973.

Sweet Charity. Staged New York, 1966. New York: Random House, 1966.

They're Playing Our Song. Staged New York, 1979. New York: Random House, 1980.

"Visitor from Forest Hills" (part one of Plaza Suite). Staged New York, 1968. New York: Random House, 1969.

_____. New York: Samuel French, 1969.

_____. In Best Short Plays of the World Theatre 1968-1973. Ed. Stanley Richards. New York: Crown, 1973.

_____. In The Comedy of Neil Simon. Ed. Neil Simon. New York: Random House, 1971.

"Visitor from Hollywood" (part two of Plaza Suite). Staged New York, 1968. New York: Random House, 1969.

_____. New York: Samuel French, 1969.

_____. In The Comedy of Neil Simon. Ed. Neil Simon. New York: Random House, 1971.

"Visitor from Mamaroneck" (part three of Plaza Suite). Staged New York, 1968. New York: Random House, 1969.

_____. New York: Samuel French, 1969.

_____. In The Comedy of Neil Simon. Ed. Neil Simon. New York: Random House, 1971.

_____. In Modern Short Comedies from Broadway and London. Ed. Stanley Richards. New York: Random House, 1970.

"Visitor from New York" (part one of California Suite). Staged Los Angeles and New York, 1976. New York: Random House, 1977.

_____ (condensed). In The Best Plays of 1976-1977: The Burns Mantle Yearbook. Ed. Otis L. Guernsey, Jr. New York and Toronto: Dodd, Mead, 1977.

"Visitor from Philadelphia" (part two of California Suite). Staged Los Angeles and New York, 1976. New York: Random House, 1977.

_____ (condensed). In The Best Plays of 1976-1977: The Burns Mantle Yearbook. Ed. Otis L. Guernsey, Jr. New York and Toronto: Dodd, Mead, 1977.

"Visitors from Chicago" (part three of California Suite). Staged Los Angeles and New York, 1976. New York: Random House, 1977.

_____ (condensed). In The Best Plays of 1976-1977: The Burns Mantle Yearbook. Ed. Otis L. Guernsey, Jr. New York: Dodd, Mead, 1977.

"Visitors from London" (part four of California Suite). Staged Los Angeles and New York, 1976. New York: Random House, 1977.

_____ (condensed). In The Best Plays of 1976-1977: The Burns Mantle Yearbook. Ed. Otis L. Guernsey, Jr. New York and Toronto: Dodd, Mead, 1977.

II. FILM

After the Fox, 1966.

Barefoot in the Park, 1967.

California Suite, 1978.

Chapter Two, 1979.

The Cheap Detective, 1978.

The Goodbye Girl, 1977.

The Heartbreak Kid, 1972.

The Last of the Red Hot Lovers, 1972.

Murder by Death, 1976.

The Odd Couple, 1968.

Only When I Laugh, 1981

The Out-of-Towners, 1970.

Plaza Suite, 1971.

The Prisoner of Second Avenue, 1975.

Seems Like Old Times, 1980.

The Sunshine Boys, 1975.

Sweet Charity, 1969.

III.   TELEVISION

A Quiet War, 1976.

Garry Moore Show, 1959-1960.

Phil Silvers Show, 1948, 1958-59.

Sid Caesar Show, 1956-1957.

Tallulah Bankhead Show, 1951.

IV.   NONFICTION

"As Time Goes By."   Introduction to The Collected Plays
    of Neil Simon. New York: Random House, 1979.
    Pp. 3-10.
        Simon describes, somewhat defensively, the crit-
    ical indifference to his work, despite its popularity
    with the public. He takes comfort in being "under-
    rated."

"Portrait of the Writer as a Schizophrenic." In The
    Comedy of Neil Simon. New York: Random House,
    1971. Pp. 3-9.
        Simon provides some autobiography, recalling
    his boyhood fondness for The Shadow, Joe Di Maggio,
    and Charlie Chaplin's Modern Times. He explains
    that one part of him (the Monster) wants to pry into
    the lives and motives of people whereas his other
    self (the Human Being) merely wants to love mankind.
    This personal conflict contributes to his compulsion
    to write new plays.

V.   TRANSLATIONS

BAREFOOT IN THE PARK

    Pieds Nus dans le Parc. Tr. André Roussin. L'Avant
        Scène, 58, 15 February 1965, pp. 10-40. French.

    Bosa v parku. Tr. Dušan Tomše. Ljubljana: Zveza
        Kulturnoprosvetnih organizacj Slovenije, 1975.
        Serbo-Croatian.

    Bosý v parku. Tr. Eva Galundová. Bratislava:
        Diliza, 1965. Slovene.

    Bosé nony v parku. Tr. Ivo Havlů. Praha: Dilia,
        1964. Czech.

THE ODD COUPLE

    Drole de Couple. Tr. Albert Husson. L'Avant Scène,
        July 1967, pp. 1-37. French.

_____. In Plaisir de France (Supplément Théâtrical)
   No. 356 (August 1967). French.

Nepárney Pár. Tr. Igor Lisý. Bratislava: Diliza,
   1969. Czech.

Podivný Pár. Tr. Ivo T. Havlu. Praha: Dilia, 1967.
   Czech.

Zares Cuden Par. Tr. Dusan Tomse. Ljubljana:
   Prosvetni servis, 1968. Serbo-Croatian.

PLAZA SUITE

Hotel Plaza. Tr. Dusan Tomse. Ljubljana: Scena,
   1971. Serbo-Croatian.

Pokaj Císlo. Tr. Ivo T. Havlu. Praha: Dilia, 1970.
   Czech.

PRISONER OF SECOND AVENUE

Vezen na Druhé Avenue. Tr. Ivo T. Havlu. Praha:
   Dilia, 1976. Czech.

THE SUNSHINE BOYS

Mládenci do popuku. Tr. Karol Dlouhý. Bratislava:
   LITA, 1974. Czech.

Sonny Boys. Tr. Gerty Agosten. Staged Stuttgart and
   Wurtemberg, Staats Theater, Schauspiel, 1975.
   German.

VI. INTERVIEW

Kanfer, Stefan. "Neil Simon: The Unshine Boy: Interview."
   Time, 15 January 1973, pp. 58-59.
      Kanfer remarks that "in nine years Simon has be-
   come a theatrical legend," and, on the other hand,
   that he has had his moments of depression like "a
   character in a Neil Simon play." The interview
   takes the shape of a dialogue, where Simon's comments are a parody of his own style. Asked what he
   writes, he replies "comedy. Based on character." Yet
   he insists: "I don't start out to write comedy. I
   begin by studying all the tragic aspects of my characters." Simon adds: "My work is growing, it is more
   openly 'serious.' I couldn't write Barefoot in the
   Park again if you held a gun to my head."

SECONDARY SOURCES

I. CRITICISM

Berkowitz, Gerald M. "Neil Simon and His Amazing Laugh
     Machine." <u>Players</u> 47:3 (February-March 1972):110-13.
          Simon's success is not based on the plots of
     his plays, but on his comic technique. His lines
     often depend upon repetition for their effect. The
     key to his success is perhaps his conditioning of
     the audience.

Gottfried, Martin. "Neil Simon." In <u>Contemporary Drama-
     tists</u>. Ed. James Vinson. London: St. Martin's
     Press, 1976.
          Gottfried calls Simon "the most popular play-
     wright in the history of American theatre." He be-
     lieves that when Simon mixes humor with pain he can
     achieve depth but that "he consistently sacrifices
     his best qualities to the laughter of audiences who
     want only to be entertained and have their values
     confirmed."

_____. A <u>Theatre Divided</u>. Boston: Little, Brown,
     1967. Pp. 217, 226.
          Gottfried, in describing a theatre caught be-
     tween "right wing" (middle American) and "left wing"
     (avant-garde) forces, places Simon in the former
     category, considering him a traditional writer and
     an audience pleaser.

Hewes, Henry. "Odd Husband Out." <u>Saturday Review</u>, 4
     December 1971, pp. 20, 22.
          A comparison of Pinter's <u>Old Times</u> and Neil
     Simon's <u>The Prisoner of Second Avenue</u> reveals their
     common use of the husband as "the odd man out."
     Pinter's Deeley unsuccessfully attempts to enter in-
     to his wife's past, while Simon's Mel is "man against
     the city." Both men end in frustration, but Pinter's
     play more adequately evokes man's predicament.

Hughes, Catharine. <u>American Playwrights 1945-1975</u>.
     New York: Pitman Publishing, 1976. Pp. 92-96.
          Hughes attempts to account for Simon's financial
     success, noting that he even owns the theatre in
     which his major "hits" are produced. His earlier
     plays she finds inconsequential, though effective,
     but she concentrates on the later comedies with seri-
     ous overtones. Simon's insights, according to
     Hughes, are of "the more facile kind" and his percep-
     tions, like his jokes, are "one-liners." There is
     compassion in Simon's portraits, but his presentation
     is heavy-handed. His humor is not a natural part of

his characterization; it is formulaic and impersonal. She concludes that Simon will never become a serious playwright unless he stops "playing to the box office."

McGovern, Edythe M. Not-So-Simple Neil Simon. Van Nuys, California: Perivale, 1978.
     McGovern argues that Simon is a more complex, deliberate playwright than his detractors would admit. She points to his inexhaustible supply of witty phrases, his insights into American sociological complexities; she admires the vast scale of his undertakings, frequently more perceptive and revealing of the human condition than many plays labeled complex dramas. She analyzes 15 Simon plays.

_____. Neil Simon: A Critical Study. With Notes from the Playwright. New York: Ungar, 1979.
     An update of her previous book, with notes from Simon.

McMahon, Helen. "A Rhetoric of American Popular Drama: The Comedies of Neil Simon." Players 51 (1976):11-15.
     McMahon believes that Simon's success has resulted from his astute perception of the needs of middle-class audiences.

Meehan, T. "The Unreal, Hilarious World of Neil Simon." Horizon, 21 (January 1978):70-74.
     Meehan calls Simon the "wealthiest playwright in the history of the known universe," with a net worth of ten million dollars. Simon "constructs comedies out of the stuff of his own life." Simon's well-crafted plays are free of troubling ambiguities. Meehan considers his simplicity, the "lack of political and intellectual comment in his works," an asset. Simon's plays affect us like "happy dreams."

"Party." People, 27 March 1978, pp. 69-70.
     This is an attempt to account for Simon's popularity among show people.

"Second Thoughts." Horizon, 20 (December 1977):33.
     Although Simon is criticized for his "tendency to trivialize his subjects," his latest works, especially the play Chapter Two and the movie The Goodbye Girl, are seen as evidence of a new depth and maturity.

Simon, Ellen V. "My Life with a Very Funny Father." Seventeen, November 1979, pp. 154-57.
     This is a personal appreciation of the playwright by his daughter.

II. DISSERTATION

Bernardi, J. A. "The Plays of Neil Simon: The First Dec-
    ade of Dramatic Development." _Dissertation Abstracts_
    37:6149A (Denver 1976).
        Bernardi argues that Simon's plays are a valu-
    able indicator of American preoccupations from the
    1960s to the present and that he has more technical
    proficiency and thematic integrity than critics have
    generally granted him.

III. REVIEWS

BAREFOOT IN THE PARK

    New York Times, 24 October 1963, p. 36:2.

    Time, 1 November 1963, p. 74.
            Barefoot is called "detonatingly funny."
        Dealing with the problems of newlyweds, it
        starred Robert Redford and Elizabeth Ashley.
        Simon is praised for his ubiquitous wit though
        his plot is seen as "middle of the rut."

    New Yorker, 2 November 1963, p. 93.

    Newsweek, 4 November 1963, p. 62.

    Saturday Review, 9 November 1963, p. 32.

    Commonweal, 15 November 1963, p. 226.

    America, 7 December 1963, p. 753.

    Theatre Arts 48 (January 1964):68.

CALIFORNIA SUITE

    New York Times, 11 June 1976, III:3:1.

    New Yorker, 21 June 1976, p. 85.

    Kroll, Jack. _Newsweek_, 21 June 1976, p. 55.
            Kroll comments: "Assuming that Simon has
        once, or several times, done _something_, then
        whatever that something is, he hasn't done it
        again in _California Suite_." The four playlets
        that compose the _Suite_ are all about culture
        shock in the Golden State, but the critic finds

226

them inferior to the earlier <u>Plaza</u> <u>Suite</u>, which Kroll also dislikes.

<u>Time</u>, 21 June 1976, p. 43.

<u>New</u> <u>York</u> <u>Times</u>, 30 June 1976, II:7:1.

<u>Nation</u>, 3 July 1976, p. 30.

<u>New</u> <u>Republic</u>, 3 July 1976, p. 20.

<u>New</u> <u>York</u> <u>Times</u>, 10 September 1976, III:1:5.

<u>New</u> <u>York</u> <u>Times</u>, 26 December 1976, II:3:1.

CHAPTER TWO

<u>New</u> <u>York</u> <u>Times</u>, 9 May 1977; 4 December 1977.

<u>New</u> <u>Yorker</u>, 12 December 1977, p. 91.

<u>Newsweek</u>, 19 December 1977, p. 86.

<u>Time</u>, 19 December 1977, p. 96.

<u>Nation</u>, 24 December 1977, pp. 699-700.

<u>America</u>, 31 December 1977, p. 485.

Kauffmann, Stanley. <u>New</u> <u>Republic</u>, 7 January 1978, p. 25.
Kaufmann considers <u>Chapter</u> <u>Two</u>, which deals with Simon's loss of his first wife and subsequent remarriage, slight and somewhat embarrassing entertainment.

<u>Saturday</u> <u>Review</u>, 4 February 1978, p. 45.

COME BLOW YOUR HORN

<u>New</u> <u>York</u> <u>Times</u>, 23 February 1961, p. 31:3.

<u>Time</u>, 3 March 1961, p. 60.

<u>New</u> <u>Yorker</u>, 4 March 1961, p. 93.

<u>New</u> <u>York</u> <u>Times</u>, 5 March 1961, II:1:1.

<u>Nation</u>, 11 March 1961, p. 222.

Hewes, Henry. <u>Saturday</u> <u>Review</u>, 11 March 1961, p. 38.
Hewes likes this play about overprotective

Jewish parents and their twenty-one-year-old son.
The stock device of a doorbell that heralds an
unexpected intrusion works predictably and the
pace of the production is lively.

America, 20 May 1961, p. 355.

FOOLS

New York Times, 16 April 1981, III:17:1.

New York 14 (20 April 1981):54.

Gill, Brendan. New Yorker 57 (20 April 1981):133.
    Gill describes Fools as an extended modern
joke, a series of one-liners about peasants in
the village of Kulyenchikov, who are too stupid
to learn anything. It seems that they are under
a curse. A schoolteacher, well played by John
Rubinstein, "spouts nonsense to the effect that
stupidity can be cured by self-respect which,
in turn, is engendered by love." Apart from
noting some good performances, Gill generally
dislikes the play.

Time 117 (20 April 1981):63.

New Leader 64 (4 May 1981):20.

GINGERBREAD LADY

Barnes, Clive. New York Times, 14 December 1970,
    p. 58:3.
    Simon's first serious play, though as
humorous as ever, is a complex work. Simon has
discovered how to "express the emptiness be-
neath the smart remark and the shy compassion
that can be smothered by a wisecrack." In addition, Barnes notes: "The wit is self-pitying,
and self-destructive and self-deprecating, and
it has enabled him to create a larger-than-life
yet still credible human being."

New Yorker, 19 December 1970, p. 96.

New York Times, 20 December 1970, II:3:7.

Newsweek, 28 December 1970, p. 61.

Time, 28 December 1970, p. 27.

Nation, 4 January 1971, p. 29.

Saturday Review, 9 January 1971, p. 4.

New Republic, 16 January 1971, p. 22.

GOD'S FAVORITE

New York Times, 12 December 1974, p. 59:3.

New York Times, 22 December 1974, II:5:1.

New Yorker, 23 December 1974, pp. 53-54.

Newsweek, 23 December 1974, p. 56.

Kalem, T. E. *Time*, 23 December 1974, p. 46.
Simon has written a play on a "highly
unlikely subject: The trials and tribulations
of Job." Yet perhaps Simon has been dismissed
too often as the casual "confectioner of gags,"
when, in fact, he "has an intuitive understanding of the comic process that runs far deeper
than one-liners." In this updated version of
Job, the messenger of the Lord "arrives with
a big G on his sweatshirt" and "the wisecracks
wing across stage like machine-gun fire." The
protagonist, however, represents the playwright's serious side, his "bedrock decency and
abiding affection for beleaguered humanity."

America, 18 January 1975, p. 36.

New Republic, 22 February 1975, pp. 33-34.

GOOD DOCTOR

New York Times, 28 November 1973, p. 36:1.

New York Times, 9 December 1973, II:3:1.

New Yorker, 10 December 1973, pp. 111-12.

Newsweek, 10 December 1973, p. 118.

Time, 10 December 1973, p. 88.

Nation, 17 December 1973, p. 669.

National Review, 18 January 1974, p. 90.

New York Times, 10 July 1974, p. 44:1.

I OUGHT TO BE IN PICTURES

New York Times, 4 April 1980, III:3:1.

New York, 14 April 1980, p. 86.

Newsweek, 14 April 1980, pp. 106-07.

Time, 14 April 1980, p. 112.

Kauffmann, Stanley. Saturday Review 7 (May 1980):56.
    "This is about a fading Hollywood writer of
    films and T.V., visited unexpectedly by his
    Brooklyn daughter of 19, whom he hasn't seen
    since she was three when he left her mother."
    Kauffmann, unamused, finds the play an uncon-
    vincing sit-com. The character transformation
    that takes place is not believably motivated and
    the occasionally clever quips about Hollywood and
    show business are not enough to salvage the pro-
    duction.

LAST OF THE RED HOT LOVERS

New York Times, 29 December 1969, p. 37:1.

New York Times, 4 January 1970, II:1:1.

New Yorker, 10 January 1970, p. 64.

Newsweek, 12 January 1970, p. 73.

Time, 12 January 1970, p. 64.

Lewis, Theophilus. America, 17 January 1970, p. 55.
    Lewis feels that this comedy of a fumbling
    "would-be philanderer" benefits greatly from
    Simon's deft touch at comedy writing. Simon is
    seen as showing a new side, too, "as a diffident
    commentator on moral values." This new comedy
    is "thoughtful as well as amusing."

Saturday Review, 17 January 1970, p. 28.

Nation, 19 January 1970, pp. 60-61.

New Republic, 14 February 1970, p. 25.

Commonweal, 20 March 1970, pp. 38-39.

LITTLE ME

New York Times, 19 November 1962, p. 41:3.

New York Times, 2 December 1962, II;1:1.

NO, NO, NANETTE

New York Times, 9 November 1972, p. 58:1.

THE ODD COUPLE

Taubman, Howard. New York Times, 11 March 1965,
p. 36:1.
Simon's skill continues to rely on his
faultless ability to find the incongruous. Art
Carney is about to be divorced, moves in with
the already divorced Walter Matthau. Carney is
the perfect homemaker, which drives the other
half of this "odd couple" wild.

Time, 19 March 1965, p. 66.

. New Yorker, 20 March 1965, p. 83.

New York Times, 21 March 1965, II:1:1.

Newsweek, 22 March 1965, pp. 90-91.

Saturday Review, 27 March 1965, p. 44.

Commonweal, 2 April 1965, pp. 51-52.

Nation, 5 April 1965, pp. 373-74.

Life, 9 April 1965, pp. 35-36.

Vogue, May 1965, p. 142.

America, 29 May 1965, pp. 810-11.

Catholic World 201 (August 1965):343-44.

New York Times, 17 October 1972, p. 32:1.

PLAZA SUITE

New York Times, 15 February 1968, p. 49:1.

Time, 23 February 1968, p. 54.
Simon, director Mike Nichols, and performers
George C. Scott and Maureen Stapleton combine for
an enormously funny production in this trio of
sketch-like playlets. The evening's high point,
"Visitor from Forest Hills," shows "how Simon and
Nichols can take a situation no bigger than a
snowball and dislodge an avalanche of hilarity."

New Yorker, 24 February 1968, pp. 75-76.

New York Times, 25 February 1968, II:1:1.

Newsweek, 26 February 1968, p. 56.

Saturday Review, 2 March 1968, p. 29.

Nation, 4 March 1968, p. 317.

Vogue, April 1968, p. 132.

America, 20 April 1968, p. 552.

Commonweal, 6 September 1968, p. 597.

New York Times, 14 December 1968, p. 61:1.

New York Times, 22 March 1970, p. 90:3.

PRISONER OF SECOND AVENUE

New York Times, 12 November 1971, p. 55:1.

New Yorker, 20 November 1971, p. 111.

New York Times, 21 November 1971, II:1:1.

Newsweek, 22 November 1971, p. 86.

Time, 22 November 1971, p. 93.

Nation, 29 November 1971, p. 573.

Saturday Review, 4 December 1971, p. 20.

New York Times, 19 December 1971, II:5:1.

Saturday Review, 26 August 1972, p. 66.

Weales, Gerald. Commonweal, 4 May 1973, pp. 215-16.
    Weales sees both Prisoner and the concur-
rently running Sunshine Boys as good examples
of dark, "survival humor" prevalent on Broadway.
He writes that "the comic material of Prisoner
consists mainly of the impossibility of living
in New York in the face of pollution, crime, and
the countless small indignities of the environment." He recommends Act I as this new sort of
comedy at its best.

PROMISES, PROMISES

    Barnes, Clive. New York Times, 2 December 1968,
       p. 69:3.
          This lively new musical, an adaptation of
    the film The Apartment, is successful in the
    originality of the book and the beat of the
    music. The amoral hero, Jerry Orbach, lets the
    top executives of his life insurance firm use
    his apartment for their girlfriends in return
    for the "key to the executive washroom."
    Through Orbach's direct addresses to the audi-
    ence, Simon has created a protagonist who,
    though we disapprove of him on principle, has
    our sympathy. His true-to-life jokes make the
    play "crackle with wit," along with its empha-
    sis on the facets of "sad and wry humanity."

    New York Times, 22 January 1971, p. 17:2.

STAR-SPANGLED GIRL

    New York Times, 22 December 1966, p. 38:1.

    Time, 30 December 1966, p. 45.

    New Yorker, 31 December 1966, p. 59.

    Newsweek, 2 January 1967, p. 66.

    New York Times, 8 January 1967, II:1:5.

    Hewes, Henry. "Aromatic Spirits." Saturday Review,
       14 January 1967, p. 98.
          Though The Star-Spangled Girl has perhaps
    a less sketchy plot than previous Simon plays,
    it is less successful. The gags are more forced
    and predictable. Ultimately, its "tepid and
    unflagging wisecracking" is unsatisfying.

    Vogue, February 1967, p. 60.

    America, 18 February 1967, p. 264.

SUNSHINE BOYS

    New York Times, 21 December 1972, p. 31:1.

    New York Times, 31 December 1972, II:1:6.

    Saturday Review of the Arts 1 (1973):59.

    Newsweek, 1 January 1973, p. 52.

    Time, 1 January 1973, p. 64.

<u>Nation</u>, 8 January 1973, p. 61.

<u>America</u>, 20 January 1973, p. 41.

Kaufmann, Stanley. <u>New Republic</u>, 27 January 1973,
p. 26.
Kauffmann has been calling Simon a mere
sketch-writer for years, and feels that <u>The
Sunshine Boys</u> proves his point. Simon is clever
and talented, but his plays do not stand up to
those of his predecessor, George S. Kaufman.

<u>Vogue</u>, February 1973, p. 78.

<u>National Review</u>, 16 March 1973, pp. 316-17.

<u>Commonweal</u>, 4 May 1973, pp. 215-16.

<u>New Yorker</u>, 30 December 1973, p. 47.

SWEET CHARITY

<u>New York Times</u>, 31 January 1966, p. 22:1.

THEY'RE PLAYING OUR SONG

<u>New York Times</u>, 22 May 1979, p. 31:1.

<u>New York Times</u>, 30 May 1979, III:18:4.

10 LANFORD WILSON

Born April 13, 1937, Lebanon, Missouri

Beginning his career in the Off-Off Broadway coffee houses of New York in the early sixties, Lanford Wilson worked as an actor, director, and set designer, as well as a playwright. The success of <u>HOT L BALTIMORE</u> in 1973 earned Wilson a place in the Off-Broadway avant garde, but not until 1980 was he able to succeed on Broadway. <u>Talley's Folly</u> combined commercial success with critical recognition as the Pulitzer Prize-winning play of 1980. As one of the founders in 1969 of the Circle Repertory Company and its resident playwright, Wilson has fortunately been able to thrive Off-Broadway. His plays reflect a close working relationship with the company's actors and its director, Marshall Mason, another of the founders. Roles, such as Matt Friedman in <u>Talley's Folly</u>, have been created for specific actors in the company. Wilson relies upon his roots in the Ozarks for the settings of two seminal works, <u>This Is the Rill Speaking</u> and its later full-length version, <u>The Rimers of Eldritch</u>, although many of his plays have a city backdrop, often New York. <u>Lemon Sky</u>, in which Alan narrates the story of his trip from the Ozarks to visit his re-married father in San Diego, is clearly autobiographical, and Wilson has returned to the Ozark setting for his most recent plays, <u>Fifth of July</u>, <u>Talley's Folly</u>, and <u>A Tale Told</u>, which are the first three in a possible five-play series about the Talleys of Lebanon, Missouri. Wilson's characters yearn for meaningful relationships in the present along with a sense of heritage. Family, history, fables, old buildings, all are valued and their extinction is mourned. His interesting use of language to penetrate plot is often referred to as "collage style" or "verbal layering." From Tennessee Williams, with whom he collaborated on a new version of <u>Summer and Smoke</u>, he learned to create psychologically complex characters, and from Thornton Wilder he has frequently borrowed the narrator-stage manager device. Like both of the older playwrights, he has a penchant for expressionistic devices and highly theatrical effects.

236

PRIMARY SOURCES

I. STAGE

Balm in Gilead. Staged New York, 1964. In Balm in Gilead
    and Other Plays. New York: Hill and Wang, 1965.

Brontosaurus. Staged New York, 1977. New York: Drama-
    tists Play Service, 1977.

Common Thyme. A Reading in New York, 1981.

Days Ahead. Staged New York, 1965. In The Rimers of
    Eldritch and Other Plays. New York: Hill and Wang,
    1967.

The Family Continues. Staged New York, 1972. In The
    Great Nebula in Orion and Three Other Plays. New
    York: Dramatists Play Service, 1973.

5th of July. Staged New York, 1978, 1980 (as Fifth of
    July). In Ten Best Plays of 1978. Ed. Otis Guernsey.
    New York: Dodd, Mead, 1979.

The Gingham Dog. Staged Washington, D.C., 1968; New York,
    1969. New York: Hill and Wang, 1970.

The Great Nebula in Orion. Staged Manchester, England,
    1970; New York, 1972. In The Great Nebula in Orion
    and Three Other Plays. New York: Dramatists Play
    Service, 1973.

Home Free! Staged New York, 1964. In Balm in Gilead and
    Other Plays. New York: Hill and Wang, 1965.

_____. In The Madness of Lady Bright and Home Free!
    London: Methuen, 1968.

HOT L BALTIMORE. Staged New York, 1973. New York: Hill
    and Wang, 1973.

Ikke, Ikke, Nye, Nye, Nye. Staged New York, 1972. In
    The Great Nebula in Orion and Three Other Plays.
    New York: Dramatists Play Service, 1973.

Lemon Sky. Staged Waterford, Conn., 1968; Buffalo and
    New York, 1970. New York: Hill and Wang, 1970.
    In Clive Barnes and John Gassner, eds., Best American
    Plays, 7th Series 1967-1973. New York: Crown,
    1975.

Ludlow Fair. Staged New York, 1966. In Balm in Gilead
and Other Plays. New York: Hill and Wang, 1965.

The Madness of Lady Bright. Staged New York, 1966.
In The Rimers of Eldritch and Other Plays. New
York: Hill and Wang, 1967.

_____. In The Madness of Lady Bright and Home Free!
London: Methuen, 1968.

Miss Williams: A Turn. Staged New York, 1967.

The Mound Builders. Staged New York, 1975. New York:
Hill and Wang, 1976.

No Trespassing. Staged New York, 1964.

The Rimers of Eldritch. Staged New York, 1967. In The
Rimers of Eldritch and Other Plays. New York:
Hill and Wang, 1967.

The Sand Castle. Staged New York, 1965. In The Sand
Castle and Three Other Plays. New York: Dramatists
Play Service, 1970.

Serenading Louie. Staged Washington, D.C., 1970; New
York, 1976.

Sex Is Between Two People. Staged New York, 1965.

Sextet (Yes): A Play for Voices. Staged New York, 1971.
In The Sand Castle and Three Other Plays. New York:
Dramatists Play Service, 1970.

So Long at the Fair. Staged New York, 1963.

Summer and Smoke. (An adaptation of a play by Tennessee
Williams.) Staged St. Paul, 1971; New York, 1972.
New York: Belwin Mills, 1972.

A Tale Told. Staged New York, 1981.

Talley's Folly. Staged New York, 1979. (Pulitzer Prize).
New York: Hill and Wang, 1980.

This Is the Rill Speaking. Staged New York, 1965. In
The Rimers of Eldritch and Other Plays. New York:
Hill and Wang, 1967.

Untitled Play. Staged New York, 1967.

Wandering: A Turn. Staged New York, 1966. In The Rimers
of Eldritch and Other Plays. New York: Hill and
Wang, 1967.

_____. In _The Sand Castle and Three Other Plays_. New York: Dramatists Play Service, 1970.

II. FILM

One _Arm_, 1970 (scenario), adaptation of a Tennessee Williams story.

III. TELEVISION

The _Migrants_, 1975 (CBS Playhouse 90).

Stoop. New York, 1969. In _The Sand Castle and Three Other Plays_. New York: Dramatists Play Service, 1970.

Taxi, 1978 (Hallmark Hall of Fame).

SECONDARY SOURCES

I. CRITICISM

Berkvist, Robert. "Lanford Wilson--Can He Score on Broadway?" _New York Times_, 17 February 1980, II:1: 33.
    Berkvist presents a thorough background of the playwright and his plays, leading up to the Broadway production of _Talley's Folly_, Wilson's first successful Broadway production. _Talley's Folly_ is a "romantic comedy about the wooing of a hesitant spinster." Berkvist provides a fairly extensive biographical sketch and explores the possibility of Wilson's being a "regional" playwright who is always looking back to his roots in Missouri.

Gussow, Mel. "Lanford Wilson on Broadway. (_Talley's Folly_: A Valentine's Hit)?" _Horizon_, May 1980, pp. 30-36.
    This article provides one of the most thorough short analyses of Wilson's career so far. Calling Wilson's plays "a unique tapestry of America" Gussow offers a brief biography, summarizes some of the dramatic highlights of Wilson's Talley family saga, and includes some of the playwright's own remarks, such as his observation that "I'm earthbound but Shepard [Sam Shepard] lifts you off the ground." Gussow compares Wilson to Thornton Wilder, Tennessee Williams, and Arthur Miller, who also won the Creative Arts

achievement award. Immediately following Gussow's
article there is an insert (p. 37) by Peter Benchley
profiling the Circle Repertory Company, which has
performed so many of Wilson's plays.

Sainer, Arthur. "Lanford Wilson." In Contemporary
Dramatists. Ed. James Vinson. London: St. James
Press; New York: St. Martin's Press, 1973. Pp. 872-
73.
This is a general discussion emphasizing Hot l
Baltimore, The Madness of Lady Bright, Lemon Sky,
The Sand Castle. Sainer characterizes Wilson's
plays as busy, "peopled" worlds and maintains that
Wilson's plays suggest a sense of innocence about
life, that there is no bitter grappling with "one's
own devils, with the subconscious powers of dark-
ness." He remarks that there are no evil forces in
the plays; most of the stage time is spent in
"chatter or rumination about the nature of things."

Winter, Helmut. "Lanford Wilson: The Rimers of Eldritch."
In Das amerikanische Drama der Gegenwart. Ed.
Herbert Grabes. Kronberg: Athenäum, 1976. Pp.
20-137.

II. REVIEWS

THE FAMILY CONTINUES (Three New Plays by Lanford Wilson)

New York Times, 22 May 1972, p. 43:3.
This review discusses the Great Nebula in
Orion, Ikke, Ikke, Nye, Nye, Nye, and The Family
Continues.

FIFTH OF JULY

New York Times, 31 October 1980, III:2, 3.

New York, 17 November 1980, p. 65.

New Yorker, 17 November 1980, pp. 172-73.

Time, 17 November 1980, p. 109.

Newsweek, 24 November 1980, p. 129.

Nation, 29 November 1980, pp. 588-99.

Brustein, Robert. New Republic 184 (23 May 1981):26.
Brustein calls Wilson "Peter Shaffer minus
the literary syllabus" and "a shrewd tactician
who has learned how to introduce homosexual

relationships, seedy revelations, bold language
and raunchy situations in a manner calculated
to offend no one." Brustein calls the story of
a decaying family, the Talleys, a kind of <u>Cherry
Orchard</u> for the tourist trade.

GINGHAM DOG

<u>New York Times</u>, 13 October 1968, II:18:6.

Hewes, Henry. <u>Saturday Review</u>, 26 October 1968, pp.
32, 67.
Hewes refers to the "total honesty" of
several scenes in this play that deals with a
failed marriage. He admires the naturalism and
the wild humor of this thoughtful play.

<u>New York Times</u>, 24 April 1969.

<u>New Yorker</u>, 3 May 1969, p. 107.

<u>New York Times</u>, 4 May 1969, II:1:5.

THE GREAT NEBULA ON ORION (Three New Plays by Lanford
Wilson)

<u>New York Times</u>, 22 May 1972, p. 43:3.

HIM

<u>New York Times</u>, 20 April 1974, p. 16:1.

HOME FREE

<u>New York Times</u>, 11 February 1965, II:45:1.

<u>Newsweek</u>, 22 February 1965, p. 93.

THE HOT L BALTIMORE

Gussow, Mel. <u>New York Times</u>, 8 February 1973, p.
37:3.
This play reminds Gussow of Saroyan and
Wilder in its presentation of idiosyncratic
characters, all unwanted people down on their
luck. The seedy hotel which provides a setting
is a kind of microcosm for contemporary society.
The overlapping conversations give the play a
musical flow.

<u>New York Times</u>, 4 March 1973, II:3:1.

<u>New York Times</u>, 23 March 1973, p. 21:1.

IKKE, IKKE, NYE, NYE, NYE (Three New Plays by Lanford Wilson)

New York Times, 22 May 1972, p. 43:3.

LEMON SKY

New York Times, 18 May 1970, p. 40:1.

New Yorker, 30 May 1970, p. 72.

Clurman, Harold. Nation, 1 June 1970, p. 668.
Lemon Sky reminds Clurman of Sherwood Anderson in its realism. A young boy's encounter with the rather boorish father who abandoned him has touching moments and the play "is fluently and honestly written." Sentimentality and banality are avoided through a clever scrambling of the time sequence.

Time, 1 June 1970, p. 63.

New Republic, 13 June 1970, p. 18.

New York Times, 3 March 1976, p. 28:4.

LUDLOW FAIR

New York Times, 23 March 1966, p. 43:1.

New Yorker, 2 April 1966, p. 124.

THE MADNESS OF LADY BRIGHT

New York Times, 23 March 1966, p. 42:1.

New Yorker, 2 April 1966, p. 124.

Commonweal, 29 April 1966, p. 178.

THE MOUND BUILDERS

New York Times, 3 February 1975, p. 35:2.

THE RIMERS OF ELDRITCH

New York Times, 21 February 1967, p. 53:1.

Time, 3 March 1967, p. 52.

New Yorker, 4 March 1967, p. 132.

America, 11 March 1967, p. 354.
Wilson is called a "less-discerning"

Thornton Wilder and his scene "a mid-Western Peyton Place." The rape of a crippled girl in a small town leads to exposure of dark secrets in the lives of the townspeople.

Saturday Review, 11 March 1967, p. 30.

New York Times, 6 April 1976, p. 30:1.

SERENADING LOUIE

New York Times, 6 May 1976, p. 30:1.

A TALE TOLD

New York, June 22, 1981, pp. 46-47.

Kroll, Jack. *Newsweek*, 22 June 1981, p. 64.
        Continuing the saga of the Talley family, this play is set on July 4, 1944, the same day as *Talley's Folly*. Kroll asserts that Wilson combines the "openness and candor" of America's heartland "with the sophistication of New York," although he feels certain details do not ring true, such as Lottie's dying of radium poisoning from licking the brush with which she paints clock faces. In this "portrait of a family whose day is done," the abstract dynamics are more interesting than the events or characters, Kroll notes, and most of all he admires Wilson's dialogue: "He [the playwright] adores and honors language and he can shape it to the music of anguish, tenderness or nutball humor."

Time, 22 June 1981, p. 48.

TALLEY'S FOLLY

New Yorker, 3 March 1980, p. 62.

Newsweek, 3 March 1980, p. 53.

New York, 10 March 1980, p. 87.

Nation, 15 March 1980, p. 316.

Commonweal, 28 March 1980, p. 182.

Brustein, Robert. *New Republic*, 5 April 1980, p. 28.
        Brustein does not like *Talley's Folly*, which he feels is a waste of Wilson's "fastidious craftsmanship on such a shallow situation," that of a mismatched couple who eventually marry.

New York Times, 6 July 1980, II:3:1.

THIS IS THE RILL SPEAKING

Pasolli, Robert. Nation, 4 April 1966, pp. 403-04.
The play is "a re-creation of daily life
in a small town in the Ozarks, which purports
to be kaleidoscopic and microcosmic of rural-
rooted America." The setting has clear autobiographical overtones, and although Pasolli
objects to "Wilson's literalness," he finds
the story "eloquent and frequently moving."

New York Times, 12 April 1966, p. 43:1.

WANDERING

New York Times, 9 May 1968, p. 55:2.

INDEX

This index includes authors (and co-authors) of secondary sources, including interviews, criticism, dissertations, and reviews. Numbers refer to pages.